ANALYSING PATIENTS WITH TRAUMAS

ANALYSING PATIENTS WITH TRAUMAS
Separation, Illness, Violence

Franziska Henningsen

KARNAC

First published in German in 2012 as *Psychoanalysen mit traumatisierten Patienten. Trennung—Krankheit—Gewalt* by Klett-Cotta

First published in English in 2018 by
Karnac Books Ltd
118 Finchley Road
London NW3 5HT

© 2012 Klett-Cotta—J. G. Cotta'sche Buchhandlung Nachfolger GmbH, Stuttgart

For the English language version translated by Andrew Jenkins
© 2018 Bernd Henningsen

The translation of this work was made possible thanks to generous funding by the Sigmund Freud Foundation, Frankfurt

The right of Franziska Henningsen to be identified as the author of this work has been asserted in accordance with §§ 77 and 78 of the Copyright Design and Patents Act 1988.

All rights reserved. No part of this publication may be reproduced, stored in a retrieval system, or transmitted, in any form or by any means, electronic, mechanical, photocopying, recording, or otherwise, without the prior written permission of the publisher.

British Library Cataloguing in Publication Data

A C.I.P. for this book is available from the British Library

ISBN-13: 978-1-78220-335-3

Typeset by Medlar Publishing Solutions Pvt Ltd, India

Printed in Great Britain

www.karnacbooks.com

Note

For ease of reading, throughout the book "she" is used for the therapist and "he" for the patient, the victim, or the child, but, at any point, the opposite gender can be substituted.

CONTENTS

ACKNOWLEDGEMENTS   xi

ABOUT THE AUTHOR   xv

FOREWORD   xvii
by Werner Bohleber

INTRODUCTION
The rift in the ego   xxi

PART I
SICK CHILDREN—SICK MOTHERS

CHAPTER ONE
"No sick children in my house today":
death fears in children   3

CHAPTER TWO
"That's my mother's trauma, not mine":
concretistic fusion, acting-out, symbolisation   21

CHAPTER THREE
"We aren't starving yet": silence in withdrawal
   and communicating in images   43

CHAPTER FOUR
Splitting and fusion   65

PART II
SEPARATION TRAUMAS

CHAPTER FIVE
"This is *my* daughter. Take good care of her!"
   From objectless anxiety to separation anxiety   81

CHAPTER SIX
"Everyone knows my mother. Everyone except me."
   Concretistic fusion and denial of object loss   97

CHAPTER SEVEN
"The greatest danger comes from myself":
   destruction and guilt   109

CHAPTER EIGHT
Acting out and compulsive repetition   133

PART III
EXPERIENCES OF VIOLENCE AND
ABUSE IN CHILDHOOD

CHAPTER NINE
A helper in search of help: splitting and psychic reality   143

CHAPTER TEN
"I want no part of this hell": en route to perversion   161

CHAPTER ELEVEN
"I can look after myself": destruction and consolation
   in one and the same object?   179

CHAPTER TWELVE
Love and hate   197

PART IV
EXPERIENCES OF VIOLENCE AND ABUSE IN ADULTHOOD: TORTURE AND WAR

CHAPTER THIRTEEN
Post-traumatic stress disorder   209

CHAPTER FOURTEEN
Negative countertransference: depletion and resilience   223

PART V
CONCLUSION

CHAPTER FIFTEEN
Consequences for psychoanalytic technique   241

CHAPTER SIXTEEN
Trauma in society and politics: an outlook   257

REFERENCES   267

INDEX   281

ACKNOWLEDGEMENTS

In my work as an analyst, encountering young children with very serious illnesses fully focused my attention on the psychological repercussions of traumatic experience. Engagement with the consequences of those repercussions for therapeutic procedure was the basis for further reflection on the matter. The fact that I can now present my experiences in book form is something I owe to my patients and my supervisees, including those who are not referred to expressly in the following pages. From one session to the next, all of them gave me the opportunity to look into their own special worlds, share their experiences, and thus enhance my understanding.

Special thanks go of course to the patients who have permitted me to report on their cases here in anonymised form. I asked most of them for this permission about two years after completion of therapy. The open-mindedness with which they responded to my request greatly facilitated my work. No one refused point blank. One woman patient said spontaneously: "Yes, of course. It would be great if others could profit from what we achieved." I explicitly pointed out to my patients that of course I could only give *my* version of the analysis. If *they* were to report on it, a different version would be the result. I offered to show them what I had written before sending it off to the publishers; we could then arrange appointments giving them the chance to talk to me about the text. All of them agreed spontaneously; in the end about two-thirds of them took advantage of my offer to read what I had written and then talk to me about it, either in person or on the phone. I found these exchanges deeply moving: the trust that had developed during the sessions was still there, reminding me vividly of the analytic encounters themselves. They also enabled me to improve some passages of the book.

The refugees I had been asked to assess for trauma-patient status released me from my confidentiality obligations. I assured them that the scientific evaluation and potential publication they were consenting to would only come to fruition several years after they had filed their applications for asylum.

Some chapters of the book are based on earlier articles for psychoanalytic journals. They have, however, all been revised and recast to fit in with the issues addressed here.

I also owe a debt of gratitude to my colleagues in Berlin and Munich, who were always willing to discuss my ideas with me during the long years we worked together side by side. My participation in the supervision group headed first by Ignes Sodre and Martha Papadakis, later by Claire Cripwell and David Miller, gave me the courage and confidence to follow through with my ideas. I also received valuable impetus from the trauma research group of the European Psychoanalytic Federation (EPF) headed by Sverre Varvin and its investigations on the psychic conditions prevailing in traumatic situations. Membership of the group whose job it was to elaborate "Standards for the assessment of individuals with traumas" (SBPM) involved me in a process of interdisciplinary exchange that greatly helped me to sharpen my ideas. But that was not all. The group elaborated a curriculum as part of the certification process for assessors dealing with traumatised refugees applying for rights of residence. In this way, our joint deliberations were transformed into concrete political action. The curriculum was recognised both by the Federal Chamber of Physicians and the Federal Chamber of Psychotherapists.

Some parts of the manuscript have been read by Werner Bohleber, others by Tomas Plänkers. Their comments have helped me to give greater precision to a number of passages. Ferdinand Haenel and Gisela Scheef-Maier have taken a critical look at the sections dealing with posttraumatic stress disorder (PTSD). Publishing editor Heinz Beyer was generous with valuable advice in the early stages of the project. I also greatly appreciated Oliver Eller's professionalism in reviewing the finished manuscript.

The book is an attempt on my part to understand my patients' severe traumatic experiences and to draw upon modern psychoanalytic theory and its neighbouring disciplines to grasp the meaning of what they entrusted to me. Another aim of the book is to demonstrate the immense explanatory potential that present-day psychoanalysis possesses and the astounding curative energies that people can summon up when they feel understood. At the same time, all these cases show us that the best we can hope for is to get somewhere near the true significance of the events in question. In an interview with Heinrich Detering, Hans Keilson looks back on his analytic career as a traumatologist and the many case histories he has authored and gives us his personal view of the relativity of psychoanalytic knowledge: "I've become very careful with psychoanalysis in the course of time. The best parts of my work are not my interpretations but my patients' knowledge that they have someone to listen to them. Listen to them properly. I'm not really a smoker, but occasionally during the sessions I have smoked a pipe. So that I don't rabbit on too much" (Keilson, 2011, p. 125).

Berlin, May 2012
Franziska Henningsen

The week before her death in February 2015, Franziska was able to sign the contract with Karnac of London for the English-language edition of her book. Many colleagues had encouraged her to take this step, chief among them Werner Bohleber, who has also read the English version. Co-operation with the translator, Andrew Jenkins, was invariably gratifying and effective. Agnes Katzenbach has done an excellent job preparing the reference section for the English edition. A warm vote of thanks goes to the Sigmund Freud Foundation, Frankfurt for its generosity in co-funding the translation.

Berlin, August 2016
Bernd Henningsen

ABOUT THE AUTHOR

Franziska Henningsen, PhD, was a member of the German Psychoanalytical Association (DPV) and a training and supervising analyst at the Karl Abraham Institute in Berlin. She published numerous articles on psychoanalytic theory and practice with adults and children, especially on psychosomatic diseases, psychic trauma, homosexuality, East–West dialogue, and the assessment of traumatised refugees. She took many important positions in the German Psychoanalytic Association (DPV) and was the secretary of the DPV 2000–2004. She was the chair of the IPA Committee for outreach and interdisciplinary dialogue from 2004 to 2006. She was a member of the programme committee for the IPA Congress 2013 in Prague. She was engaged in the development of psychoanalysis in East-Germany and Eastern Europe. She chaired, for a long time, the DPV East–West committee and was a member of the IPA Moscow sponsoring committee. She died in February 2015.

FOREWORD

Werner Bohleber

Franziska Henningsen has written a remarkable book; this English translation will make it available to a much wider audience. The focus is on detailed case histories of patients with severe traumas. She takes us through the successive stages of analysis and gives us a graphic impression of the progress of her diagnostic and therapeutic insights into traumatic processes and their treatment. She enlarges on her psychoanalytic technique, her interpretations, and the way the analytic process evolves anew with each individual patient. Her main interest is in the development of the transference/countertransference relationship. Traumatic experience has to be actualised within that relationship if it is to be treated successfully; only in this way can therapeutic change become a feasible proposition. Henningsen is outstandingly good at discerning traumatic microprocesses and trauma-sequel phenomena in transference and countertransference and equally good at conceptualising them in psychoanalytic terms. The cases described in this book enable us to look over the shoulder of an immensely gifted psychoanalyst and observe her at work.

In encounters with traumatised patients, the therapist's constant awareness of her own countertransference is especially significant because in the confrontation with traumatic material we therapists are liable to respond with a defence reaction that is usually preconscious in its effect. This reaction springs from a desire to evade the violence, horror, pain, and anxiety of the traumatic events in question so as not to have to imagine and engage with them in our own minds. The incisive thrust of traumatic memories and the frequently appalling nature of the events involved threaten to overwhelm the psyche. Accordingly, we may tend to partially phase out or play down traumatic events in order to make them more manageable for ourselves. Once we have understood these connections between trauma and emotional countertransference and realised that the defence mechanism sets in for our own protection, we will be better able to correct for that mechanism and to bear the full brunt of the patient's traumatic experience(s).

The treatments central to the book provide an excellent fund of material for reflecting on these problems. In Part I, Henningsen reports on her experience in treating child cancer patients with conditions serious enough to require hospitalisation. Part II focuses on separation traumas in early childhood and their repercussions on later personality development. The patients in this section of the book are all adults. The third part investigates experiences of violence and abuse in childhood and the effects on further development, while the fourth part focuses on traumatic experiences of violence and torture in wartime contexts. Here again the patients are adults.

While it is of course true that psychoanalysis has always been concerned with the consequences of early traumas (cf. Freud's treatment of the Wolf Man), we have very few psychoanalytic investigations that proceed from a present-day understanding of early traumas to discuss their specific implications for personality development. Patients of this kind embarking on psychoanalytic treatment rarely see a connection between their past traumas and their present distress and disorders. Naturally, the significance attributed to events in childhood will depend on the analyst and her explicit or implicit theoretical knowledge. We still know very little about the lifelong consequences of early trauma, and this state of affairs makes Henningsen's book extremely important in scientific terms. Early trauma stunts the development of autonomy. Self- and object representations cannot establish themselves independently but are inextricably embroiled with one another by fear of abandonment. The telling concept coined by Henningsen for this constellation is "concretistic fusion", a reference to the trauma-conditioned fusional nucleus of the patient's abortive attempts at a separation between self and object. The way the author conceptualises this clinical phenomenon and describes how it reveals itself in the therapeutic relationship and becomes susceptible of treatment is unique in the entire body of psychoanalytic literature as we know it so far. In short, Franziska Henningsen's book is a genuinely original contribution to psychoanalytic research on trauma.

INTRODUCTION

The rift in the ego

It was the horrors of the First World War that prompted the pioneers of psychoanalysis to turn their attention to the sequels of traumatic experience. In his lecture "Fixation to traumas—the unconscious", Freud defines trauma as an experience "which within a short period of time presents the mind with an increase of stimulus too powerful to be dealt with or worked off in the normal way, and this must result in permanent disturbances of the manner in which the energy operates" (Freud, 1916/17, p. 275).

In 1918, the theme chosen by the organisers for the Fifth International Psychoanalytic Conference in Budapest could hardly have been more topical: "The psychoanalysis of war neuroses" (cf. Ferenczi, Abraham, Simmel, & Jones, 1921). The meeting attracted a high degree of public attention and helped to make psychoanalysis a talking point. This interest was however short-lived because the acute symptoms of most war neurotics were fast disappearing. Today, we know of course that this had nothing to do with spontaneous healing, nor had the disorders in question simply run their natural course. The distressing symptomatologies were warded off at the expense of serious restrictions to the ego, and trauma sequels will certainly have had a latent effect on the men who had been through the torments of battle.

The condition referred to as "war neurosis" and described in detail by Freud (1901b, pp. 114–115) and by Sándor Ferenczi, Ernst Simmel, and Karl Abraham (Ferenczi, Abraham, Simmel, & Jones, 1921) was later renamed post-traumatic stress disorder and duly found its way into the ICD-10. The brief heyday of psychoanalysis inspired by the Budapest conference and the charismatic impact of Sándor Ferenczi are still widely considered crucial for the later development of psychoanalytic trauma research.

In his essay on the "Confusion of tongues between adults and the child" (1949), Ferenczi describes the impact of external reality both on the relationship between analyst and analysand and between parents (or other referential figures) and children and discusses the significance of this for the origins of neurosis. Taking sexual abuse as an example, he describes the interplay of dependence, fear, helplessness, and guilt and explains how the victim automatically identifies with the perpetrator, a figure that then mutates into an internal threat: "Through the identification, or let us say, introjection of the aggressor, he disappears as part of the external reality, and becomes intra- instead of extra-psychic" (Ferenczi, 1949, p. 228). In this process, the child introjects the guilt feelings of the adult. This may result in the child's ego being split into an observing and a defenceless part and/or in pathological precocity.

Freud also discusses the introjection of an external danger and the way this can lead to a split in the personality or an "ego conflict":

> The war neuroses, in so far as they are distinguished from the ordinary neuroses of peace-time by special characteristics, are to be regarded as traumatic neuroses whose occurrence has been made possible or has been promoted by a conflict in the ego. [...] The conflict is between the soldier's old peaceful ego and his new warlike one, and it becomes acute as soon as the peace-ego realizes what danger it runs of losing its life owing to the rashness of its newly formed, parasitic double. [...] Apart from this, the war neuroses are only traumatic neuroses which, as we know, occur in peace-time too after frightening experiences or severe accidents, without any reference to a conflict in the ego. (Freud, 1919d, pp. 208–209)

Later, Freud was to deliver a more precise definition of the splitting of the ego triggered by traumatic situations (at this early juncture he refers to the constellation as the ego and its "parasitic double") and thus consolidate the foundations for the evolution of analytic theory and practice (1940e). Freud insists that a splitting of the ego is inconceivable without some traumatic event. "We can assign in general and somewhat vague terms the conditions under which this comes about, by saying that it occurs under the influence of a psychical trauma" (Freud, 1940e, p. 275) The consequences are permanent. "This success is achieved at the price of a rift in the ego which never heals but which increases as time goes on" (Freud, 1940e, p. 276). His views on the splitting of the ego were adopted by many later authors, such as Melanie Klein (1946, 1952), Otto Kernberg (1975), and others for whom concepts associated with trauma otherwise play a subordinate role. With reference to numerous examples, I intend to show that splitting is a crucial defence mechanism that can help us to understand traumatic processes. These processes can differ widely in their nature. Genetically they can begin very early but also at a later stage they can relate to affects, objects, or reality. In each individual case they take on a different guise.

Today, psychoanalytic trauma research has made further progress and has proved its pertinence in many different fields. But if we want to identify the effect of a traumatic event in childhood, we still need to investigate the mutually conditioning factors described by Freud as a progressive series. They are reciprocal and they interact with one another. "Early trauma—defence—latency—outbreak of neurotic illness—partial return of the repressed. Such is the formula which we have laid down for the development of a neurosis" (Freud, 1939a, p. 80). In retrospect, the individual case makes it possible to determine the progressive impact of a traumatic event more precisely (cf. Sandler, Dreher, & Drews, 1991; Dreher, 2000). In the early stages of child analysis and developmental psychology, infant traumas were graphically described and systematically investigated, notably by Anna Freud and Dorothy Burlingham (1942, 1943), John Bowlby (1973), and René Spitz (1965). Their work has lost none of its relevance and is now being supplemented by psychoanalytic research on infancy and by neuropsychology (e.g., Schore, 2003; Stern, 1995). Physical pain, traumatic separation, and object loss are the most frequent causes of infant trauma. Prevailing opinion, notably in connection with infant development, is that traumatic *relations* are internalised, they cannot be recalled and expressed in images or language but are stored in the implicit procedural memory and mark an individual's subjective experience and behaviour for life (Bollas, 1987; Kernberg, 1992; Schore, 2003).

The horrors and the consequences of the Nazi era were (and still are) another reason to reflect on the effects of traumatic external reality on the internal reality of the individual. The transgenerational identifications (Bergmann, 1982; Gampel, 1994; Kestenberg, 1989; Kogan, 1990) of the descendants of Holocaust victims were recognised as such in psychoanalysis and not infrequently occasioned new approaches to psychoanalytic thinking and practice. Another wave of clinical trauma research resulted from the necessity of providing therapy for the mentally afflicted veterans of the Vietnam War. A traditional psychoanalytic approach was not suitable for these people. Neurologists, psychiatrists, pharmacologists, behavioural therapists, ergotherapists, and many others engaged with the severe disorders they displayed. The terrain became increasingly interdisciplinary and psychoanalysis had difficulty asserting its claims. In the 1970s and 1980s, mainstream analysts adhered to their concern with internal reality, focusing notably on the investigation of narcissism (cf. the Kohut-Kernberg debate), the internal world of objects, and to some extent with Freudian Marxism. Accordingly, the prospects held out by the consideration of trauma were neglected. It was a time when psychoanalysis was very much in the ascendancy and, as we have seen, its chief concern was the internal world of the individual. For many analysts, this preoccupation was diametrically opposed to an engagement with trauma, which they relegated to the sphere of external reality, thus justifying the avoidance of the psychoanalytic issues posed by trauma sequels.

Psychoanalysis is a branch of learning dedicated to the investigation of internal reality. Explicitly declaring psychic traumas to be a legitimate object for psychoanalytic involves a heightened awareness of external reality. This in its turn implies that the effects of political, societal, and historical factors and conditions on the individual must be taken into consideration. For many analysts this was a difficult undertaking; indeed some may have felt it to be at odds with the very principles of psychoanalysis itself.

Occasionally, there appeared to be a real danger of losing sight altogether of the realisation that psychoanalytic reflection and insight are invariably located in a field of tension existing between internal and external reality. One of the most vocal critics of this tendency was Ilse Grubrich-Simitis. She showed that Freud had discussed both models—drive and trauma—and that there was no implicit "either-or" behind them. Her conclusion is:

> We should continue explicitly, and henceforth relieved of ambivalence, to try and integrate the traumatic factors in pathogenesis into the genuinely psychoanalytic etiological formula, that is, into the drive model. If we get no further on the ontogenetic level, we should not hesitate to consider the phylogenetic dimension. (Grubrich-Simitis, 1988, p. 29)

In her later work, she demonstrates that Freud invariably incorporated the traumatic aspects of neurosis into his deliberations, albeit with an occasional degree of ambivalence prompted by his fear that the perspective on the unconscious might otherwise be vitiated (Grubrich-Simitis, 2007).

Recognition of the traumatic effect(s) of reality is a necessary precondition for access to psychic spaces where destructive experience can be mourned, assuaged, or even integrated. Frequently the analyst must first call things by name and/or show the patient that he has at least an inkling of the shame felt by being the victim or the extent of the possible catastrophe. Only then can the patient feel secure, develop trust, and turn to face the ravages within (Bohleber, 1997, 2007, 2010; Grubrich-Simitis, 1981, 2008; Oliner, 2010).

The approach that I pursue in this book is geared to my own personal social and clinical experience. The individual complexity of all the cases I discuss here is left unadulterated. Each of them calls for a specific kind of access, which I both describe and provide theoretical substantiation for. In all of them, a traumatic factor plays an essential role for the understanding of the patient, which in turn calls for the use of a technique specific to the situation in question. Psychic trauma is invariably embedded in a form of personality development that I discuss in terms of the psychoanalytic conflict model (Mentzos, 2009). From the variety of perspectives there emerge a number of focal insights that give rise to ongoing theoretical considerations. This is why each of the first four parts closes with specific ideas on theory and clinical practice that are related to the cases discussed in that part. These discussions of the focal insights build on one another and draw attention to the perspective that was particularly helpful in understanding the given case, although it was not of course the only one conceivable.

Occasionally the course of the analyses makes it necessary to home in on developments taking place from one session to the next. These microprocesses are described and discussed in detail. But the holistic perspective is essential. The structure of the book is a function of the wide-ranging nature of the cases discussed. Part I focuses on illnesses and disorders experienced as traumatic: leukaemia, premature birth, a severe physical disability of the patient's mother, depression of the mother, stomach ulcers on the part of the father. These disorders, of the parents or the child, traumatised the patients in a specific way and in early infancy aroused death fears that the patients were unable to come to terms with and that turned into fixation points in their later development. Annihilation is at the heart of the matter. In the stressful mother–child relations, the mother's anxiety is the child's anxiety and vice versa. Frequent is a fusional form of defence that has to be worked on later in transference analysis. Following the case discussions, this characteristic is discussed in detail with reference to the concept of "concretistic fusion" and the splitting processes involved. Crucial implications for psychotherapeutic practice are indicated throughout.

The second part focuses on traumatic separation. The cases discussed revolve around separations experienced as traumatic (being consigned to a six-day crèche as of the sixth week of life, death of the mother when the patient was two years old, mother's suicide at the age of eight). While object loss of this kind also led to splitting processes and fusions, a prominent feature in these cases (depending on the nature and pathology of the pre-traumatic stage) is the quest for the lost and/or dead object. After the description of these cases and with reference to the theoretical conclusions on splitting and fusion arrived at earlier, the tendency to acting out and compulsive repetition is conceptualised and subjected to critical scrutiny. The most alarming sequel of traumatisation is interpersonal violence. The next two parts are devoted to this topic. Part III focuses on patients on whom violence was inflicted in childhood, causing them to develop a special predisposition for perverted identifications and/or psychosomatic disorders. At the same time, most of these patients had failed to come to terms with severe separation traumas (death of the mother at age one, father's absence in the Second World War, displacement). Experiences of violence exacerbated the situation, leaving their mark on defence structures and survival strategies in the form of identification with sadistic objects. Subsequently, I discuss issues connected with the relation between love and hate, investigating their potential relevance for approaches to treatment.

Part IV revolves around political violence, torture, war, and refugeeism. These patients suffered Freud's "rift in the ego" in adulthood, leading to post-traumatic stress disorder (PTSD). A modified form of psychoanalytic treatment was appropriate.

The volume closes (Part V) with a discussion of consequences for psychoanalytic technique and thoughts on the implications and responsibilities involved in the relations between politics, society, and the traumatised individual.

PART I

SICK CHILDREN—SICK MOTHERS

CHAPTER ONE

"No sick children in my house today": death fears in children

When a child faces imminent death or has a potentially fatal illness, this normally represents an intensely traumatic situation for the entire family (Henningsen, 2002). Few parents are able to talk to their children about the situation. Siblings are often left alone with their fears, and sick children themselves usually sense that their immediate environment has placed a taboo on their illness, a veil of silence that cuts them off from the moral support and consolation of their closest relatives. The excessive strain vitiating the supportive role of the family—psychoanalysts refer to this role as the "container function"—frequently leads to dissociations on the part of all those involved. The parents are no longer able to integrate their feelings and this cuts them off from the symbolic language required to maintain emotional contact with the sick child. Accordingly, psychotherapeutic aid is extremely important for these families. Children very often express themselves nonverbally, especially when they sense that the parents are no longer capable of verbal exchange. In my experience, children also invariably know how serious their situation is—if only at a preconscious or unconscious level—and indicate this to their environment, albeit in a species of sign language that needs to be recognised as such and translated.

Part I is dedicated to case examples involving children with traumas caused both by the actual course of the illness itself and by the frequently drastic medical interventions required to deal with it. It is designed to indicate how they represent their psychic situation in the course of therapy and how helpful it is for them to be properly understood. The children in question are girl patients I treated at Munich University's children's outpatient clinic some thirty years ago (Henningsen, 1980; Henningsen & Ullner, 1981).

In adult analysis, traumatic childhood experiences often play a major role. The encapsulated traumas are unconscious, the patients are normally unable to talk about them. Nor can these patients symbolise their traumatic experience. In the analytic situation the traumatic constellations are very often brought to the surface by enactments, after which they can be worked on via transference interpretation and integrated into the self (Part II). In the treatment both of adults and children I regard these enactments as helpful, a form of unconscious thinking that can be understood by means of interpretation and translated into symbolic language. In the case of children in acutely traumatic situations, the interpretive technique has to be adapted to the child's stage of development. In adults, it is possible to arrive at conclusions about the degree of dissociation and pre-traumatic personality structure, which in their turn tell us a great deal about the patient's symbolisation capacity and define the interpretive technique to be used.

In my dealings with adult patients suffering from traumas, my experience in treating severely or fatally ill children at the Munich University clinic has often been helpful when the trauma is re-enacted in transference. Children have a special capacity for making use of play and creative activity to express nonverbally what is going on in their minds. When verbal communication breaks down in the critical stages of adult analysis, it is frequently essential to mobilise this capacity in order to understand the transference.

First vignette: Marion (age four years, six months)

Four-year-old Marion was in hospital undergoing treatment for lymphoblastic leukaemia. Her family doctor had had her transferred to hospital, as she had been diagnosed for the disease two days earlier.

At our first session, Marion was pale. She took a good look at the room. After we had established initial contact, I told her that while she was in hospital she could come to my room to play and we could talk about how she was feeling. She said she wanted to draw, immersed herself quietly in her activity and produced a drawing of a house (Figure 1).

> When I asked her: "Does anyone live in the house?" she replied: "No, there's nobody living in the house." I said: "I can imagine it's rather a sad house, if no one lives in it." Marion: "Yes, it's very sad," adding vehemently: "And the tiles on the roof are all red!" After a brief pause, I said: "Those tiles on the roof look like blood stains!" Marion (relieved): "Yes!"

With this picture and her comments on it, Marion was telling me about her state of mind. The empty, uninhabited house covered with the big red roof-tiles was a self-portrait. One could also "read" the picture as representing a body with legs. My interpretation of the roof-tiles as blood stains was an attempt at translation from the picture on the paper to the child's body-self. In this situation I functioned as a mirror, showing my little patient that I could sense how threatened she felt. At the same time, this exchange took place in a quiet, relaxed atmosphere that instilled trust and reassurance in the child.

Figure 1. Spontaneous drawing by a four and a half-year-old girl with acute leucosis. Striking features are the emptiness of the house and the way the red tiles on the roof resemble blood stains.

In the first few days, Marion was very despondent and also very suspicious of the hospital surroundings. In my presence, however, she engaged actively with her suspicions. She investigated all the cupboards and drawers in my office and asked me what some of the things she found there were for. I tried to show her that it was very important to know where she was and what kind of things one comes across in a hospital, what the doctors would be doing in her case, etc. In accordance with her age, Marion attempted to come to terms with her fears by means of intensive role play.

> Doctor–patient games were a part of every session. Identifying with the aggressor, Marion was always the doctor, I myself, or dolls, were the patients. Marion sometimes wore my white coat, "genuine" utensils from the ward were there for her to use: injection needles, "jabs", plaster, bandages, spatulas, and a stethoscope. She gave me a jab, took blood from my finger, and said: "Okay, you'll feel a slight prick, it won't hurt at all." Then she would look into my mouth: "You've got bad teeth." She examined my throat and said: "There are swollen bits." (That was how her leukaemia had been identified!). She used the stethoscope to see if my heart was still beating. She asked me about earlier illnesses, gave me prescriptions, and then stated quite sternly that I was ill: "Tell your mummy you won't be coming home yet." I responded with sadness and asked her what mummy would do. We agreed that mummy would go to work and come to the hospital during the evening visiting hours, etc. In the doctor games, Marion was extremely cruel to the dolls. Sometimes her doll was the good doll and mine was the bad one. The bad doll was constantly crying and "piddling in her pants" because "she's ill and her mummy's not there". The good doll was always co-operative and never in pain.

Marion's scenic play indicated how she inwardly performed a splitting into good and bad objects in the way Kernberg (1975) describes as a condition for borderline states. My interventions were an attempt to show her that there is nothing wrong in saying when something hurts, that it can be helpful to tell others about it. I remarked that the bad doll did not cry all the time and that I had noticed how hard she was trying to be brave and that she wanted nothing more than to be like the "good" doll. But if she cried because something was hurting her, other people would still like her. Later Marion used playing with the dolls to address the fact that she was losing her hair. Then we played "radiation therapy", which is an especially stressful situation for children because no one can be with them during treatment. To simulate the radiation situation, she took the lamp on my desk and crawled under the table with it, imitating the sound of the heavy doors closing behind her with a threatening "boom-boom". In all these play scenes it was relatively easy to create parallels with her own situation. After our sessions together, Marion was always greatly relieved and made sure that they were never postponed. For example, she would not let the doctors give her injections of methotrexate before our play sessions had taken place because she knew that after these injections she would have to spend twenty-four hours lying down.

In play she also expressed her death fears. Here it was important that I only played them through with her and never offered any interpretations. Marion's development was in line with her age; fantasy and reality were interchangeable and not yet separated by superego development. If I had confronted her with interpretations she was too young to understand, I would have destroyed her creative potential for working on what she was going through.

One game we played was "the wolf and the seven little kids". Marion wanted to be the little kid that hid in the grandfather clock. I was the mother who warned her children about the wolf before going off to the shops. The other kids were dolls. The wolf appeared in the guise of my brown armchair and devoured all the kids (Marion put all the dolls under a cushion). When I (the mother) got back home, all my children were gone. I called out to them and was just about to despair when I heard someone knocking on the desk (the grandfather clock). We rejoiced at our reunion. She told me what had happened and we cut the wolf's stomach open. Then we took the dolls out and filled his belly with building blocks. We pushed the armchair over and the wolf fell into the well.

As Marion spent more time in hospital and our relationship steadied, her games became more regressive. In one of them, she was the baby and I was the mother giving her the bottle. When the baby was sleeping, noisy children would wake her up and I had to scold them and make sure that peace and quiet was restored and the baby could sleep. Marion's inner satisfaction was obvious. Every play-therapy session gave her strength that helped her get through the following days. One reason why I played such a significant role for her was that she had a single mother who could only visit her in the evenings.

Second vignette: Antje (eight years, six months)

Antje was in hospital for aplastic anaemia. At this point in time she knew nothing of the imminent bone-marrow transplant, although her parents had already agreed to the doctors' proposal. The marrow was to be donated by her younger sister Monika (five years, ten months). My role was to help prepare both sisters for the operation. Monika will be the third vignette in this chapter; for the moment however we will focus on Antje.

Antje was a very serious, taciturn, and rather slow child whose development up to the outbreak of the illness had been largely unremarkable. She still found it difficult to feel that she was a girl and was unhappy not to have such nice long luxurious hair as her sister Monika and her room-mate Kalli.

Figure 2. Scene with dolls arranged by an eight and a half-year-old girl with aplastic anaemia. The patient puts herself on the lap of her late grandparents in the reclining chair. The mother is on the left (standing).

Reports by the doctors treating her later on an outpatient basis indicate that her subsequent development was favourable. She regained her health and was not found to be psychologically abnormal in any way.

In our initial psychotherapeutic sessions, Antje was very fond of arranging scenes with the dolls she was given (Figure 2). The following is an extract from a session protocol:

> At the outset, Antje says: "Today there are no sick children in my house, they're all perfectly healthy." She gives me detailed explanations, describing the activities of the individual dolls. Then she says: "There's a nasty smell in the flat because he's been sick. He won't stand up. He must go to bed. If he can't stand, he must be ill. None of the dolls have had any sleep, they've been awake all night, they won't go to bed." After that, she puts the princess and the baby to bed. The doctor is called in to examine the children: "That one in the reclining chair is my favourite grandma, that's my granddad. I never saw him, he died before I was born. And that's my girlfriend Petra [princess lying on a fur rug] ... That's Monika [sister] and that's me [girl on her grandparents' lap in the reclining chair]. Although I haven't got long hair ..."
> My comment: "But you'd like to have long hair."
> Antje: "Yes ... And that's mummy and daddy."
> "What do you think? Which of the dolls is best off?"
> Antje: "Petra, because grandma has given her a lovely long dress and because she has long hair."
> "And which of them is worst off?"
> Antje: "No one. No, grandma because she's ill. Our grandma died of cancer, she was really ill. Actually, grandad shouldn't be in the game because I don't know him. Grandad's going for a walk now, it's too warm for him in here. Mummy's best at standing, isn't she? This one can't really stand, he's not very well. And the little baby's got diarrhoea."

Subsequently a very intensive conversation developed between Antje and me about her grandmother. She was very, very fond of her grandmother, who was not very old when she died. Other grandmas live to be eighty. Do people always die when they're seventy or eighty? But her grandma died of cancer, and it was better for her to die because she was in such awful pain. Antje is only eight years old and in the daytime she is not in pain. But they have to give her so many injections and tablets and she can't go home. It's all pretty bad, but not as bad as it was when grandma was so ill, says Antje.

Important here is the way in which at the beginning of the game the child mobilises her powers of defence and denies her illness: "Today there are no ill children in my house." But she cannot keep this up for very long, the children have to be put to bed because they have diarrhoea, cannot stand properly, etc. Antje puts herself in the lap of her late grandparents. For all its drama, however, the game also indicates considerable trust. Antje was "very, very fond" of her grandma, and mummy is "best at standing", which probably means: "I can rely on my strong mother, although I can sense that there are awful things in store for me, plus my dear grandma is dead, so I wouldn't be alone if I went to heaven." In this game, Antje reveals what is going on in her unconscious mind. The signals were helpful in counselling the parents and in looking after the child in the isolation period. During the critical phase in which the transplant may be rejected by the patient, the parents were able to talk to their child about the fact that she might die and had to promise that they would put her favourite soft toy (a large dog) in the coffin with her. The prospect of joining her grandma in heaven was a great consolation for Antje. My psychotherapeutic task was primarily to help the parents recognise and understand the signals coming from their daughter so that they could stand by her and feel less insecure about giving her the right kind of support.

Third vignette: Antje's sister Monika (five years, ten months)

Bone-marrow transplants invariably extend the relevant families to the limits of what they can take. The situation demands a makeshift type of family life with the members shuttling to and fro between home and the haematological centre and the parents having to cope with considerable vocational repercussions. In addition, of course, all the family members live in fear of what might happen to the child faced with the operation. One common outcome of this critical situation, in which the actions of parents and relatives are geared almost exclusively to the sick child and her prospects of survival, is that the psychological situation of the bone-marrow donor—often a sibling—tends to be neglected. Antje's sister Monika gave me a vivid impression of the way in which these mortal fears are experienced and dealt with from the viewpoint of a sibling and bone-marrow donor.

At the time of the transplant, Monika was five years and ten months old. She was the last of three children and generally felt to be a fairly uncomplicated child, perhaps with a slight tendency to exploit her position as youngest girl. There were frequent tempestuous quarrels between her and her older sister (the eight and a half-year-old patient), who was always orderly and sensible. In the run-up to the transplant, Monika spent two and a half months with her aunt and uncle, who lived a long way away. Her parents could only visit her occasionally, her father had to work, her mother was looking after Antje (the patient) in Munich. Due to infections, Antje's hospitalisation in Munich had to be postponed twice, so that Monika had no way of knowing when the separation of parents and siblings would come to an end. During the first three weeks with her relatives she was happy and lively enough, but as time went on she became increasingly depressed and despondent.

When Monika came to Munich, she was told that, as she already knew, her sister Antje's blood was ill. She could help by giving her some of her own blood, which meant that Monika would be given an injection to put her to sleep. While she slept, some of her blood would be taken from her. After that she would probably have to stay in bed for a few days. Because children that age have little idea of what bone-marrow is and the transplant itself looks like blood, the whole process was referred to as "giving blood". Monika agreed to the procedure, although a child that age can hardly be described as capable of taking such a decision. The pressure she sensed became apparent in the subsequent examinations and in psychotherapy.

The psychological examination

As is customary, in-depth psychological anamnesis was conducted with the parents; the child was examined with the aid of projective procedures. In contrast to what the parents had said initially, Monika was very quiet during the examination and made a hesitant and timorous impression. All the tests indicated how much she had been suffering from the depressive mood in the family and the long separations. At the same time, she was able to express her despair and anger, a favourable factor for the prognosis. Her response to the "enchanted family" test is representative of the test outcomes as a whole (cf. Figure 3):

> Monika first drew a dog (her mother), then a snake (her sister), then herself as a spider, her father as a chicken, and finally her brother as a ladybird. "The spider has a thread there," she said and drew a thread hanging down to the snake. "The snake and the spider have the best of it because the snake can give you a good bite and the spider can stop you going any further because

it can make a web. Worst off is the chicken because it's so slow and can't bite." Monika would have liked to be the snake "because it can give you a nasty bite, but not the ladybird because it can't do anything at all." When I asked her whether the animals she had drawn ever did anything together, she said: "No, they don't do anything together."—"Does that make them sad?"—"Yes, but the chicken is saddest of all because it's so slow and has such a big fat tail."—I say: "One thing I've noticed is that the thread connects the spider and the snake much more closely than the others."—"Yes, that's how it is."—"What are they doing?"—"They're on the phone to one another."—"And what are they talking about?"—"They're saying that they're sad because they're not doing anything."—"I can well imagine that they're sad."—"Maybe they're giving blood," said Monika finally.

In my view, Monika gives a very clear picture of the way she experienced the atmosphere within the family. Her big brother was relegated to the wings, he was affected least by what was happening. Her father was also more on the sidelines, there was not much he could do, he had to go to work. Monika drew her sister as a snake, probably feeling that there was plenty of poison in her. At the same time, her sister is the one causing all the trouble at the moment. As a spider, she herself

Figure 3. "Enchanted family" by a girl of five years, ten months shortly before donating bone-marrow.

can stop the others from going any further. Obviously she had a very clear awareness of how much depended on her blood, on what she was doing for the family. On the one hand, she was sad because she missed the contact with her sister, on the other she obviously felt angry. The "phoning" also refers to the contact situation with her sister. Antje was already isolated and Monika could only get in touch with her through the intercom.

Psychotherapy

In the period in which Monika was confined to bed, I visited her for an hour every day while the parents went off for a meal. Her parents were advised not to send her back to her relatives immediately after the transplant because she had suffered so much from the separation. Once she was able to get up, she came to the psychosomatic counselling centre about three times a week for outpatient psychotherapy.

When Monika awoke from the anaesthetic, she cried a lot. At this stage, it was important for someone to be with her. At lunchtime she suffered greatly from the separation from her parents and we made a clock so as to have a clearer idea how long it would last before her mother returned.

> Frequently she would look across to her sister lying in the next room (there was a connecting window between the two rooms). Her expression as she did so was usually sad, sometimes angry. In response to this I once said: "Yes, the things you have to put up with for your sister's sake!" When Monika came back to our play hour for the first time after the operation, she bared her midriff full of horror and said: "Look at the needles they stuck in me, all over my belly!"—"That's really awful!" Subsequently Monika spontaneously drew another picture of the enchanted family. Before the operation she had probably made contact with her inner objects by drawing the family members as animals and now she was able to fall back on this important experience (cf. Figure 4).

She had this to say about the picture:

> She is the big fat snake, the ladybird is her mother, the spider her father, the dog her brother, the chicken her sister. When I asked her about the picture, she said that as the snake she was best off because she could bite,

"because I'm a poisonous snake". This is why she wants to be the snake "because it can bite and it's poisonous and has a poisonous fang." But then she suddenly developed quite strong fears, left the picture where it was and reached for the paint box.

The formal structure of the picture reflects her inner chaos. Now she identified with the snake, the poison was in her. At an unconscious level this is probably a representation of the fear or unconscious desire of poisoning her sister with her own blood. After all, she has often been angry with her sister. Here projection and identification intermingle. The magic thinking typical of children this age will probably have been operative in generating this fantasy. In Monika the transplant had triggered a series of oral-sadistic fantasies manifesting themselves in the repeated references to biting. In contrast to the first picture, the family members are barely identifiable; while she was drawing and explaining the drawing, her references were highly nebulous. If I had asked her a few minutes later, she would probably have assigned different family members to the animal figures. At the bottom of the page lurks the big black snake, her sister, the illness, death, she herself. The curving lines linking top to bottom resemble a beak, as if all the animals in the upper part of the picture had gelled into one body and with these

Figure 4. "Enchanted family" by a girl of five years and ten months after the transplant operation.

beak-shaped lines were offering the ill snake some kind of connection (blood perhaps?). These lines are reminiscent of the phone connection in the first picture (before the transplant). At the same time, this beak might signify that the snake has devoured the whole family. Inside and outside, projection and introjection are both present and interchangeable. If we decide to view the picture as an image of the internal objects and the state they are in, then the patient in this session is functioning on a psychotic level, her fear is unbearable.

> In the following months, Monika painted a lot of pictures with a great deal of blood in them (cf. Figures 5 and 6). The first time she painted the house with the bird and the birdhouse (or flower), she added the red background right at the end. She told me that there was a lot of rain falling, the angels were pouring lots of rain down from heaven. I remarked that the rain was red and asked whether the angels were sending red rain or possibly even blood down from heaven.—"Yes, it's all blood, all of it." We talked a lot about blood, giving blood, pain, and the fact that the idea was for the blood to become part of Antje and help her grow, much as the rain makes flowers grow. Monika was enthusiastic about her pictures and fascinated by the painting process. She spent many hours producing similar pictures, all with a red background.

Figure 5. House with bird and flower. Blood rains down from the sky.

Figure 6. House with sun, bird, and flower. Blood rains down from the sky.

One day she asked me to paint a red picture as well. I agreed and she told me what to paint. Each of us was to paint "her blood" on "her sheet of paper"; the atmosphere was highly regressive. In my countertransference I felt profoundly moved, I sensed my impotence, thought about how I could help Monika and how she in her turn could help her sister. Everything depended on blood, a vital fluid without contours. We used the same paint box with a pot of red. My blood was her blood, hers was mine, just as she had turned into the snake when she gave her sister blood. When the two sheets were soaked in red, she wanted each of us to write our names on the painting and then "put a box round them" and "underline" them (Figure 7).

This was another expression of the transference situation. While the joint blood-painting had a fusional character, the names and the underlining of them were a delimitation. In this way, Monika put an end to the fusion. With the help of my interpretations she had understood that now everyone had their own blood, their own body, and their own name. There was no way of predicting whether the donation of blood would help the recipient.

In this session Monika was once again confronted with her fears of death and had entered into a fusional attachment with me. Our joint

Figure 7. Two paintings with names in boxes, the upper by the analyst, the lower by the patient.

painting and my interpretations helped her to come back out of regression. In the fusion we were connected by our feelings. Later, this experience frequently helped me to understand traumatic processes in the treatment of adults. Time and again one can observe how in the traumatic situation a split-off feeling will lead to a fusion between subject and object that in the course of individual development hardens into a structure and in the transference taking place during analytic therapy manifests itself as a "concretistic fusion" (Henningsen, 2005, 2008; cf. Chapters Two, Four, Five, and Six in the present book).

Figure 8. "A picture without blood".

In one of the last few sessions before Monika was able to return home, she painted a picture "without blood" (cf. Figure 8). This picture, and her play behaviour as a whole, indicated that Monika had started to overcome her conflicts. In the very last session we also made ourselves hats (it was carnival time). Monika asked me to give her hat to her sister, whose survival was now probable but who was still isolated. This way, her sister had the same as she had, but she could still keep hers. This enactment completed her psychotherapy with a very healthy and constructive donation for her sister.

Follow-up

One year after Antje's discharge from hospital, the parents participated in a follow-up examination where Monika was asked to take the same tests a second time. The psychological examination indicated that Monika had indeed overcome the conflicts connected with the blood donation. This is best illustrated with reference to the "enchanted family" picture she painted during this follow-up session (cf. Figure 9).

> Monika portrayed her sister as a snail, her mother as a butterfly, her father as a bird, herself as a hare, and her brother as a stork. She wanted to be the

hare because she was so small and could sometimes hop "all over the place, on the playground, and in the flat!" She had painted her sister as a snail "because she always looks so grim". Her father is a bird "because he'd like to fly and throws me up in the air like a balloon". Her brother was a stork "because he's so big", her mother a butterfly "because it has feelers and eyes". The animals are all in the best of spirits and playing hide-and-seek.

Monika was now in a position to experience the roles of the individual members of her family as clear and well-defined. After the successful transplant, her sister looked "grim" and was wound in on herself like a snail. Monika obviously sensed that Antje still had a lot to come to terms with. The parents are above her, they are presumably the strong ones because they can fly. At the same time, this is an allusion to the fact that the parents are the ones who can go away.

In the follow-up interview, the parents report that in their view Monika has completely got over the trauma of the operation. She is proud of the fact that her sister has her blood. She spends little time thinking about hospital and the outpatient clinic. However, Monika frequently reacts touchily or apprehensively when her parents leave the house. These ongoing fears of separation indicate that the trauma still casts a shadow on her life. Antje was as well as could be expected, but she was still very quiet and one could tell that she had been through a lot.

Figure 9. "Enchanted family" by a blood donor—a girl of six years, ten months—one year after the transplant operation.

CHAPTER TWO

"That's my mother's trauma, not mine": concretistic fusion, acting-out, symbolisation

My experience of patients with traumas from infancy drew my attention to a phenomenon that I found to be operative both in the initial transference offer and in the analytic process itself. It can best be described as a variety of fusion with the object that contains an aspect of the traumatic experience that is susceptible neither of mentalization nor (consequently) of symbolisation and that remains bound up with the object (Henningsen, 2008). This "concretistic fusion" is a trauma-specific defence mechanism arising from dissociations. Without remission it will develop a life of its own. It binds part of the self to the object and prevents separations and progress towards autonomy. It leads to transference figures that directly address the analyst's unconscious and invite projective countertransference identifications (Grinberg, 1991). Potentially, its genetic roots are legion. With reference to ideas proposed by Ilse Grubrich-Simitis in her paper "From concretism to metaphor" (1984), I call this "concretistic fusion".

In traumatic processes, the essential transference figure in the individual case derives from the intersection of two dimensions, the topographical and the genetic. In the following I first give an outline of these two dimensions before drawing upon two case examples to discuss my views on this point and the theoretical implications involved.

The topographical perspective: Freud describes the traumatic event as the trigger situation for splitting processes. The success of trauma defence is "achieved at the price of a rift in the ego which never heals but which increases as time goes on. The two contrary reactions to the conflict persist at the centre-point of a split in the ego" (Freud, 1940e, p. 276). This process has been observed and described by many authors either as an intrusion, a suspension of the boundaries between internal and external reality (Amati, 1990; Bohleber, 2010, pp. 75–100; Oliner, 1996) or as a "fusionary self-object switch" (Scharff, 2002). Kernberg describes the "fixation to the trauma" in a similar manner. Traumatising events lead to primitive fusions, with hatred as the dominant affect. The resulting attachment to the traumatising object leads to "identifying [...] with the *relationship*" (Kernberg, 1992, p. 27, emphasis added), "unconsciously they [the patients] become their own persecutory objects while sadistically attacking their victims. They cannot escape being victim and perpetrator at the same time" (ibid., p. 28; see also Chapter Seven).

The genetic perspective: alongside the nature and intensity of the trauma, the extent of these fusions also depends on the stage the victim has reached in his development. Traumas and splitting processes attack the human self in a specific way if, for example, no satisfactory separation between subject and object has been achieved because the individual is either very young or displays a corresponding pre-traumatic personality structure (e.g., a borderline structure).

Infant research findings indicate that neonates can already distinguish between stimuli from the outside world and internal events. In the symbiosis with the mother, a newborn child is a causally active subject from the outset (Gergely, 2000). In successful cases, the mother's mirror activity is equivalent to a good container; in pathological cases distortions occur if the mother, say, projects her own anxieties on to the child instead of mirroring the child's anxieties, or if instead of mirroring them she merely reproduces them, thus returning the anxiety undigested to the child, leaving him on his own and unable to form the necessary internal representations. This condition lays the foundations for the development of a symbolisation disorder. The child's feeling remains identical with the mother's feeling, and no uncoupling can take place (Bion, 1962, Chap. 5; Fonagy & Target, 2002).

The range of pathological affect-mirrorings is wide indeed, but the various disorders all have one thing in common. Inadequate containment with a traumatising effect always involves a disturbance in the development of self-representations. It leads to fusions between self and object that seriously impair mentalization and symbolisation processes. As I shall demonstrate later, the special features of traumatic experiences in early childhood frequently take on the character of cumulative traumatisations (Khan, 1974). In the analytic process they have a specific effect on transference.

Trauma-conditioned fusions materialising later (i.e., after the development of object constancy or after overcoming the oedipal phase) need to be evaluated differently. In such cases, a repertory of symbolisation capacities and secondary representations from repeated affect-mirrorings has developed in the pre-traumatic years (cf. Gergely, 2000, pp. 1209–1210). While these functions are no longer available in connection with the encapsulated trauma, they may still be effective in other segments of the personality and can be reactivated relatively quickly with the help of therapy.

Interpretation of the splitting is an implicit injunction for the patient to extricate themselves from the fusion. This involves jeopardy for the patient (or the analytic process) because the self-object fusions have given the patient a more or less conscious feeling of security deriving from the fact that the destructiveness has been partly bound up with the object. As I see it, extrication from the object is connected with many small projection/introjection steps. The affects thus released must be named and acknowledged. In this process, acting-out plays a crucial role. Only when the analyst has interpreted the acting-out in transference can the patient develop a feeling for the emotional dimension of his/her action. Emergence from the fusion is regularly connected with the acknowledgement of shame and guilt (Amati, 1987; Henningsen, 2004c; Chapter Seven). In the initial phase of analysis it is thus especially important to ensure that a trusting transference relationship is established.

Ms R

Ms R (Henningsen, 2008), a young adult, came to me because she had had a mental breakdown. Over a period of eighteen months she had been unable to face sitting the second part of her final examinations.

Trauma history

Ms R suffered initial traumatisation right at the beginning of her life. Before pregnancy, doctors had given her severely ill mother a maximum of ten years to live and had strongly advised against pregnancy because she would not survive it. But the mother quickly accepted her (unintentional) pregnancy and spared no effort to find a doctor willing to look after her. At the time, both parents were undergoing analysis. The mother's analyst terminated the analysis because he interpreted her pregnancy as acting out. The father had broken off his analysis because he could no longer stand his analyst's accusations that he was living in a "sibling marriage".

The parents had never discussed the dangers of the pregnancy. They were both committed academics, and success in their professional careers was very important for them. Unconsciously they had resolved to negate depression or helplessness. Analysis revealed that throughout her development, the patient's function had been to compensate for her mother's physical deficits and act as a living antidote for depression. With her unusual intellectual gifts she represented for the father an ideal self. Illness and helplessness were taboo, warded off via projective identification. But they would lavish their help on others, often to the point of total exhaustion.

Their daughter was born prematurely via caesarean section and had to spend the first six weeks in an incubator. She learned to speak very early and immediately expressed herself in complete and grammatically immaculate sentences. This pattern repeated itself during a sojourn abroad at the age of four. After arriving in Paris, the patient was mute for six months and then suddenly surprised her family with perfect French. Wherever she appeared in her childhood and adolescence, she was respected and marvelled at as the epitome of a child prodigy. At an early stage, she unreservedly adopted the intellectual and moral values that her parents stood for. The warm-hearted and comradely attitude she displayed both to people outside the family and her parents ("I always had a friendly relationship with them") bestowed on her a large circle of friends.

The patient went through a second trauma sequence at the age of six. Her parents' marriage broke down, her father went abroad. Her mother had to go to hospital and was looked after by various friends of her parents. "What a good thing you know so many people you can stay with," she was told. The people around her failed to register the fact that she no longer felt at home anywhere, suffered from severe depression, and rapidly put on weight.

Depression, inner distress, and profound loneliness were her constant companions, but all these things were taboo and had to be kept under wraps in her unconscious. After her parents' separation she hardly ever saw her father. She and her mother repeatedly quarrelled; neither of them could explain the fact. The patient sat her school-leaving examinations at an internationally renowned boarding school. Here she entered into a sexual relationship with one of the teachers, who was impressed by her unusual gifts. Unconsciously, she had incestuously revitalised her relationship to her intellectually stimulating but constantly absent father. Only in the course of analysis did it dawn upon her that with this relationship she had sexualised an unsatisfied longing from her childhood. The parents never noticed the crisis their child was going through.

Diagnostic considerations

The abortive attempts undertaken by the parents to come to terms with their conflicts via analysis indicate that neither they nor their therapists succeeded in verbalising their wartime childhood traumas in a way that would make them susceptible of analysis. The "unsayable" in the story of this patient lies, to my mind, in the exclusive unity of life and death, dying and being born, an entity that was beyond the comprehension of the participants, compelled splitting processes, and prevented symbolisation.

The splitting processes triggered by the traumas are the starting point for the patient's psychoneurotic development. They can be specified as follows: anger and despair over her severe physical deficits drove the mother to fight doggedly and successfully against her illness and to achieve many things that others had thought to be too much for her. Dependence and helplessness were associated with mortal danger, and manic defence was the only available choice. It is probable that even before her birth, Ms R functioned as the mother's narcissistically cathected manic self, that is, the mother carried her physically undamaged self in her womb. This fantasy can however only be upheld if aspects of reality, such as physical boundaries, dependence, and helplessness, are split off. With the birth of her daughter, the mother had triumphed over mortal danger, but at the same time this surviving part was she herself, that is, self and object had to fuse for all time in order to keep each other alive. Part of the patient's self could not be born, it had to remain split off and concretistically fused with the mother's warded-off depression. The victorious, surviving part could then develop into a gifted, committed, and helpful individual. The unresolved conflicts between mother and daughter can be interpreted as abortive attempts at (self-) delimitation. The profound loneliness bound up with this only manifested itself in adulthood, when the parents divorced after thirty years of separation, started preparing for old age, and the patient finally had no choice but to embark on a career, that is, when the inevitability of separation and death became reality again. The patient's breakdown shortly before the conclusion of her professional training precluded autonomy and served to perpetuate the fusion.

The patient had been forced to spend the first six weeks of her life in intensive care; in that period it was impossible for mother and child to attune to one another satisfactorily. The patient's early, autodidactic language acquisition may well be another indication that she was able to adapt to the needs of the objects at a very early stage without sharing a transitional space with them. Her later development into a school achiever sharing and defending her parents' ideals with rhetorical skill will no doubt have consolidated the evolution of a false self (Winnicott, 1953).

The parents' separation in the oedipal phase and the excessive pressure exerted by the achiever role at school are repetitions and/or cementations of existing relational constellations of a traumatic nature. On a split-off, unconscious plane, all three (parents and daughter) were fused with one another; at the conscious level, each of them was autonomous, intelligent, and helpful, looking after themselves, bearing each other's warded-off depression in themselves. Actually feeling the deadly loneliness was taboo.

Establishing concretistic fusion in transference

In the first two years, Ms R's analysis took place on two planes, as described by Freud in his article "Splitting of the ego in the process of defence" (1940e). In immaculate German, Ms R gave an account of her biography, complete with highly complicated interpretations of various conflict situations. There were no dreams. ("I never dream.") The individual events were cogent, invariably pertinent and important, but the sequence was chaotic. I tried various ways of getting to grips with the unconscious topology of these belligerent and apparently chaotic texts, I made copious notes, did memory-training exercises, discussed them in an intervision group. All this was accompanied by an incessant flow of tears on the patient's part, which she initially appeared not to notice. The first thing I did was to buy a substitute cushion for the couch; a saturated cushion was something I could hardly expect the next patient to put up with. These tears were the tears of "little Sonia", the fragile infant born too early and hungering for love, a figure that the adult, eloquent Sonia would have no truck with, that same Sonia who once told me that I was her analyst and that on no account would she allow herself to see me as a person, as that would "interfere with the projections and transferences". Her tears flowed at every session, from the first minute to the last, without affecting the intonations of her voice or the enunciation of the words she was using.

Transference splitting quickly became apparent. The official, controlled (but false) self that she customarily used for communication purposes made contact with me via speech. I tried to follow as best I could, but I sensed that I was not reaching her in any essential way. I felt strained and tired.

After about three months of analysis, I committed a serious error. I fell asleep during the session. I was very ashamed; this had never happened to me before. Ms R noticed that I had nodded off and immediately did her best to let me down lightly: "It could happen to anyone." But I was deeply ashamed of myself and felt disastrously guilty. It occurred to me that in my capacity as an analyst I had failed just as abysmally as Ms R's mother had failed as a mother. Ms R had been just as quick to play down my lapse as she had probably been quick to reassure her sick mother. I also sensed how tempting it was to let her convince me that nothing really serious had happened (cf. Zwiebel, 2010).

My extreme countertransference reaction brought about by projective identification helped me to understand the processes involved and, in the years to come, to interpret them accordingly. A fear of failure had been aroused in me before the analysis proper actually began, a fear analogous to the anxiety the mother had attempted to ward off in pregnancy and birth. My unconscious enactment gave me an inkling of the distortions in the mirroring of her affects that Ms. R had experienced as an infant and small child. In the session I had lapsed into a depressive mood that had caused me to fall asleep. I bore the depression of the patient and her mother in me, and this combination had deprived me of my powers to fulfil the function of an analyst. Instead, I was fused with the patient in her distress. The mortal threat assailing mother and child at the time of conception and birth set off a circular process of projective identification with the doomed part of her own self, a process that manifested itself via concretistic fusion. At the action level, the replacement cushion I had bought ensured for the time being that the patient could weep. In the subsequent years, the essential thing was to work on the split-off part of the self in transference so that the patient could experience it as part of her psychic reality.

At a manifest verbal level, the patient was fighting a battle on various sites of conflict where she acted out her traumas. These attempts at a solution failed repeatedly; again and again Ms R was operating on the verge of a disaster. In this phase of analysis, my interpretive activity largely took the form of a species of translation. "Quotations of trauma" (Henningsen, 1990; Lipin, 1955) were identified and designated in transference and in secondary transference areas. The defence configuration started to crumble.

Getting out of the fusion

Parallel to these developments, the patient began to discover me as a person. When she was once again fighting for her life in her career, she once forgot to pay me and was very surprised by my interpretation of her behaviour. I said that she wanted me to help her bear her guilt (German has the same word—*Schuld*—for guilt and debt). I was supposed not to have any needs of my own but to show my solidarity by dealing with the things that were important for her. Vacations were another topic. I planned my holiday without consulting her beforehand, displaying the same behaviour as her father, who had gone off without telling her, even fathering a child with another woman without asking her opinion on the subject. The fallible sides she discovered in me were an initial shock to the omnipotent defence system in which she had been unconsciously united with me. This was the onset of the painful and dangerous process of breaking out of her fusion. The patient began to remember how as a child she had denied her loneliness, fantasised about forming an inextricable unity with her mother, and was unable to confide her anxiety and helplessness to either her father or her mother. Outwardly she was always strong. She was now able to describe her mother's physical infirmity, something she had never referred to before. She never "saw" it in her mother. But in her gait—and in her infancy—she had assumed a posture that resembled her mother's handicap. Feelings of guilt and shame had prevented the patient from facing up to her mother's physical deficits and actively soliciting her father's attention after he had left the family. He parents had always looked after her well, but emotionally they had steered clear of her. Now, as then, she can only reach her mother—and me—in worst-case disasters.

Professionally she was concerned with mothers who were "exasperated by wailing babies" and on the spur of an affect harmed or even killed their children. Here too she was found wanting. I was able to show her that unconsciously she *was* both the squalling child and the killing mother, she was the bearer of her mother's unhappiness, a mother who was under constant pressure to perform, who wanted to live and could not accept her unhappiness. The general conviction was that without her, her mother would never have lived so long, and the patient began to feel what a burden this had been.

This insight was an extreme shock for Ms R, and she threatened to disintegrate. She left the work with dead babies to others, swallowed all kinds of psychoactive drugs at random, thus demonstrating to me that I could not support her either.

P: I can't take any more of this.
A: Perhaps no one could take it. I think that at the moment we are dealing with feelings your parents couldn't have stood up to either.
P: I find it difficult to acknowledge that.
A: The insight is extremely hurtful for you.
P: It must have been dreadful, first I was in an incubator, my mother's life may have been at stake, they wouldn't let my father come and see me properly, only through a window. ... Leaving a child to cry is for me the worst thing a mother can do. I see now that when you console a child, you are consoling yourself, my mother still does that. ... I know I can be sure I was a wish-child ... But my parents never talked about what it means to bring a child into the world when you haven't got much longer to live. They were terribly rational, maybe they didn't want to think about it ... I believe that what I fear now is that my mother really might die soon.

Once again an abundance of parallels with her present situation and her psychic reality were drawn: she was the squalling baby I could not put up with; I would either "go to pieces" or "give her a real telling-off as I changed her nappies". Gradually she sensed that I was prepared to share her helplessness.

After two years of analysis, she confessed that she experienced me as a "partner": "There's a land-line from here to the outside, good or bad." It was the first session in which no tears flowed, her affects no longer had to be evacuated. Ms R was now able to perceive me not only with the rational but also with the split-off, emotional side of her personality. The process was linked with the first steps towards a disengagement, an emergence from the fusion; she was able to see how she had avoided creating an image of herself. "The land-line to me" can be understood as an initial attempt to symbolise our relationship, including, as it did, both the good and the bad.

In the next three years we were able to work on the patient's severe depression. She sensed that it was connected with deep-lying traumatic points in both parents. The analytic process was reflected in a variety of somatic issues. Ms R developed skin trouble.

A: I believe your skin is flaking because you are emerging from the unity with your mother to have a skin of your own.

Unconsciously and split off, Ms R had lived with her mother in one skin, a physical unity. Only now could she stand back and look at this unity because she was going through the painful process of leaving it behind. My summer vacation was approaching, her skin went on flaking, the fusion—not only with her mother, also with me—was coming to an end. The patient also had a painful constriction and inflammation of the vocal cords.

A: You are angry because I'm going on holiday and leaving you alone, but you're afraid to scream at me because screaming babies drive their mothers to distraction. Whatever comes from inside you is taboo.

Ms R felt that I was a support for her and very gradually began to understand that the negative affects (anger, helplessness, hatred) were bound up with the fusion and now had to be acknowledged if the attachment to the traumatic object was to be dissolved.

Ms R was debating whether to take a driving test but could not bring herself to do so because she feared killing someone on the road.

A: Again and again you fear your own autonomy ... Being born means killing your mother.

Shortly before my vacation—this was in the third year of analysis—she reported her first dream, in which, after an odyssey in a taxi, she finally succeeded in contacting a woman she was trying to reach. It was of course a dream about us. Could she reach me—and I her—at the point where she was most authentic? Would we not lose each other in the vacation interval? The "land-line" appeared to be working; the dream was a symbolic realisation that helped her get through the time when I was away on holiday.

Subsequently, the transference relationship took on a latent tinge of homoeroticism. Essentially, however, we continued analysing her re-enactments in very small stages. The unhappiness she shared with her parents became increasingly apparent; the patient achieved a degree of distance, displayed greater understanding for her parents' behaviour, and made contact with them more often.

In the course of their conciliatory exchanges, the patient had promised her mother to ensure that she and the family would have a nice Christmas. Unfortunately this never happened, because her mother died suddenly. The patient was deeply shocked and maintained telephone contact with me. When we resumed the analysis after the funeral, Ms R was suffering from insomnia. My comment was: "Mourning for your mother and being alone is such a strain for you, you're probably afraid to go to sleep and give yourself up to your dreams." The insomnia persisted for a long time, but one day the patient come to the session with a dream that had helped her and that also indicates how her capacity for symbolising difficult experiences had progressed.

> I had a sick little bird with me, in a clay vessel with a hole in it. I was dreadfully worried about what was wrong with the bird. I became more and more desperate. You were there and tried to help me. You said I should try to get the bird to come out of the hole, then we would see what was wrong with it and whether it could fly. You advised me to open the window and I did. I held the opening of the vessel in the direction of liberty. Finally the bird emerged but veered off to the right. It did not fly into the pane, it was clever enough not to do that, but it didn't fly out of the window either. Again and again I half caught it with the vessel in an attempt to bundle it through the window. I became more and more desperate. Finally I succeeded. The bird flew away and I felt elated.

After the patient had recounted her dream, with a high degree of emotional involvement, she was very uncertain: the metaphors were "so banal", she said.

A: Do you know the children's song this is an allusion to?
P: Yes, but I can't remember the words. Can you remind me?

A: A bird comes flying, sits down on my foot, has a letter in its beak, a greeting from my mother. Dear bird, fly off again, take my greeting and a kiss. I can't go with you, because I have to stay here. ... Your mother is dead, you can't go with her anymore.

Ms R wept. In the session I had tried to do the same thing as in the dream—persuade her that she had to let go. I had translated her symbolic language in the dream and transposed it to the interpersonal relationship between us. The "clever" bird was her sick part, the part bound up with the mother. At the same time the dream was about her birth, the window pane was an allusion to the incubator. She said no one had ever sung her such a simple old children's song. She sensed that I was a consoling object and was subsequently able to give the individual stages in her work of mourning greater depth with the help of various dreams. The focal point was her anger and the guilt feelings associated with it.

Working through her separation anxieties took a very long time. We repeatedly established connections with the traumas. Gradually, Ms R managed to find a language in which to express her experiences. While this was going on, she entered into a love relationship and got married. In contradiction to her prophecies at the beginning of the analysis ("I don't need a child"), she now desired nothing more than to have a child, and finally got pregnant. The transference deepened and in my countertransference I again experienced the whole plethora of anxieties connected with the health of mother and child. Once again, we engaged with the worries and anxieties of her parents, which she had internalised, and mortal fears gained the upper hand (Stern, 1995). At the same time, the patient was assured by her husband (and by me) that we were prepared to accompany her and help her bear the uncertainty about the baby's health. She was not abandoned. Before the birth, the patient recalled the "bird dream" and my response to it. Only now did she understand what had moved me so much at the time. She sensed the emotional bond between us, which was able to withstand not knowing. The analysis was terminated after seven years. Genuine separation from the analytic process could only begin after the birth of her child and had to be worked on at less frequent intervals.

Mr V

Mr V (Henningsen, 2008) was twenty-six years old. He was unusually small, slender, and slightly built. When I first saw him, he reminded me of my fifteen-year-old son, except that my son was a little taller and more virile. I sensed that the patient was subject to enormous pressure. He was extremely eloquent; if he had been able to, he would have liked best to "sublimate his problems away". For more than six months he had been suffering from severe conjunctivitis; he could neither read nor write and for that reason was unable to take advantage of a doctoral grant he had been awarded.

> P: When I was six years old, I injured my left eye and it went blind … This was never a problem for me, but it is now. I'm afraid of going totally blind, I suffer from bouts of anxiety and can't sleep. I've been to five doctors, none of them could find anything wrong. My fears are out of all proportion, there must be something else.
> A: Maybe there's something in your life you don't want to see?
> P: When I was between four and seven, I had leukaemia, but I only know that from my mother, I have no memory of it. Maybe I now have to cope with all the fears I didn't have at the time … But that's my mother's trauma, not mine. My girlfriend left me six months ago, for me that's a trauma.
>
> After he had described the separation from his girlfriend, he told me about her panic attacks and her severe illness.
>
> A: You were telling me just now about the way your leukaemia was a trauma not for you but for your mother, she was the one who was really scared. And when you and X were a couple, you could see the fear in her face. Now there's no one close to you with such fears, but you feel the anxiety in yourself.

This first session had greatly affected me: twenty years before, I had acted as a psychotherapist for dying children and their families (Henningsen, 1980, 2002; Henningsen & Ullner, 1981). The patient not only physically resembled my own son, I was also immediately reminded of *my* "leukaemia children". For a moment I hesitated, uncertain whether I wanted to be confronted once more with fears for a dying child, but then I offered him psychoanalytic treatment. In countertransference, his attitude ("that's my mother's trauma, not mine") was a warning, reflecting my intense response at the first session.

Trauma history

The accident in which the patient lost the sight of his left eye happened when he was six, shortly after his younger sister's birth. For that reason he had to spend two months in hospital alone. His good eye was bandaged in an attempt to reactivate the vision in its injured counterpart. When he was hospitalised for leukaemia, his mother was with him most of the time, his grandmother looked after the other children. He was given chemotherapy for three years, total body irradiation only once because his mother could not stand it. She suffered a nervous breakdown and would not consent to further radiation treatment. He tells me that on the phone his mother can still sense how he is feeling before he has said a word.

In his childhood the patient had a severe eating disorder. His parents could only persuade him to accept food by reading exciting stories to him at the same time. He could read and write before he went to school, but he was so frail that his grandmother had to take him there and pick him up afterwards because he could not carry his satchel.

The risk of infection was too great for him to attend kindergarten. The accident happened when he had left his parents' garden, which hardly ever occurred. Neighbour children had told him he could only play with them if he rang the bell at another boy's house and asked his mother if he could come out to play. After he had done that, they made him repeat the process, saying that if he didn't, they'd shoot him with an arrow. He had often played role games with his cousin in which they fantasised about shooting arrows at each other, so he did not believe they would actually do this and refused.

He had never been in a fight with other boys. Up to his twelfth year he had to undergo regular lumbar punctures to check on the progress of the leukaemia. Because of the screaming fits he had as the time for these punctures drew nearer, his parents would wait till morning to tell him that he had an appointment that same day. His anxieties prevented him from getting to sleep, so he had a bed in his parents' bedroom until he was twelve. His own impression was that puberty began at the age of sixteen. He was a very gifted scholar, his father gave him an unusual amount of intellectual coaching.

At the beginning of analysis, he had no memories of his illness whatsoever. In connection with the lumbar punctures, he did remember the painful pressure on his back caused by the insertion of the cannula, but the accompanying scene in hospital could only be reconstructed and recalled in the course of the analysis. Mr V had no image of his illness. In this connection, the anxieties assailing him when he was supposed to go to sleep are important. They prevented the nightmares that would have confronted him with an image of the terrors he was going through. At home, reference to his illness was taboo; there are no photos of him without hair after chemotherapy. I cannot go into the parents' narcissistic attachment to their son; they were greatly distressed to have such a sick boy. But it is worth noting that his mother was an identical twin and therefore particularly predestined to develop an alter-ego relationship with her ill son. Mr V also suffered from urinary pressure and occasional inflammations of the bladder. He was prone to head colds, and later he admitted to nail-biting and sexual problems.

Diagnostic considerations

Mr V's trauma history begins at four, an age when—in comparison with Ms R (who suffered initial traumatisation right at the beginning of life)—the capacity for symbolic thinking is more developed. Prior to that, his development had been unremarkable, except that, as their only son, he had been the object of marked narcissistic cathexis for his parents. The possibility cannot be ruled out that at the age of six his parents had given up all hope of his survival and the function of the later sibling was to replace him. The diagnosis was probably the starting point for the development that culminated in splitting. The inconceivable (imminent death) was kept away from the child; his mother functioned as the receptacle of pain and concern for his life. In this way, a negative hallucination was built up in the child preventing the recognition of reality and designed to protect him from being overwhelmed by mortal fears (Freud, 1890a, p. 296, 1901b, p. 109; cf. also Scharff, 2002, p. 606 et seq.). When at the first session Mr V said: "That's my mother's trauma, not mine", he was attempting to hold on to this defence but probably had an unconscious inkling that it would hardly be feasible if he wanted to achieve adulthood and autonomy. This part of his personality remained bound up with the mother in the form of a self-object fusion.

Establishing concretistic fusion in transference

Mr V suffered greatly from his eye condition; outside therapy he lay in his darkened flat with cosmetic pads on his eyes. At the weekends he was assailed by panic attacks and rang me up so as not to get his mother involved again. Just as his mother could "read" the mood he was in before he said a word on the phone, I could always tell at the end of a session whether Mr V would get some sleep the next night. I was never wrong. I had quite concretely taken the place of his mother and he wanted me to protect him from another breakdown. However, his ability to dream remained unaffected. In his dreams we were able to identify quotations from the various traumatic experiences he had been through in childhood.

He could neither remember what the hospital entrance looked like, nor could he find personal access to me in transference or to his mother in reality. All these three relation points were potentially traumatic and had to be avoided. Soon, however, his eye symptoms disappeared during the week, returning only at the weekends. Obviously there was a relationship with me after all, and he feared he might become dependent on me. He was the apple of his mother's eye; his mother was the container that protected his eye; this container had been destroyed. He had never lived alone in his body. In his conscious perception I was an abstract thing, but at an unconscious level I was his mother (Segal, 1957). After we had worked on the following dream, he achieved a degree of understanding for his unconscious relationship with me, and his conjunctivitis cleared up completely.

> I'm in a room. Below me, slightly to one side, I see my body. It is the body of a fifty-year-old woman, and it is my body. The woman wears a ribbon in her hair and has four eyes. Four eyes in a row. The middle ones are covered with cotton wool, cotton wool pads. I want to take them off, they are under the eyelids, but then I wake up.

This dream symbolises the concretistic fusion and outlines the programme for the analysis. Separation and integration processes will loom large. His body is mother's body, his body is my body. We look at his body with four eyes, two of them sound, two of them sick. He is disturbed in his sexual identity. The fusion of the bodies also has an incestuous component. Physical separation from me—the mother—is supremely dangerous; the eye accident happened outside the garden, it was dangerous to stray away from mother's protective influence. In the dream he is not outside me, but as soon as he attempts separation, his eyesight is at risk and he has to return. The necessity of getting away from the fusion announces itself in this dream. Unlike Ms R, Mr V is able, from the outset, to represent aspects of his constellation of object relations with the help of dreams. He very quickly reminded me of my two earlier patients (Chapter One); he had obviously retained some of the gifts he had when he was a four-year-old boy.

Getting out of the fusion

On the one hand, transference healing made him very optimistic. Opting for analysis had obviously been the right thing to do. On the other hand, and because of this success, his unconscious, incestuously tinged dependence on his mother (on me) became clearer. I was the one who had come up with the right interpretation, therefore I was the one who had power over his body, his illness, and his health. Lying on the couch meant torture, lumbar punctures, chemotherapy. He was afraid of "going mad", as the following dream indicates.

> I look into the mirror, my face falls off, it is radiation-damaged. I have the tatters of my face in my hand.

Mr V fell in love with a woman called Inga. For six months she found it impossible to choose between him and another man. Mr V had always been impotent. In transference he showed me that he could not have a face, no skin of his own. He feared that I might discontinue the analysis in the same way as his mother had terminated his chemotherapy. But I did the opposite. For a few weeks I offered him a fifth session. This change of setting was a signal that I was willing, at a concrete level, to go on providing support and resisting the danger. We were thus able to continue working on the material we had. With the mirror he began to create a vis-à-vis for himself in the dream and to extricate himself from the fusion. In my countertransference I felt highly depressive; sometimes I had the fantasy that the patient's profound regression might cause the leukaemia to return. His immersion in me, in my room, in my wall hangings that he so admired evoked in him a profound yearning and at the same time enormous fears that he might disintegrate or lose his identity. When he observed himself outside of me (mirror = my face, my eyes), he began to fragment his face and lose his skin. Or, vice versa, when he separated himself off from me, things became mortally dangerous for me (as for his mother); there was the risk of decompensation. This dream showed once again the danger that separation meant for him. It was a question of physical dispossession. Memories of earlier medical operations surfaced. In the sex act he was never sure who his body belonged to. "Perhaps the impotence is your body protecting you from belonging to anyone else." His impotence began to disappear, and Inga soon decided in his favour.

Lack of space prohibits a description of the further course of this six-year analysis. Mr V married Inga and in the subsequent years worked on his anguish and the irreversible consequences of his illness. He re-enacted many painful details which in transference he was then able to understand, mourn for, and integrate.

Discussion

The cases described here are representative of experiences that I have been through with other patients suffering from early childhood traumas. They show how closely the traumatisation(s) of the patients are bound up with the object. Split-off parts of the subject fuse with the object, and this structure stands between subject and object like a numbing kind of putty that stunts all development. The child's trauma is the mother's trauma and vice versa, it must not turn into psychic reality and accordingly has to be split off. In my patients it was the unavoidable stages of development in early adulthood that triggered the breakdown. First-time job experiences and issues posed by genital sexuality unsettled the development of the patients' identities and challenged their defence against the traumas (fusion with the object for all time). Abortive separation in this part of the self prevented complete representation of the absent object in the subject. Accordingly, the trauma could not be symbolised. The "objectless anxiety" affect has to be warded off for as long as one lives.

In both patients, the vehemence of acting-out and somatisation was equally marked, as it was in those of my other patients whose psychoneurotic development was triggered by traumatic experiences in early childhood. There was however one essential difference between Ms R and Mr V. In Mr V's case, the concretistic fusion could very quickly be symbolised as a transference figure, whereas Ms R needed two and a half years of analysis to reach the same point. Comparison with other analyses of patients with traumas confirms the conclusion that suggests itself: the earlier traumatisation occurs, the longer concretistic fusion is needed in transference. The logic behind this conclusion is fairly straightforward: the more incomplete the separation between subject and object is, the longer it takes in analysis to make that separation possible.

In the first phase of analysis, my interpretive technique was largely descriptive. I talked about what was going on in analysis and related it to the traumatic scene. This translation work gradually made defence ego-dystonic. I avoided causal interpretations as far as possible, so as not to put too much pressure on the patients' feelings of shame and guilt right at the beginning of analysis.

The specific form taken by the concretistic fusion was always closely bound up with the nature of the trauma. Central in both cases (Ms R and Mr V) on the level of the false self was the blotting out of physical impotence and limitations. On the plane of the traumatised self, on the other hand, everything was physical, and in transference I was responsible for the bodily side of things, making sure that Ms R could weep as much as she needed to and in Mr V's case simply knowing how he was feeling. The essential thing was to recognise and give a name to the traumatic experiences split off in the fusions.

Causally the fusions are bound up with the disruption of psycho-somatic unity, the form of which becomes clear when we look at the pathological nature of the affect-mirroring involved (Fonagy & Target, 2002; Fonagy, Gergely, Jurist, & Target, 2002). Ms R's mother was unable to mirror her child's feelings in any well-defined way (Fonagy & Target, 2002; Fonagy, Gergely, Jurist, & Target, 2002). She probably projected her own unconscious death fears on to the child and merely reproduced the child's other impulses, thus thwarting an uncoupling from one another. Emotionally, mother and child remained fused in this depressive part; a fusion core formed that from the outset was instrumental in the later development of a symbolisation disorder. Whereas in the case of Ms R it is appropriate to speak of a (depressive) fusion core linking two pseudo-autonomous persons, in the case of Mr V we have two persons in one body (McDougall, 1989).

Mr V's mother had also projected her own death fears into the child, but Mr V was four years old at the time and had already developed a number of self-representations that enabled him to think symbolically. True, even during pre-traumatic infancy the relationship with his parents had been narcissistically tinged, and this may have encouraged the formation of the fusion. But Mr V had various secondary representations at his disposal and in analysis these could be activated relatively quickly.

In my view, these dissimilarities explain the different course taken by therapy in each case. Only successively and at a very late stage could

Ms R symbolise her traumatic experiences in analysis, whereas Mr V was fairly quick to represent his pathological separation anxieties in dream form. To the end, Ms R remained an analysand with very little dream activity. By contrast, Mr V enriched the analytic process from the outset with an abundance of dreams casting light on what was going on in transference.

In the cases we have been discussing, I think it especially important to see how these fusions relate to the patient's respective development and to trace the way in which these structures are perpetuated and consolidated and in critical situations bring about serious illness. When these fusions are resolved in transference, there is a danger that the affects thus released—affects of objectless anxiety and fear of destruction—may jeopardise the therapeutic relationship. Accordingly, it may make sense to increase treatment frequency for a limited space of time. Normally the experiences in question can only be verbalised at a later stage.

Both these patients (and the others) developed transitional homoerotic phenomena in phases of integration, notably at the beginning, when they sensed how the unsayable, the unspeakable threat, could be retained within the therapeutic space. Here the reality of the trauma is revealed in the psychic effect it has. The experience of being held led to massive arousal that was bound via sexualisation. Like my other patients with early traumas, Ms R had had transient homoerotic experiences in adolescence or early adulthood, at a time of extreme uncertainty. In Mr V's case, the issue of homosexuality permeated the entire analysis. He had an incestuous bond with his mother and established a similar attachment in transference. In analysis, the requisite separation processes called for work on the destruction and guilt that appear to be indissolubly interlinked as a result of the trauma and the helplessness bound up with it (cf. Henningsen, 2004c; Chapter Seven).

Another factor that played a major role in all patients was attachment to the primary family, although they were outwardly separated from their parents' homes and lived elsewhere. As is the case in child therapy, initial analytic progress, usually powered by transference, prompted the parents to urge their children to discontinue analysis. Unconsciously, the depth of the relationship that the patients were establishing with me will probably have seriously alarmed the parents. They too sensed the very real danger that incipient separation from their children was liable to endanger their defence against their own traumas. Later, after the patients had found a new language for verbalising their traumas, they also regained access to their parents, which was helpful for both sides.

As our two cases demonstrate, the readiness to fuse displayed by the patients at the beginning of treatment frequently leads to swift transference healings. Ms R and Mr V were soon able to resume work and Mr V's eye disorder quickly cleared up. But as in all such cases, work on psychic structures requires high-frequency, long-term analysis. In my experience, extricating oneself from the fusion is the essential and the most difficult process in treatment because at this point the patients are especially unstable and endangered. This stage of treatment releases the objectless anxiety from its former bindings. All kinds of responses are conceivable: psychosomatic reactions like the skin disorders of my two patients; temporary impotence; thoughts of suicide; tendencies to discontinue therapy; or psychotic reactions. In these critical phases, the essential thing is to use interpretation of the process to make the symptoms understandable in transference. Usually, the trusting relationship that has been established and the work done on the history of the trauma—albeit on a purely cognitive plane up to this point—are of major significance in the instigation of symbolisation processes.

CHAPTER THREE

"We aren't starving yet": silence in withdrawal and communicating in images

Hanna

Hanna is a thirteen-year-old girl with a history of severe anorexia. I have published an account of my work with her under the title "… *aber die Gespräche mit Ihnen waren so interessant*" ("… but talking to you was always so interesting"), a quotation from what Hanna said at one point in her treatment (Henningsen, 1988). At that time, I did not fully understand the extent to which the girl's traumatic experiences in early childhood had conditioned the genesis of her illness. For that reason I intend to revisit the case here.

First contact

Hanna (thirteen years, three months) is the youngest of four children in an unremarkable family. The father is an official in a small Bavarian village, the mother is a housewife. Twice a week, the mother does some cleaning for a nearby company to earn a little extra money. Hanna attends a secondary modern school. She is a very average schoolgirl and is generally considered "ungifted". Before she came to our clinic in Munich, she spent a number of weeks at another hospital where she was treated for anorexia nervosa. She put on a little weight and no further psychotherapeutic measures were taken. Back home she lost weight again and ate nothing at all, thus prompting her parents to turn to the psychosomatic counselling centre of the University Children's Hospital in Munich.

Hanna is a pale girl with long dark-blond hair that hangs down over her face and almost prevents eye contact. Her handshake is extremely slack; after every greeting I automatically stretch my fingers so that I can feel them again. In the first few days in hospital she displayed no affects whatsoever and made no kind of contact with others. For hours she sat in a corner of the hospital yard, staring in front of her with a vacant expression on her face. Her bearing at the time was such as to arouse suspicion of an incipient psychosis (catatonia); today it would certainly be appropriate to inquire into the possibility of reactive autism. But the psychological examination suggested a severely depressive condition. Hanna was five foot tall, which was in line with her age, and weighed 37.3 kg, which according to Köhle and Simons (1982) was 10 kg or twenty-seven per cent underweight (today BMI: 16.58). She suffered from constipation and used laxatives every day. Before the onset of amenorrhoea, her menstruation had been irregular. The classical symptoms—physical overactivity and ambition—were absent, but this is nothing new (Thomä, 1961; Mahler & Thomä, 1964; Sperling & Massing, 1970).

Anamnesis

While Hanna is undergoing her medical check-up, I meet her mother for a preliminary talk. It quickly becomes apparent that the parents are at their wits' end. Hanna's mother is a large, strapping woman with a loud voice. Her description of the situation reveals the state of despair she is in. She makes a massive impression on me, her narcissistic attachment to her daughter dominates our conversation. She finds it more or less impossible to talk about her daughter's development from Hanna's point of view, only from her own: what it was like for her when Hanna was born, etc. She is also frequently unable to distinguish between her daughter's feelings and her own, as if they were one person. But if I confront her with this or help her by asking a question, she is quick to adjust and able to carry on from there.

Like all the children in the family, Hanna was an "accident". The parents had little money and the paternal grandmother, who lived in the same house, frequently criticised the mother during her pregnancies. "I hope you suffer," she would say, "then there won't be any more kids." She also "accused" Hanna's mother of "wanting too much sex" from her son, Hanna's father. Up to the wedding, the grandmother had shared the parental bed with Hanna's father and later "made a lot of trouble" during their marriage. The mother will hardly have been able to assert herself. When she was carrying Hanna, she cried a lot and felt pressurised by the neighbours and her mother-in-law. In her desperation she went out and bought an entire trousseau for the baby to show that she could manage on her own. "We're not starving yet," the mother said to me.

She says she had never needed to spend much time looking after Hanna because the other children were there (two, four, and six years older). Hanna had always been docile, except on one occasion when her mother had to go to hospital. Hanna was fourteen months old at the time and refused to look at her mother for four weeks after she returned home. Even today, the mother feels very hurt by her daughter's behaviour and cannot acknowledge the child's separation trauma. Aside from that, Hanna's development had been normal. Up to the onset of anorexia some six months ago, Hanna was an unusually sunny child, but now she has no more contact with anyone and even neglects her pets, a miniature rabbit called Charlie and two dogs, Susi and Strolchi. Hanna would like a job looking after animals when she has finished school. The mother refers to her marriage as good. Of course there were sometimes differences of opinion, but the parents never quarrelled in front of the children. The bone of contention is usually that she is too lenient and the father too strict. Though the mother-in-law no longer lives in the same house, the family often feels that she is breathing down their necks and this frequently involves them in deception, for example, when the family plans to go camping at the weekend without her. The children are also instructed not to tell the truth. This is explained to them as a white lie. Hanna's mother was never given any proper sex education. "That's what puts you in a fix when it comes to having children yourself. I got it wrong four times, didn't I?" Her conjecture is that Hanna knows what her period means, but they have never talked about it. As regards food, the mother says she wouldn't mind trying out other dishes but the family menu repeats itself every two weeks "because they all want the same stuff. They're very picky and choosy, my posh children, they get that from their father." Since his own father's death, Hanna's father has suffered from recurrent ulcers; four years ago two-thirds of his stomach were removed.

In the quest for the clinching factor triggering the anorexia, there are two things to go on. Two siblings had finished school and left home, so Hanna was alone with her brother, who was hoping to do his *Abitur* (school-leaving exams entitling him to go to university). Hanna's sister, four years older than Hanna, had always been a real companion for her. Also, last summer Hanna had a traumatic experience on a camp site where the family has a caravan. She saw a man having a heart attack, who shortly after died in the community rooms on the camp site. Her mother says she was profoundly disturbed by the experience but cannot say any more about it.

Diagnostic considerations

The exchange with the mother is an adequate basis for initial hypotheses about the genesis of her daughter's disorder and her present conflict situation. The mother's mixture of self-commiseration and possessiveness plus her egocentric view of things had a numbing effect on me at various points in our conversation. I had to "key myself up" to confront her and/or divert her attention to her daughter. My depressive countertransference feelings may reflect those of her daughter. In addition I was probably sensing the depression the mother was fending off. The father plays almost no conscious part in the proceedings at all. The mother presents herself as the centre of the family. Her feelings are reality for everyone. Her present conviction that Hanna was "riled" when she refused to look at her after her spell in hospital reveals an empathy disorder that almost certainly asserts itself whenever separation, ambivalence, and aggression(s) are up for discussion.

In the background, however, the father and his mother are important figures. There was obviously an incestuous attachment between them. The recurring ulcers starting after the death of the grandfather can be regarded as a psychosomatic correlate for his unconscious and unaddressed oedipal conflicts (Henningsen, 1976). The mother had next to no support from her husband and probably clung symbiotically to her youngest daughter, the family pet. It is safe to assume that Hanna followed her mother into depression and that here a fusion core took shape that was bound to crack open with the onset of sexual maturity in puberty and triggered the anorexia.

The recent separation from her sisters will have exposed Hanna to her mother even more radically and effectively hampered individuation. Hostile feelings were projected on to the grandmother and on to the repulsive/seductive sides of sexuality. Thus each pregnancy turns into a "blunder" and has little to do with love or pleasure in life. The scene on the camp site may have awakened sexual fantasies in Hanna and brought the family's fended-off, forbidden "incest" myth to the surface.

In addition, we need to ask to what extent Hanna identifies with the father, who like her is very fussy about what he eats and is generally very choosy. Does she feel neglected as a result of her father's illness and is this her revenge? Or is she using the illness (like the father?) to flee from the engulfing arms of her mother? Is her refusal to eat a protest against the mother?

The time in hospital

During the first two weeks, the parents were not allowed to visit their daughter. Hanna's mother found the separation extremely difficult to bear. There were repeated instances in which the mother flew in the face of what the doctors were doing, phoning her daughter to tell her that she didn't have to eat if she didn't want to and that she weighed enough. Or she would flout all agreements and suddenly turn up at the hospital laden with cakes and bags of apples. The hospital staff did their best to react to the mother's behaviour calmly, repeatedly bringing home to her the demands posed by the situation.

Hanna was put in the general ward of the children's polyclinic. My agreement with the nurses and doctors was as follows: no coercive measures were to be undertaken. Hanna was given the same meals as the other children. If she refused to eat, the food was taken away again after half an hour without comment. She was weighed twice a week and told about her weight. The ward doctor was fully and solely responsible for her physical care. My regular visits and the weekly nurses' conference enhanced my contact with the staff of the ward, where I was providing psychotherapeutic care for other children as well. Should there be no signs of improvement after the first week, we would get together and discuss how best to proceed. Hanna had one analytic session a day with me (five a week).

In Hanna's case, an advising psychiatrist was called in to rule out the possibility of an incipient psychotic development. The psychiatrist prescribed low-dose anti-depressive medication for Hanna, which she took during her stay in hospital (four and a half weeks) and in the first two months of outpatient treatment. On the second day of her stay in hospital Hanna collapsed in the corridor outside the ward. She was moved to a one-bed room; the psychotherapeutic sessions took place at her bedside, later in my office. In psychodynamic terms, Hanna's faint was connected with another bag of food that her mother had brought her. That way, she could protect herself from her mother and leave it to the staff to keep her away. She delegated part of her defence to the hospital.

Throughout her stay in hospital there was a clearly discernible connection between her basic mood and her willingness to eat. On days when she was prepared to contribute something to the psychotherapeutic session she was also able to eat a little. On such days she also took an interest in objects or toys, her mood was slightly more buoyant, and she was generally less passive. In her severely depressive states—mostly in the first few days, later they receded somewhat—she had a vacant expression on her face, hardly said a word, scarcely responded to questions, and wanted me to ask her questions she could answer with "yes" or "no" so that she wouldn't have to say so much. In technical terms, her expressionless face and her silence were the biggest problem for me because it made it difficult to summon up any understanding for her. If I asked her questions, she would feel I was trying to pry or to force her into doing something, and this encouraged her paranoid mistrust. Hanna only ever spoke in terse short sentences. Usually she repeated things she had already said before. Two topics were recurrent: she wanted to go back home as soon as possible, and she was afraid of being laughed at if she put on weight. Hanna had a girlfriend who was very thin and constantly boasted about it. She often said to her: "Come on, fatso!" Hanna had frequently felt hurt and annoyed by this. In this context it also seemed significant that Hanna felt that the doctors who urged her to eat (against our agreement) were not taking her seriously. Only towards the end of her stay in hospital did it start to dawn on her that, while it is right to stop people from laughing at you, starving yourself half to death is perhaps not the wisest course to pursue. I told her that as a psychotherapist I was there to help her find other ways of defending herself against scorn and mockery. This fear of mockery reveals Hanna's narcissistic sensitivity. Of course I asked myself what was behind it all. Did she feel inferior because she was a girl (castration anxieties)? Or did she have feelings of rejection bound up with her early trauma (the pathological attachment to her depressive mother and the mother's hospitalisation)?

Another stereotypically recurrent subject was her desire to go home. She kept on asking how much she would need to weigh in order to be discharged. In the first few days, when her depressive states were at their worst, she felt rejected and let down by her parents. Her terse comment was: "They don't want me." Soon after, her mother came to visit her for the first time. After this visit, Hanna confessed to me that she would never have thought that her parents would worry about her so much. "They do want me," she said. Her desire to go home also had to do with her pets. She told me about them, but in general she was unable to express her longings in terms of specific ideas and well-defined wishes.

Hanna realised that by refusing to eat she was missing out on something. Basically she enjoyed her food. Also, she was penalised for her refusal: her parents rejected her, and the doctors did not stick to the agreement and tried to make her eat, which meant they didn't really take her seriously. Once she had understood this, she appeared to be willing to eat again, a development accompanied by slightly greater interest in her surroundings. Once, when I made an appreciative comment about a carpet she was making, she responded with the stony, expressionless gaze she had displayed earlier. I said to her: "You don't know whether to be pleased or not." Then she started crying bitterly. After a while, she was able to talk to me about painting and handiwork and I sensed that she took an interest in these things. I felt some slight hope that a working alliance had established itself between us. After four and a half weeks (twenty-three sessions), I decided that taking her out of hospital would not have any adverse effects.

Outpatient treatment

After her discharge, Hanna came to Munich once a week for psychotherapy. This involved a train journey of an hour and a half. The first nine months of treatment were very difficult indeed because she hardly ever said a word the whole time. In these sessions I was so affected by the depressive feelings the girl was warding off that I started seriously doubting whether there was any point in continuing. The sessions always took the same course. Hanna entered the room, gave me a friendly handshake, and as soon as she sat down, all contact broke off. Her hair hung down before her eyes like a curtain, her gaze became stony and vacant. She said nothing of her own accord. She wanted me to ask her questions but she never answered them. There was practically no hope of getting her to talk about her feelings or experiences. I inquired, interpreted, fell silent, in line with my ideas and my countertransference. My efforts had no appreciable effect. I drew parallels with her oral greed, she was hungry for my questions, wanted me to feed her with my sentences. She rejected exchange with me as rigorously as she spurned food at home. After the sessions I was drained and felt the need to stride up and down in my room, probably to work off the tension that had accumulated. Before Hanna arrived, I let in fresh air or drank strong coffee or tea to steel myself against the fatigue I knew was bound to come.

I experienced her negative transference alternately as aggression and helplessness, and interpreted it as such. At the same time, I had the feeling that I would just have to stick it out. I suggested we could paint, make things, play games, or make music together, but she invariably refused. At this stage in the proceedings, some sessions did not take place. In retrospect, this was the result of inexplicable misunderstandings. Via projective identification, Hanna lived out her mother's depressiveness for me, the mother she was bound up with. She was the inferior, rejected, unloved child I could make no progress with, just as the mother saw herself in her child. The fusional core between mother and child consisted of depression and silence and became manifest between us.

But outside the sessions she gradually started getting better. She played with her pets and made contact with her school friends. At Christmas, it became evident that despite her rejective attitude she also identified with me. She had said she wanted a round table for her room like the one I had in my office. In the sessions, we soon had a topic we were able to exchange views on, albeit in a fragmentary way: Hanna's pets. After her discharge from hospital, her entire problem was re-enacted with reference to her pets.

Shortly before Hanna's first stay in hospital, her poodle Susi had given birth to puppies, one of which was extremely weak and had to be fed by Hanna with a bottle. In Hanna's absence, the young dogs developed to an age at which they could either be sold or put in a dogs' home. So that she could see at least one of them, Hanna's parents kept

Strolchi, the runt of the litter. One week after discharge from the polyclinic he too was given away. Hanna's reaction was to shed bitter tears and refuse to eat until her parents finally agreed to bring him back home again. Hanna was very fond of the dog, and when she left the house he invariably "cried". She felt less alone when he was there. A number of parallels suggested themselves between this situation and the state she was in in hospital. Hanna was very much alone, very weak, and had to be nursed back to health by others. Later it transpired that Strolchi was a mongrel: "It happened at my cousin's confirmation party." Asked how the family and her sisters felt about him, Hanna said her sisters had wanted to keep him but her parents had still given him away. Her grandmother said his feet were too long, it was too much work looking after him, and he was too expensive. Hanna described in detail the games she played with Susi and Strolchi. An interpretation suggested itself for Hanna's identification with the dog. He had been put in the dogs' home like she had been put in hospital. Like herself, Strolchi had been a "child" looked upon above all by her grandmother, but also by her mother, as the product of dirty sex. When she had been separated from her mother at the age of fourteen months, Hanna had not been able to express her distress in an understandable way.

At this stage in the proceedings, Hanna had probably understood quite a few things at the purely cognitive level. But emotionally there was no resonance at all, the affects were split off. All in all, this period was also marked by lifelessness and rigidity.

When our exchanges had petered out once again and it was time for me to ask questions to keep the ball rolling, I wanted to know whether Hanna's mother asked her as many questions as I did. She said yes, and it became apparent that Hanna disliked this. Her mother was always asking her about school. Thereupon I said: "Then your silence with me makes sense. It's good for you to be able to say no to these eternal questions, if you don't let me interrogate you like your mother and give polite answers even though you don't want to." In the subsequent sessions Hanna talked a little about handicrafts and complained about her overweening grandmother. She was the one who said that dog food was too expensive. I said: "All right, but up till recently you certainly didn't cost your grandmother much in the way of food." Hanna laughed a little and in the next few sessions agreed to do things with me, painting and batiking. Of course, I had tried similar or even identical interventions before, but they had never had any visible effect on her behaviour.

What I believe to be essential is that at this point in the therapy I had a better understanding of my countertransference. Hanna constantly rejected me and my efforts. I had the feeling that I was physically present but not really there. That was the way she treated her body. Her powerful anger and oral greed were clearly split off and projected on to me. I realised that as long as she turned me into nothing in transference, this had no negative impact on her general physical state; in fact it remained stagnant or even improved a little. I believe that this realisation stopped me from being annihilated by her destructive transference offer. At the same time, I had no expectations of Hanna. Harold N. Boris describes the countertransference problem with anorectic patients in a similar way:

> The anorexia [...] is designed to elicit countertransferences by stimulating substantiations for the projections the anorectic characteristically makes. The analyst is to be discovered as greedy, intemperate, enslaving. These discoveries will in turn imply defects and flaws: if the analyst wants the breast so much, he cannot therefore have one; if he hasn't a breast or penis (or whatever) of value, he needs neither to be desired nor envied; he is a no-thing. This is the anorectic solution. (1984, p. 437)

The pictures

Our joint activities established between Hanna and me an "intermediary space" (Schacht, 1987; Winnicott, 1953) in which Hanna was able to relinquish her nothingness position. The atmosphere changed appreciably. I no longer felt so strained by the therapy. Initially she was shy and insisted she had no ideas. She wanted to use finger paints but I was to tell her what to paint with them. And she wanted me to paint on the same paper she was using (the paper was very large, A3).

In Picture 1, I was the one who suggested painting flowers but soon we understood each other implicitly and the suggestions and ideas came from her. I keep my painting restrained so as not to influence or impair her development. For Hanna it is important that I am with her, taking part.

In the second picture we move our fingers across the paper, make contact, and then part ways again. This picture reveals an essential juncture in the transference situation. As the lines on the paper intertwine, the

Picture 1

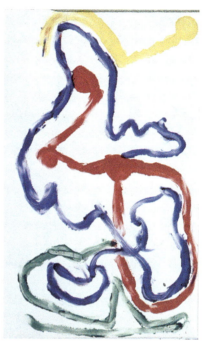

Picture 2

Picture 3

Picture 4

Picture 5

Picture 6

Picture 7

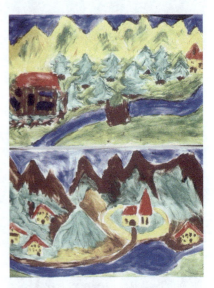

Picture 8

Picture 9

Picture 10

Picture 11

Picture 12

Picture 13

Picture 14

Picture 15

56   ANALYSING PATIENTS WITH TRAUMAS

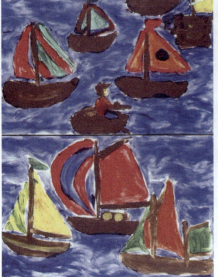

Picture 16

Picture 17

Picture 18

Picture 19

illusion of fusion materialises in the relationship (Milner, 1952, 1969), as if our limits were suspended, as if she were a part of me and I of her.

After that, we paint a clown (Picture 3). I remember very clearly that Hanna painted the closed eyes and the big mouth. They reminded me of her shut-off face and split-off greed. Before the outbreak of anorexia, she too had been a jokester, a clown fending off melancholy with the role she was playing. It was impossible to talk to Hanna about such things. She wanted to express herself by her deeds. At times we also made music. I would play a tune on the xylophone and Hanna would repeat it, or vice versa. Or one of us would play the start of a tune and the other had to finish it. Sometimes we also played simple children's songs, with me sometimes accompanying Hanna on the flute. Then she wanted to paint again.

Two dogs appear on the paper, done in Indian ink (Picture 4). Hanna paints the dog on the left and the bowl of dog food. I ask her: "Is that Susi and Strolchi? Or is it the two of us?" A smile flits across her face. She feels understood. The six dog biscuits are presumably the six members of her family. One can also see the two dogs as a couple. The food and the red floor also suggest that these may be oral-sexual fantasies.

When we paint our horse picture, I only have room for an anorectic foal. The picture expresses the transference and countertransference situation discussed earlier. My role is that of the needy foal, hers that of a powerful horse that reminds me of her mother. I sense the dynamism of Hanna's horse, in stark contrast to her own physical appearance and her limp handshake. We talk about this.

At the next session Hanna wants me to paint on paper of my own. Here Hanna enacts a separation. Her contact with me becomes more objectal and begins to consolidate itself. Hanna's reaches for the finger paints and the big sheets of paper. She suggests we both paint a house. I am to paint the same thing as her but separately, on a sheet of my own.

The next subject is the window of a "jeans shop". Details such as the hooped T-shirts are to be found in both pictures. She adopts ideas of mine. We also both paint father, mother, daughter. In Hanna's picture, the daughter is not standing on her own two feet but perched on a kind of clothes rack, expressing her insecurity about her female identity. Hanna's daughter figure has no face; here she is showing the side of herself that has turned away from life. In a personal communication, Wolfgang Loch proposes the following interpretation of the clothes rack: on a symbolic plane Hanna is expressing an initial externalisation of her male introject. Loch sees a second step in this direction in Picture 15, where Hanna paints a man "from top to toe".

In our fairground pictures we both revel in the abundance of the material. They illustrate an essential aspect of our relationship. I tend to be as open as I can to win Hanna round, whereas she prefers to close herself off.

In the mountainous landscapes of her home, the striking features are the bright, friendly mountains and the bridge across the river. I no longer recall which of us first painted the river and the bridge. I ask myself whether the river, as a natural boundary, represents the living transitional space (Winnicott, 1953), the middle realm between external and internal reality. Here the task of therapy is to build a bridge. Marion Milner (1952, 1969) refers on various occasions to art and play as a "bridge between inner and outer, self and not-self."

The mute fish in Picture 10 shows Hanna becoming progressively more lively and imaginative. The same is true of the bird of paradise in Picture 12. Its big bushy tail is a sexual symbol. Reserve or restraint has been thrown to the winds.

The next painting is of a camp site (Picture 11). Hanna's is fenced-in and quiet. The many fences are presumably an equivalent for reality but also allude to the incest barrier. She has even painted the house the man with a heart attack was moved to. We talk about the fears she had at the time.

In her picture of the Ferris wheel (it is the *Oktoberfest* season in Munich) Hanna expresses the flurry and the dynamism of the turning movement (Picture 13). I am happy to see her so strong and expressive.

The same applies to the "scary ghosts" (Picture 14). The faces of Hanna's figures clearly display fear and terror, but no aggression on the part of the ghost. Her ghost is kneeling, it can neither escape nor come rushing to the foreground. What is she telling us? If we look at the last three pictures in sequence, we will understand why she proceeded as she did. The hypothesis expressed earlier that the man's cardiac arrest on the camp site had triggered sexual fantasies and conflicts in Hanna's mind is confirmed. In my view, the Ferris wheel also expresses orgasmic turmoil and the ghost pictures Hanna's fears. After she had painted the camp site, we talked both about her experiences at the time and about the lack of space in the caravan, with everyone sleeping in the same area. Subsequently she was able to display her feelings in the pictures.

The traumatic situation on the camp site is for Hanna an equivalent for the primal scene and was probably centrally operative in the outbreak of her illness.

Our pictures become increasingly different from one another. I am more and more strongly convinced that Hanna will find her way. When we painted the two Red Indians (Picture 15), Hanna came to the session with a new haircut, her fringe cut short "so one can see the face better". Her mother accompanies her to the next session, I had not seen her for 18 months. She asks me to talk to Hanna and persuade her to do her O-level examinations. Her teacher had said she was doing well in school and had what it took to pass the exams. Hanna told me she would like to go on attending school and become a children's nurse. "That's great," I said. "If those are your plans, I'll keep my fingers crossed for you." Hanna's American Indian impresses me particularly because here she has painted a man in full.

With the sailing boats it is Hanna (!) who paints a human figure (Picture 16). After that she wants different material to work with. We agree to try out reverse glass painting at the next session.

Hanna arrives at the session with preconceived ideas. She wants to paint flowers (Picture 17). The impression I have is that in the meantime she has read up a few things about rustic-style painting and wants to paint in that style. Important is the red flower in the middle, an expression of her emotional side and her sexuality.

When we have finished our first work, she wants to continue with reverse glass painting. First she suggests "morning" and "evening". Without talking any further, I begin a morning picture, while Hanna paints two owls (Picture 18). When she has finished her picture, she compares it with mine and says that her sky is too light for an evening picture and scratches some of it away so that she can make the moon shine more brightly and turn it into a sun. Here she is presumably painting the mother–child situation she had always wanted and also the transference relationship: two cheerful owls, in no way reminiscent of brooding, depressive nocturnal birds.

At the next sessions, she resumes her original plan and produces an evening picture. She paints a well. With the well and the red bucket in the middle of it, Hanna is once again expressing her genitality. The red centre of the picture recalls Picture 17, in which all the flowers circle around the large red blossom. In the picture of the well, the oval shape resembles a window (Picture 19). The view from darkness into light and the three trees may be an expression of the inner position Hanna has arrived at. It is a view of a three-part constellation, perhaps a reference to the oedipal situation. Important is the fact that she is now able to paint on her own and independently of me. She gives the picture a shape of her own.

At the final sessions she says repeatedly that she thinks that soon she won't have to come any more. She insists that she is just fine. Although there are many things we haven't talked about, I think she's right. She then paints a winter landscape with snow and a frozen lake with children skating on it. I could not take a photo of her last picture because she took it home with her. Hanna terminates the treatment after twenty months. Her weight is average. She is now fifteen years old and five foot five. She has her period, but it is still irregular.

Of course, I attempted to feel my way into the situation and the topics Hanna wanted to paint and was less concerned to produce "nice pictures". Our pictures are often complementary. When one of us paints something bright and open, the other produces a picture that is dark and forbidding (Pictures 8, 9, 19), when one of us paints something mute and still, the other produces something more lively and vibrant (Pictures 6, 10, 12, 13) and so forth. Here, complementarity needs to be understood as the smallest move away from imitation (Gaddini, 1998) and/or identification. In her pictorial expression, Hanna ultimately becomes more liberated and light-footed, and my pictures have increasingly little to do with hers. The many fences she paints (Pictures 5, 6, 9, 12, 19) are a counterpoise to the symbolic tendencies perceptible in the complementarity. Hanna sets herself off from me in order to discover her individuality. Alongside this self-demarcation there are also commonalities. Hanna repeatedly takes up details in my pictures, like the hooped T-shirts (Picture 7), the potato sacks (Picture 8) and the oval frame (Picture 19). The relationship Hanna establishes with me via the paintings is characterised by self-demarcation and identification alike.

Two and a half years after the conclusion of therapy, I invited Hanna back for a follow-up interview. She came with her parents. The parents expressed their gratitude, said that since treatment Hanna had been a new person, and then left. Hanna had turned into a pretty young girl, her gaze was clear-eyed and awake, and she even gave me a firm handshake! She said she was doing fine, her period was usually regular. She enjoyed going to a discotheque with friends from school. She was not "going steady" with anyone, she preferred to be part of a group and not to commit herself yet. She had done her O-levels with a "good" average grade and was looking forward to starting her training as a children's nurse.

Asked what she could remember of her experiences in our interviews, she said: "I didn't like it in hospital. But the conversations with you were very interesting." She obviously did not know that she had been silent most of the time. But our communication took place via the paintings; in therapy she was able to communicate with a good internal object.

Discussion

In terms of symptomatology and family constellations Hanna appears to be almost a "classic case". Her father is chronically ill, her grandmother dominant, and her mother helpless (Sperling & Massing, 1970; Thomä, 1961, 1981; Köhle & Simons, 1982), she had been teased and called "Fatso" without being particularly corpulent (Bruch, 1978; Thomä, 1981). If we take our bearings from Köhle and Simons, Hanna was certainly a patient with a favourable prognosis although at the time of hospitalisation her weight was considerably lower than it should have been (Köhle & Simons, 1982, p. 533). But her illness began in early puberty; at the onset of treatment she had not been ill for very long. And a traumatic experience had preceded the outbreak of anorexia (cf. also Bruch, 1978).

The long initial phase of treatment, Hanna's silence and total refusal to co-operate, might prompt one to think of the Parisian school (Marty, 1958; de M'Uzan, 1977) and later the affectlessness of psychosomatosis patients described by Christel Schöttler (1981) and Stephanos (1981). Another approach would be to interpret Hanna's silence as an autistic phenomenon. The two-stage form of illness described by Frances Tustin (1986, p. 1 et seq.) can be found in Hanna's anamnesis: close attachment to the mother and traumatic physical separation in early childhood. In Hanna's case, one would then need to take account of the fact that this early-childhood trauma was encapsulated, with the capsule bursting and leading to anorexia in puberty when the girl was once more confronted with physical separation after exposure to the primal scene.

At all events, the essential factor is the splitting-off of the affect in the traumatic scene. The course taken by therapy indicates that Hanna's rigidity was a reaction to an ongoing conflict. We can regard the cardiac arrest suffered by the man on the camp site, and the camp site situation in general, as the operative factor. Primal-scene fantasies reduced Hanna to silence. Sexual arousal and fear will have been exacerbated to the point of intolerability, causing massive ego-regression with attendant "asceticism at puberty" (A. Freud, 1937, p. 153). Hanna denied the existence of her environment and her own body. In my countertransference I sensed the destructive affects, a sign that by means of splitting and projection Hanna was able to involve her vis-à-vis. I was able—with varying degrees of success—to take my bearings from my countertransference. Later, Hanna was able to express her feelings in her paintings. Their vividness and the wealth of ideas in them suggest that she was able to develop a language for her feelings. This development tends in her case to contradict the presence of autistic phenomena.

In Hanna's case we are confronted by a specific kind of one-dimensionality that reappears strikingly in traumatic situations. The disintegration of the protective shield enables the harmful external world to impinge on the psyche. Destructive influences from the outside world are no longer filtered by contact barriers, repression mechanisms, or transitional space. In transference-countertransference analysis, this leads to the almost intolerable feelings of destruction so impressively represented in anorexia.

> There is no transitional space—the not-me, but yet not-other space—that transitional phenomena require (Winnicott, 1953). The anorectic lives, as it were, without a skin. Others, in their incandescent desirability, impact on her with detonating force. And this is the problem. To solve it, the anorectic creates an 'inner' space: in-me but not of-me. She sets all her soldiers of vigilance to monitor that space. Thus employed, they do not have time or energy to notice the presence of the object, who would otherwise excite desire and envy. (Boris, 1984, p. 437)

When Hanna started painting, this created an intermediary space that made it possible to reverse this regression. The well-known equation looking=eating (Fenichel, 1932, p. 598) was confirmed via inversion: not-looking=not-eating. The course of treatment reversed this process: Hanna shows herself in her pictures and I look; I show myself in my pictures, she looks. And after she has achieved separation in transference, she looks straight at her own sexuality by ousting me from the painting with her powerful horse.

Early traumatisation at the age of fourteen months is responsible for the serious crisis in puberty. This was when Hanna's "constant historical basis" (Fenichel, 1932, p. 587)—today we would speak of her implicit procedural memory—was given its decisive imprint. It seems safe to suppose that her mother's hospitalisation took place during the practice phase or the transition from the practising phase to the rapprochement phase (cf. Mahler, Pine, & Bergman, 1975). Hanna had no adequate symbolic language at her disposal to cope with the separation from her mother, so she also reacted to the present trauma with speechlessness and depression.

Hanna's therapy was more about facilitating development processes than working on neurotic processes in the conventional sense of the term. Hanna was still very young, she was in the initial stages of puberty. She needed the presence of another to develop, and she became more independent, lively, and intelligent all the time. Her relationship with me became constantly more objectal and coherent. At the end of treatment, Hanna had acquired some of that "capacity to be alone" described by Winnicott (1958). In this way, preconditions were created that made it easier for her to get through the remaining stages of puberty. Winnicott also sheds light on the question of how we should understand the close intermesh between individuality problems and sexual conflicts:

> It could be said that an individual's capacity to be alone depends on his ability to deal with the feelings aroused by the primal scene. [...] To be able to be alone in these circumstances implies a maturity of erotic development, a genital potency or the corresponding female acceptance; it implies fusion of the aggressive and erotic impulses and ideas, and it implies a tolerance of ambivalence; along with all this there would naturally be a capacity on the part of the individual to identify with each of the parents. (Winnicott, 1958, p. 31)

Other authors would refer to this as achieving the depressive position (Britton, 1995).

Individuation and engagement with one's gender identity are two closely related developmental processes. This is as true of puberty as it is of infant development. Margaret Mahler and her associates (Mahler, Pine, & Bergman, 1975) provide ample evidence that in the rapprochement phase girls become aware of penis absence and are shaken by it. I believe that Hanna was going through a "pubertal rapprochement crisis" that needed to be worked on.

Yet many questions still remain unanswered. Why, for example, was it not possible to give clearer verbal expression to the conflicts? Pictures reveal and conceal at the same time. They lack the unambiguity of verbal language and call for interpretation. A picture is by definition a mystery, an allusion, it can refer to something else. By remaining on this plane of communication, Hanna represents her struggle for the preservation of autonomy, which she experienced as being jeopardised. In her painting, Hanna was expressing something that she had no words for and living through it with me. If we look at her paintings in sequence, we see that the first of them revolve around separation and individuation. Only after that do we come across the equivalents for the primal scene. Throughout the whole process, however, the interaction patterns of demarcation and identification described above were of crucial significance for her relationship with me.

As for the primal scene, here again we are dependent on conjectures. The shattering feelings manifested themselves in the pictures; reconstruction in the narrower psychoanalytic sense failed to materialise. In his analysis of the Wolf Man, Freud (1918b) repeatedly asked himself whether the report had to do with real events or the products of fantasy:

> I should myself be glad to know whether the primal scene in the present patient's case was a phantasy or a real experience; but, taking other similar cases into account, I must admit that the answer to this question is not in fact a matter of any great importance. These scenes of observing parental intercourse, of being seduced in childhood, and of being threatened with castration are unquestionably an inherited endowment, a phylogenetic heritage, but they may just as easily be acquired by personal experience. (p. 97)

In Hanna's case, at all events, psychic reality is the reality communicated and analysed. We know relatively little about what she actually experienced. But perhaps that is not so important.

CHAPTER FOUR

Splitting and fusion

In the cases we have been looking at, splitting played an essential role in the defence against anxiety. Accordingly, I should like to take a closer look at splitting processes and the fusions materialising in their wake. In Freudian psychoanalysis, the concept of splitting was primarily bound up with "ego-splitting" and distinguished from dissociation. Later the term was further differentiated and integrated into various theories (Krejci, 2011).

In principle, splitting as defence belongs to the group of genetically early defence mechanisms such as denial, projection, and introjection, whereas the pendant to affect-splitting at the oedipal level is isolation (Henningsen, 1990, p. 217 et seq.). In the 1960s, Lorenzer and Thomä (1965) investigated a large number of traumatic processes. In the tradition of structural theory, Lorenzer describes an "insular" compulsive-neurotic defence syndrome. The perception of the trauma is still there, the affect is denied, the energy of the affect is transposed to the unconscious, which corresponds to the defence mechanism "isolation" in a compulsive neurotic. Like Mentzos at a later stage (2009), Lorenzer emphasises that patients may display a wide range of different neurotic disorders. He stresses the pseudo-adjustment of trauma patients.

This "pseudo-normality" [...] is certainly a highly problematic pathological feature that can confuse the casual observer because here a serious type of disorder is concealed by an outwardly harmless appearance. But in the course of our considerations it will no doubt have become clear that unswerving "normality" is not an expression of stability but of rigidity strictly maintained, in line with the law of all-or-nothing, until it (eventually) collapses. (Lorenzer, 1965, p. 694)

The disorder concealed behind the rigidity is more than a compulsive-neurotic symptom. It is referred to by many authors as a "defect" located in the vicinity of a warded-off psychotic process that cannot be explained without the assumption of splitting processes (Kardiner, 1941; Lorenzer, 1965). Freud described this defect as ego-splitting and related it to traumatisation: "We can assign in general and somewhat vague terms the condition under which this comes about, by saying that it occurs under the influence of a psychical trauma" (Freud, 1940e, p. 275). The synthesising functions of the ego are disrupted. "This success is achieved at the price of a rift in the ego which never heals but which increases as time goes on. The two contrary reactions to the conflict persist at the centre point of a split in the ego" (ibid., p. 276). What Freud is primarily describing here is the phenomenon of two realities that can be simultaneously represented in the ego. Although for Freud projection naturally plays a central role, he was not concerned with the fact that parts of the ego or affects are externalised via projection and can then enter into a connection with the object, as happens in concretistic fusion and under borderline conditions (Mentzos, 2009).

Melanie Klein placed splitting at the heart of her theory of development (cf. M. Klein, 1946, 1952), understanding it as a genetically early defence mechanism necessary for development, a mechanism that materialises in the early stages of object-finding and also serves to protect good mother–child experiences from attacks. She gives us variegated descriptions of defective integration between libidinous and destructive tendencies focused on the same object (the maternal breast) and says: "The early methods of splitting fundamentally influence the ways in which, at a somewhat later stage, repression is carried out, and this in turn determines the degree of interaction between conscious and unconscious" (Klein, 1952, p. 66). Kernberg drew upon insights from Edith Jacobson, Margaret Mahler, Harold Blum, and others to develop a structure model centring on the internalisation of object relations. His definition of splitting is similar to Melanie Klein's.

> *Splitting* [...] is a mechanism characteristic of the first stages of development of the ego. It grows out of the naturally occurring lack of integration of the first introjections and is used as a defensive mechanism to protect positive introjections, [...] splitting is typically a mechanism of the early ego [...], but it can persist pathologically at higher levels of ego organization. (Kernberg, 1976, p. 44, original emphasis)

Both authors emphasise the early stage at which splitting takes place and stress the fact that despite ongoing ego maturity pathological genesis may persist. For our present concerns, this observation appears to be essential. In my view, the theories of M. Klein and Kernberg give us a model that makes it conceivable how a psychic defect can originate from traumatisation prior to the genital phase. Kernberg sees splitting as a "major defensive operation" in borderline patients (Kernberg, 1976, p. 163). Mentzos takes Kernberg's ideas up as follows:

> In one respect, however, I believe that Kernberg's ideas need to be enlarged on. It is not splitting as such that is so characteristic of the borderline condition, but rather a changing, alternating form of splitting. In this form [...] it is sometimes the self-relation that is split off, at other times the object-relation. Temporarily, the respective counterpoles are not seen but ignored. (Mentzos, 2009. p. 169)

This alternation serves to avoid on the one hand an "irreversible fusion with the object", on the other "absolute self-relatedness" culminating in total object loss (ibid., p. 170). In the transference processes of severely traumatised individuals, the pendulum-swings between intrusive fusion and narcissistic withdrawal recur frequently and need to be understood and interpreted in the analytic relationship. Very often, affective fusion contains a central element of the traumatic anguish.

Another way of accounting theoretically for the phenomenon of splitting is proposed by W. R. Bion (1962) when he adds to M. Klein's "maternal" breast the additional dimension of the "thinking breast", thus expressing earliest human experiences in terms of epistemological categories. The mother (the breast) functions as a mediator between internal and external reality, helping with the "digestion" or processing of experience, the communication of knowledge and of the Good and the True (in a neo-Platonic sense). In other words, when things go well, the mother takes over for the child at this stage the ability to tolerate not-knowing and can thus give the child protection and basic trust. But if the exchange between mother and child is traumatic or disturbed, this may instil in the child a one-sided mode of perception. Mortal fear of potential death from starvation forces the child to accept food. In the course of this, a split develops between material and psychic gratification, later between material and psychic reality. These forms of splitting are probably the most extreme we can imagine. "The need for love, understanding and mental development is now deflected, since it cannot be satisfied, into the search for material comforts. [...] This state involves destruction of his concern for truth" (Bion, 1962, p. 11).

Serious addiction disorders, anti-social tendencies, and very severe narcissistic personality disorders can be understood in this light. The main difficulty besetting the analytic process is presumably the fact that such profound splitting structures prevent the psychic exchange with others or at least greatly restrict the possibility of experiencing such an exchange. All things immaterial appear life-threatening and signify death; things material are all that count. Either that or, vice versa, immaterial thought products are all that count; earthly things do not exist.

> Fear, hate and envy are so feared that steps are taken to destroy awareness of all feelings, although that is indistinguishable from taking life itself. If a sense of reality, too great to be swamped by emotions, forces the infant to resume feeding, intolerance of envy and hate in a situation which stimulates love and gratitude leads to a splitting that differs from splitting carried out to prevent depression. It differs from splitting impelled by sadistic impulses in that its object and effect is to enable the infant to obtain what later in life would be called material comforts without acknowledging the existence of a live object on which these benefits depend. (Bion, 1962, p. 10)

Bion does not refer explicitly to "traumas", perhaps because in his time this category of human experience was bound up too exclusively with external reality. But in the passage quoted above he describes the mental state known as "depletion" (cf. Chapter Fourteen and Hirsch, 2004), which follows from infant traumatisation. This is why it is helpful to pursue this approach further and combine it with developmental theories on infancy. Internally, traumatic anguish is associated with evil and leads to a collapse of the alpha functions; the "live object" is not present, life is extinguished, there is no space for "love and gratitude" as representatives of the good.

In individuals with traumas, the pathological, integration-proof splittings established in early childhood are the basic themes of their lives and lead frequently to the rigidity and ego restriction described by Lorenzer. They are often the reason given for the indication of high-frequency long-term analysis. These patients can only be sustainably helped by means of a subtle, stepwise engagement with rapprochement and the avoidance of early object relations. Even when the patients "know" what has happened to them, it takes a long time to bring about the emotional understanding required for the integration of the split-off affects. In an essay on ego-splitting, Erika Krejci gives us an impressive account of the transference situation.

> Such patients are able to use free association in a way that runs counter to a gradually discernible centring on unconscious content. [...] The patient "does not know" (has no real awareness) that he is attempting to conceal, rather than uncover, his own—infantile—feelings, because being-seen and showing-oneself are associated with a perverted context. Being invisible is a protection against attack and condemnation. But this concealment takes place in the guise of alacritous cooperation, submission to the analytic arrangement. (Krejci, 2011, p. 17)

In the worst case, avoidance of emotional understanding—usually bound up with avoidance of some kind of anguish in the transference relationship—leads to pseudo-adjustment to the analytic process.

Traumatisation invariably involves a disruption of simultaneous psychosomatic processes. Neuroscientific studies provide impressive evidence for fundamental psychoanalytic assumptions on this point. In the treatment of a traumatised woman patient, van der Kolk (1996), for example, used imaging to show that when she engaged with her trauma the amygdala was highly active while Broca's area remained inactive. The patient "had no words" for her experience. This experiment can be regarded as proof of affect-splitting and the attendant symbolisation disorders. Emotional hyperarousal triggered by the threat prevents verbalisation and cognitive awareness (Sachsse, 2004, p. 49). In each individual case, it is necessary to investigate the intensity and chronicity of such splitting processes and to ask whether and how they are integrated into the development of personality, psychic conflicts, and capacities, or whether they lead an encapsulated life of their own. Allan N. Schore (2003) combined neuropsychological insights with psychoanalytic development theory to show that an infant trauma leads to hyperarousal and ultimately to dissociation and permanent changes in the brain. He refers to this as the formation of defensive projective identifications that are stored in the implicit procedural memory. These structures take shape in the right hemisphere, which is in charge of the processing of non-verbal affects and unconscious processes. Schore's model is highly compatible with the notion of concretistic fusion, which itself refers to an unconsciously effective defensive structure that defies verbalisation. This structure relates to the split-off affect and hence to the neurobiological foundations of psychic processes. I have described this defence as a special case of projective identification.

Highly significant factors are the point in time when traumatisation took place, how severe it is, and what the pre-traumatic development was like (Mentzos, 2009, p. 264 et seq.). Prior to trauma, the four-year-old Marion (Chapter One) was certainly a healthy, securely attached child; in the family the absent father was positively substituted for by the commitment displayed by the grandfather. Throughout therapy, I considered it an essential task to mirror Marion's feelings so as to prevent the onset of a pathological splitting process. In the initial interview, my interpretation of the roof tiles as bloodstains was a relatively direct offer of myself as an object prepared to talk to her about her anxieties. Marion could use me for a beneficial purpose. The fears and the pain repeatedly assailing Marion certainly had a recurrent traumatic effect leading to hyperarousal. But it appears—and this was confirmed by the later catamnestic encounters—that Marion did not develop any lasting dissociations and projective identifications of a defensive nature. The attendant psychotherapy was able to preclude this eventuality.

The constellation was similar for the five-year-old Monika (Chapter One). She too was able to display her sadness from the outset; my job was to strengthen her capacity for working on the problem and to name her fears and experiences so that she could feel understood. Though after the transplant her integrative capacities collapsed, she was still able to get back in touch with a positive experience before the operation and show me her inner chaos. I attempted to put a name to the split-off elements; painting all the blood pictures with the same motif enabled her to find my support, and she was gradually able to regain stability. This process culminated in the painting of blood and nothing else that she wanted us both to sign. One could hardly find clearer expression of the transference. The boxes put round the names stand for emergence from the fusion and the establishment of ego- and body-boundaries of her own.

In the case of eight-year-old Antje (Chapter One), it was also necessary to preserve her from serious affect splittings. She was able to portray her unconscious anxieties with frightening precision and made it very clear that she needed help. Her parents needed me as a translator so that they could talk to their child about the feelings and fantasies that affected them all but would have been placed under a taboo without the therapeutic interventions. Speechlessness would have condemned Antje to dreadful loneliness and this would presumably have triggered massive splitting processes. The consequences of the traumatic events were alleviated both for the children and the parents. The mothers/parents were saved from a burnout syndrome because in ongoing therapy they learned to re-extricate themselves in stages from their symbiotic identifications.

Things developed differently in the case of Mr V (Chapter Two), who came down with leukaemia at the same time as Marion. However, neither he nor his parents had ever had any psychotherapeutic support. His parents did their best to help their son in their own way, but they were unable to establish the necessary distance. Nor had they found a language in which to talk to their son about his and their concerns and fears. Mother and son were bound up with one another in their fear of the illness; a joint fusion core had formed that they were unable to forgo even when the illness was over. The mother's feeling was the son's and vice versa. Only in analysis was it possible to bring about psychic separation between mother and son.

In the case of Hanna, it seems likely that there was also a joint fusion core between her mother and herself serving—much as in the development Ms R (Chapter Two) went through—to regulate the depressive mother's affects. The coarse hostility to sexuality behind the parents' projections and the father's incestuous attachment to the grandmother were other essential factors preventing the mother's separation and leading to the onset of anorexia. The patient's silence (she hardly spoke during therapy) and the severe restrictions to her intelligence (she was poor in school) are initially reminiscent of autistic phenomena (Tustin, 1986). But the course taken by therapy indicates that in Hanna there was a living world waiting to be discovered and "hard autistic objects" had not yet materialised. Why? I would suggest that, as with my other patients, there were more favourable constitutional preconditions at work and, as evidenced by the analyses of Ms R and Mr V, "disciplining and humanizing elements of the nursing situation" (Tustin, 1986, p. 110) were able to restrict or prevent the creation of "hard autistic objects" so that an autistic development in the proper sense of the term did not come about.

As I see it, Monika and Hanna show how with the aid of an intermediary space and their creativity they were able to represent their fusion with the object and later—after experiencing a sufficient degree of mirroring and decoupling in transference—to put an end to it. From this I learned a great deal for the treatment of my adult patients. The affect—the annihilation anxiety felt by subject and object—was translated into a symbolic language by Monika's "blood pictures". In Hanna's case, the abandonment of narcissistic withdrawal began no less concretely via the sense of touch (finger paints). Touching the outer skin and the object with fingers and paints was crucial. This was followed by a long period of parallelism. By dealing with the same subjects in separate pictures, she was practising separation and identification. One might fairly refer to these children's pictures as symbols for fusions and separation processes. The affect was projected on to the paper by both subject and object and experienced a fusion. Splitting was reversed because in the pictures the affect was bound up with the content and could be put into words again.

Another essential reason why the concepts associated with autistic phenomena play only a minor role in my work may well lie in the nature of my approach. If one tries (as I do) to home in relatively quickly on the situation causing the trauma, the perception of the split-off affect (annihilation anxiety, destruction, and panic) in countertransference will be direct and immediate. The prime concern then is to recognise and acknowledge this affect, hard to bear as it is, and not to banish it from the mental space. In the analyst's mind, search motions attempt to locate the affect thus perceived. This creates a connection with the patient in which the analyst's involvement takes the form of projective identification. This attitude is the precise opposite of the function of the "hard autistic object" that cuts off all contact and serves as a substitute object. The autistic object is largely closed-off and sequestered, whereas the split-off and projected affect is more geared to openness. In fact, it indicates a potential point of contact with the patient. It may well be that the patients we are talking about here are simply less severely disturbed, but it is also conceivable that the different theoretical persuasions involved engender a different understanding of these patients, generating alternative modes of access to their psychic reality. This is quite definitely not a question of "right" or "wrong".

I use the term "concretistic fusion" to refer to a defence structure representing a specific form of projective identification derived from clinical experience via scenic understanding. We are talking here about the consequences of unconscious, objectless anxiety in early infancy. Infants or babies are dependent on self-object relations. If their needs are not satisfied by the immediate environment, organismic panic will set in and they will re-introject the outwardly oriented part of the relationship. Both dimensions—good/evil, psyche/soma—are, or remain, split. Arousal leads to auto-eroticism and serves self-preservation. A fusion core materialises to bind the panic. Structurally, these fusion cores are highly individual. In further development they retain their physical basis and cannot be mentalized. They are imprinted on implicit procedural memory (Schore, 2003) and, as we saw in the cases of Ms R and Mr V, manifest themselves in enactments, somatisations, and addictive tendencies. I shall return to these events in later chapters, where I describe the cases of Ms S (Chapter Five), Ms F (Chapter Six), and Ms O (Chapter Eleven), all of whom suffered from the consequences of severe infantile traumas.

In connection with these early processes, I would emphasise the physical basis of perception and follow Gaddini (1998, p. 83 et seq.) in referring to the baby's perceptive activity as imitation and introjection. I propose reserving the concept of identification for those processes in which self and object are separate and signal anxiety may materialise. "Imitations and introjections follow the pleasure principle, whereas identifications are geared to reality and, in the course of their stepwise progress, develop the potential for a mature object relation" (ibid., p. 84). Strictly speaking, the correct term for this would then be projective introjection (cf. Abraham, 1924; Ferenczi, 1909; Abraham & Torok, 1986).

I consider projective introjection a helpful model in explaining the effect of traumatic experiences on the inner object-world. With his interpretation of "intrusive identification" (a concept first proposed by Meltzer), Tomas Plänkers (2008) proceeds from similar premises to examine the origins of concretistic fusions from a different perspective (cf. Ebrecht-Laermann, 2009). The traumatic effect, he contends, comes from the violent intrusion into the psychic space and the establishment of an identification with the destructive introject spawned by the trauma. His ideas on introjective projection draw upon Meltzer's "claustrum" theory (1966, 1990), O'Shaughnessy (2003), and others. He regards his construct as a "bridge concept capable of debunking the nonsensical polarisation of trauma and conflict" (Plänkers, 2008, p. 42). The interactions described by Plänkers and others between traumatic and traumatised object relations on the one hand, and corresponding subjective experiences on the other, are in line with the ideas I have set out here and confirm the internalisation process involved in traumatic relations. My approach differs somewhat in the slightly greater emphasis placed (a) on the necessity of focusing on the defence against affect-splitting and the unconscious partial fusions with primary objects and (b), in individual cases, on bearing in mind that not all sectors of a personality structure will necessarily be affected by trauma introjects and defence constellations.

The development of defence structures is invariably an individual thing and in transference it establishes a direct link between the patient's unconscious and the analyst's unconscious. In contrast to autistic phenomena, the aim of these fusions is not to disrupt human relations (cf. Rhode, 2005; Tustin, 1986) but to stabilise the traumatic condition with the aid of the object. The split-off affect remains as the common denominator between two objects. This can be the starting point for intergenerational transmissions.

In Ms R and Mr V we saw how the split-off part that is fused with the object acted as a kind of putty impeding development. As such, it triggered their respective crises in early adulthood. These patients could neither live with their mothers nor without them. The mother's trauma was the child's trauma and vice versa. Ilany Kogan also considers this mode of existence to be an essential dimension in cases involving trauma patients. In her book *Escape from Selfhood: Breaking Boundaries and Craving for Oneness* (2007), she describes a (male) patient whose attachment to his mother was abruptly ended by her suicide.

Kogan gives us a graphic account of the encounter between a severely traumatised patient and his (female) analyst, an encounter in which the patient's split-off affects repeatedly fuse with the analyst's unconscious. In the course of time, the analyst recognises them, raises them to the level of reality, and understands them. In states of affective fusion there is no transitional space. The boundaries break down and the task of the analyst is to promote a triangulating perspective. I go into more detail on cases of this kind in Part III, which deals with the experience of violence/abuse in childhood.

In some ways, the concept of concretistic fusion resembles the dead mother complex (Green, 2001). In his article, Green describes the effect of maternal depression on the child. For him, the "dead mother" is a metaphor that reveals its true meaning in transference. The child simultaneously introjects and splits off the mother imago, making mourning and "burial" equally impossible. Parallel to this cathectic deprivation of the depressive mother object, the child builds up an unconscious mirror identification with the dead mother. "This reactive symmetry is the only means by which to establish a reunion with the mother" (ibid., p. 179). Splitting and introjection/identification intermesh; object and subject remain connected without engaging in any genuine emotional exchange.

Re-reading Green's work in the context of my own ideas, I initially contemplated forsaking my own concept and describing my experiences in his terms. But then I realised that the perspective that had helped me understand my patients was a slightly different one. True, because of the traumatic experiences they had undergone, the mothers of my patients were also depressive. But they were more active in warding off the psychic shocks they had suffered and they instrumentalised the children in the splitting processes. The children were by no means "abruptly deprived of all cathexis". On the contrary, they were highly cathected so as to fend off the trauma. The trauma was shared with them, tabooed, and split off. I also identify differences in the analytic process. Green gives a very graphic description of the way in which the mother is gradually "resurrected" in transference and the analyst is initially non-existent, "not quite inside, not quite outside". In the sessions with my trauma patients, I always felt that part of my self was totally "inside". With varying degrees of intensity, depending on the progress the analysis had made, I was connected with another, non-traumatised part of the patient occupied with warding off the trauma.

One can certainly regard the concept of concretistic fusion as a special case of projective identification. The extent to which the concatenation of object relations in its entirety is affected by these fusions differs from case to case. Accordingly, the concept cannot be neatly incorporated into object relation theories. It homes in on the expulsion of unbearable affects that, like intrusions, can penetrate directly into the respective other. The split-off affect cannot be worked on, it binds mother and child together. This fusion between mother and child (it is entirely possible for *parts* of the personality to be involved) knows no transitional space (Winnicott, 1971). Transgenerational identifications are frequent. The affect cannot be mentalized and leads to acting out, symptoms, and permanent defence strategies that can bind the partners together for as long as they live. Once this bond is severed and becomes conscious, the result is shame and fear of depletion. Silvia Amati (1990) has something similar in mind when she speaks of the "symbiotic bond" between mother and child and advocates that this "should not be equated with projective identification because it is not a projective or identificational relationship with an entire or partial object but the projection of a non-objectal 'core of non-differentiation' deposited in the external world" (Amati, 1990, p. 725). Bohleber's view supports these ideas: "Overwhelming excitation and intense anxiety damage the sense of self and bring about a self-object fusion as the core of the traumatic experience, which is difficult to resolve and persistently impairs the sense of identity" (Bohleber, 2007, p. 342).

Despite the undeniable phenomenological similarities, concretistic fusion is not to be confused with adhesive identification (Bick, 1968; Meltzer, 1975; Ogden, 1989). Bick and Meltzer observe the failure of very early introjections and the consequences of that failure for a development culminating in autism. The pathology they describe leads to two-dimensional object relations (cf. also Klüwer, 2005; Nissen, 2008) and excludes any kind of projective identification. In concretistic fusion, by contrast, a degree of three-dimensionality usually remains which may vary in its development and can also take the form of pseudo-adjustment. It may be similar to what Ogden terms the "autistic-contiguous position" but is not identical with it. Ogden sees the "autistic-contiguous position" as a defence structure that is not restricted to autistic phenomena but can also occur in borderline structures and psychoses and serves to fend off massive fears of disintegration and alienation. He sees this defence as a specific shaping force in the dialectical interplay between the depressive and the paranoid position. If this defence is no longer bound up with the depressive mode, a psychotic breakdown may result. The phenomena described by Ogden serve symbol-formation and disavowal of the object.

Here his concerns differ from mine. My aim is to draw attention to the fate of affects split off by the trauma. The concept of concretistic fusion is designed to indicate a specific perspective that I consider helpful for the understanding of traumatic processes and that also enables me to assess the chances of restitution. After all, not all parts of the personality structure are invariably infiltrated by the fusion cores. The affect split off by the trauma leads to a fusion structure between subject and object. This "adhesion" is a function of a traumatic relational constellation that is not susceptible of mentalization. In the case of infant trauma it has an originally psychobiological foundation and with the help of analysis can be recognised, worked on, and partly or very largely integrated or resolved, depending on its severity and the course taken by therapy. Wherever possible, understanding the fusion in the scene or symbolising it in dreams and actions is the first stage in getting to grips with the problem.

PART II

SEPARATION TRAUMAS

CHAPTER FIVE

"This is *my* daughter. Take good care of her!" From objectless anxiety to separation anxiety

Research on infancy has shown how inadequate containment with traumatic effects is a lasting impediment to the development of self-representations. The mother's face mirrors the child's experience without being identical with it. The child internalises this mirrored experience as a secondary representation. In normal development, basic trust and a naive theory of the mental will evolve in the interactional concatenation between affect modulation and affect mirroring. This enables the child to anticipate actions in the immediate environment and react accordingly. When all goes well, the mother's mirroring activity will be the equivalent of good containment and encourage sound internalisation of the object. In pathological cases distortions are to be expected, for example, when the mother cannot contain her own anxieties and projects them on to the child rather than taking up the child's anxieties and working on them. She merely replicates those anxieties and gives them back to the child undigested. The child remains alone, the ability to form the necessary internal representations is inadequate. It is here that pathological fusions and symbolisation disorders have their roots.

Object-splitting takes place when the expectations ascribed to the object fail to materialise and the integration of things perceived breaks down (Bion, 1962, Ch. 5; Fonagy & Target, 2002; Fonagy, Gergely, & Target, 2002). At a very early stage, babies and infants with attachment disorders tend to avoid the mother and her potential mirror function and to turn in upon themselves so as not to become painfully aware of the existing defect (cf. Fonagy & Target, 2002). In this way they create a negative hallucination for themselves and may develop autistic features and/or an addiction structure (Bion, 1962; Gaddini, 1998). In the case we will be looking at first, I shall attempt to show how at the beginning of analysis the patient entered into a fusion with herself (part of her self) to compensate for the absence of mirroring.

This fusion needs to be understood differently from the kind experienced by other patients with early traumas, where a potentially fatal illness (of the mother or the child) lies at the heart of the traumatic condition (Henningsen, 2002, 2008; cf. also Part I). The mothers of these latter patients are overwhelmed by the affects of the children or the affects of their own depression and as a result are incapable of mirroring. The children follow the mother into depression (A. Freud, 1937, p. 87); a fusion core with a defensive function takes shape and partially blocks further development. The child's feeling remains identical with the mother's and no uncoupling is possible. André Green has conceptualised these processes in his article on the "dead mother" (Green, 2001).

Kernberg's (1992) distinction between low-level affect states and peak-affect states points to a further dimension of fusion in affect. Experiences with low affective intensity in the symbiotic phase enable the child to develop ego-functions and an ability to think in terms of secondary processes. Experiences bound up with strong affects encourage the internalisation of primitive object relations manifesting themselves in "only good" or "only bad" memory traces. If self and object are not yet separated, structures will materialise at the core of which self-object fusions remain active. "Fused, undifferentiated, or condensed all-good self and object representations are built up separately from equally fused, undifferentiated, or condensed all-bad self and object representations" (Kernberg, 1992, p. 13).

Proceeding from the scene that presented itself to me at the first session and in the early stages of analyses with patients suffering from early traumas, I encountered a defence structure that is traceable to that early trauma and (as regards the traumatic sector of the psyche) can neither be symbolised nor mentalized. In this self-core, the development of secondary representations has been thwarted. In transference, the encapsulated trauma becomes manifest in a split-off form through acting-out and enactment (Klüwer, 1983, 1995) and has to be integrated in the course of treatment. The form taken by such a structure is highly individual, but there will always be an interpretable connection between this structure, the nature and intensity of the trauma, and the development undergone by the patient (Greenacre, 1967; Henningsen, 2003, 2008).

These defensive structures, which I refer to as concretistic fusions, are individual in their form. In transference, they establish a direct connection between the patient's unconscious and the analyst's unconscious. Ms S's trauma affected her so early that, in order to ward off objectless anxiety, she developed a "nurturing contact with [her]self" (Gaddini, 1998, p. 207 et seq.) that she could always fall back on later. She developed a (part-)fusion with herself as an autoerotic strategy for keeping herself alive. She was attempting to fend off a form of annihilation anxiety that she was unable to symbolise.

Ms S

Ms S (Henningsen, 2005, 2011a, 2011b; Thomä, 2011) is a lithe, attractive, dark-eyed young woman in her early thirties. At our first encounter her gaze was vacant and forlorn, she was unable to look me in the face. She had come to me because of severe bouts of depression, bulimia, complete lack of orientation, and various psychosomatic ailments. Her husband had taken up with another woman and was not prepared to return to her. He insisted that their child should stay with him, saying that he considered her unsuitable for motherhood. "Without my daughter I just can't go on living, I'd never be able to," she says. She was unemployed and appeared to have no fixed abode: "It's like the ground has been taken away from under my feet, the world is tottering." Ms S had started a new relationship, but the conflicts it involved quickly put an end to it. Recently she had been involved in a minor road accident and had left the scene of the accident without waiting for the police: "I couldn't stand it, I just had to get out of there." She had a university degree and before her collapse had successfully held down a managerial post in West Germany.

Biography

Ms S's parents were both very young when she was born. At the age of six weeks they entrusted their daughter to a crèche where the children could stay for the entire working week (this was former East Germany). The first photo of her is a press clipping that shows her as a baby in the care of a member of staff. Although they were never members of the ruling Socialist Unity Party and had a critical attitude to the regime, the parents shared the conviction expressed in the press clipping that the six-day crèche was a brilliant socialist achievement, ensuring and safeguarding the good of the child. Little is known about Ms S's life in the crèche, but one fact does appear to be noteworthy. At one point, the crèche changed its schedule, closing no longer on Saturday but on Friday evening, a fact that completely escaped Ms S's parents. When no one came to collect the child, one of the staff took her home with her. Ms S had always screamed in protest when she was taken back to the crèche on Monday morning. Ms S herself, however, has no memory of this. When she was three, she was put in kindergarten, which she heartily disliked and where she cried a great deal.

At school, Ms S was a group leader with the Young Pioneers (an East German youth brigade) and was universally felt to be a good comrade. Later, in analysis, she said: "I'm a proper collective child." In adolescence she developed an anorexia-bulimia problem that she was able to conceal from her parents and her later husband.

The patient's maternal grandmother died in childbed, her grandfather died in the war, and she grew up in the (loveless) care of her paternal grandmother. The patient's father first saw his father at the age of seven, when he returned from the war severely wounded. He died shortly after. Both parents were branded by traumas, unable as they were to develop any identifications with their real parents except that of having been abandoned by them. In accordance with this denied defect, they could not build up any emotional attachments to their own child that would have provided her with support and structure. They had no feeling for the significance of separation anxiety.

Establishing concretistic fusion in transference

When I saw the patient at our first session, my initial idea was to give her some support in getting to grips with her chaotic life situation and leave it at that. There seemed to be no prospects for successful analysis. Before I actually met her face to face, I got the dates for our first encounter mixed up and there was no one there when she arrived. Unlike myself, Ms S was completely unfazed by this mishap and said: "It's always like that with me." Once I had realised my error, I called her to apologise. She was overjoyed to hear from me, no one else had ever treated her like that before. It is not entirely inconceivable that my unconscious reacted to the original phone call and that without any knowledge of Ms S's biography I was enacting her dissociation from others by botching our first meeting. Before treatment had even begun, I felt so guilty about the blunder I had committed that it seemed highly unlikely that the patient could expect to benefit from my future efforts on her behalf.

I first offered her a one-hour-a-week short-term course of therapy designed to impose some kind of order on her present chaotic life conditions. In this period I was able to identify, designate, and mirror her feeling of being adrift in the present. In using sentences such as "I have no structure" or "I don't feel connected to myself" to describe the state she was in, the patient was gaining an initial (albeit purely cognitive) idea of the consequences of her earlier traumas that in her childhood had probably been partly compensated for by the rigid structures that were very much a part of external reality in the GDR. I frequently confronted her with her tendency to reduce everything to the status of trivialities.

On one occasion, Ms S left a jar of jam in the hall after our session. I discovered it at the end of the day, so I spent some time speculating about which of my patients was most likely to have left me this little gift. Later, Ms S told me that the idea had "occurred to her out of nowhere" after we had parted and she was going down the stairs to the front door. She had left the jam there without thinking twice about it. She had no inkling of this conceivably being an intentional action that might have something to do with her relationship to me. As I tried to allocate the jam to one of my patients, I felt immense pressure bearing in on me. I was obviously expected to realise precisely what it was that distinguished her from my other patients (the crèche children) and recognise the trace she had left on me. Ms S had deposited the jam in the front hall (entrance) in the same way as *she* had been "deposited" at the crèche. For her it was an unrelated act, but I was in a state of extreme tension. My countertransference feelings suggested to me that she was the one who had driven me into this state of troubled uncertainty.

As she sat opposite me, she would frequently rub her eyes in a self-tormenting manner, boring the knuckles into the cavities in such a way that all I could see was the bloodshot white pupils. It must have hurt very badly. I couldn't stand the sight of it and told her so. This was a symptomatic action, the pain she inflicted on herself was the only way she could develop any kind of feeling for herself. In my mind's eye, images took shape of the so-called "wobblers' room" at the children's hospital where I used to work. I remembered the articles by René Spitz, notably those on coprophagic children (1965). These children had given up all hope of receiving any kind of mirroring from their environment. They produced the little pellets of excrement for purposes of autoerotic stimulation. I frequently felt prompted to mirror her apparently affectless actions by assuming a committed and emotional attitude. This emphatic behaviour on my part was the only thing that enabled her to form an (albeit purely cognitive) conception of what was going on.

Ms S acted without affective participation; her feelings were "in abeyance" (this was how she was later to refer to these splittings). Two states appeared to alternate: animate versus inanimate or concrete connection versus separation. In the animate interactions I was the "carrier" of those affects of hers that I was trying to mirror. She then experienced me as a real object. In the inanimate states we were separated, I could mistake her for someone else (as in the case of the appointment error), she deposited herself as a jam jar.

In the year with the one-hour treatment scheme, Ms S had selected me as an idealised narcissistic object and was able to convince me of her desire for analysis.

When she arrived for the first session after the summer interval, she was certain that I would not accept her for analysis after all because she was pregnant. I said: "We've agreed on analysis and I would say it's already begun. Perhaps you can only come to me when there are two of you. You come to me and at the same time you've still got something of yourself within you that can't get lost." With her pregnancy Ms S had enacted a concretistic fusion that protected her from separation. At the same time she had once again envisaged a separation between us.

> Ms S was obviously relieved that I started with the analysis as we had agreed. But it was still very difficult to get in contact with her. She could not imagine being present in me, that I could form an image of her, empathise with her. She understood the remarks I made as sneering, cynical criticism of her. On one occasion she had a dream of a growing monster. When I suggested a connection between the dream and her fears of giving birth to a sick or abnormal child, she accused me of making her feel insecure and worrying her for no reason. She was unable to recognise her dreams as a

contribution serving the better understanding of her internal processes. Instead she projected the negative affect, the threat, onto me as if I had created the dream. As soon as she saw me as separate from her, my empathy turned into a threat. For example, when we continued working on the dream and she felt the support I was giving her, she said: "Ha, you got me that time!" In the first few years, processes like this recurred time and again, and we were able to detect parallels with her bulimia symptoms (which soon disappeared) and her time at the crèche.

We hit upon a comparison between my empathic incursions into her personality and the intake of food. When her withdrawal was in jeopardy, when the concretistic fusion between us wasn't functioning in a way that was in line with her unconscious fantasies, she had to disgorge me like the food she had spurned. Probably she had repeatedly withdrawn into herself so as to feel as little as possible of the pain of separation, anonymity, and otherness. With autoerotic stimulation and denial of separation she was able to maintain something approaching equilibrium. But when I tried to "invade" her with my empathy, this narcissistic withdrawal was destroyed. She wanted to "attach me to her", then she could afford to let me get closer to her because then she was sure of no longer losing me. "Then you'd be attached to me with an umbilical cord like the child growing inside you," I said. The notion that her husband or I might have an idea or an image of her in our minds appeared to be completely inconceivable for her. Her presence had been almost entirely insignificant for her mother, and in the same way she found it impossible to imagine herself being present in me or forming an inner representation of others. In my countertransference, these states were reflected in crippling fatigue, inattentiveness, and guilt feelings. When these depressive feelings started encroaching on me, I recalled photos of six-day crèches that I had come across in magazines or I saw in my mind's eye a small child cowering in the corner of a hospital ward. These images kept me awake and enabled me to stay with the patient as I listened.

For Ms S the only concrete thing in her inside world was the growing baby. And when her husband was away, the child meant that she had something very concrete from him inside herself. But what did she have of me when she left my office? At the end of every session the "point" of analysis was called into question.

Gradually the patient began to sense that although sessions came to an end and although there were weekends in between, she had an emotional attachment to me because her thoughts and ideas went on in the intervals. She told me how she kept on losing things. I was able to show her that she treated things the way she herself had been treated. She was the lost child, the one who came late, the one nobody took an interest in. Here, psychoanalysis was the exception! She never arrived late although she had a long way to come. In a rudimentary fashion she began to discover me as her vis-à-vis. In her body she felt the first movements of the child, her baby was also developing a dynamic of its own. Her dependence on me gave Ms S an initial security; she told me that this made her feel freer than before. Alongside the symbiotic transference with me there was a kind of parallel symbiosis, first with the unborn child, then with the baby.

Ms S gave birth to a normal, healthy child (Jenny) and resumed analysis within a relatively short space of time. She had given up her job to devote herself fully and entirely to her daughter. She was determined to give Jenny something she had not given her older child and had not experienced herself. Step by step the patient was able to recognise the many tiny nuances of separation and unity, destructive fantasies, and loving care, panic, and reassurance. In many sessions it was as if we were jointly rediscovering the development of the human individual "from baby to infant". Jenny made splendid progress, Ms S lived through, and worked on, many of her traumatic experiences in identification with her daughter. One thing she had to grapple with was her envy of her daughter, who fretted much less when she was separated from her mother than her mother did when she was away from her or me. She was also envious of me because I had not been so severely damaged in childhood and accordingly could look on with equanimity and optimism while she tormented herself. This envy had been a central motive in acting out.

> Plans to return to her job were acted out in a way that jeopardised the continuation of therapy. For example, Ms S suggested immediately reducing sessions to two a week without preceding this with a process of mourning and leave-taking, although there was ample time to do so. I insisted we should use the time to find out what it meant if she came less often. The point at issue was whether Ms S would succeed in accepting this (probably necessary) change in her psychic reality and symbolising it."Frau Henningsen, I can't do that, and I'll never be able to."—"If you evaded it, you would be passing up an important opportunity in your analysis." Shortly afterwards

she gave in to a spontaneous impulse and had two wisdom teeth extracted. They would have to be taken out at some point and now she had time. I said: "Soon you'll only have two sessions with me instead of four, and now you've only got two of your four wisdom teeth." After the operation she suffered from dental pain for an unusually long time, although a check-up examination indicated that everything was as it should be. Ms S had to create concrete physical pain for herself to anticipate the psychic separation pain involved in halving our sessions. She found a way of papering over the crack by temporarily coming to me three times a week instead of two.

She often asked herself how her mother had been able to stand giving her away so early. "Probably your mother was not able to *feel* what it means to have a mother because she never had a mother herself," I said. The patient worked up a great deal of anger at her parents and also discovered the emotional dimension of her mother's tragic fate. She brought me a photo of herself and her mother when she was about six years old. I gave her my impressions: "You're both very appealing on that photo, it looks to me more like a big sister posing with her little sister." Further enactments were necessary before Ms S could start extricating herself from the fusion in transference.

Incipient symbolisation of hatred and annihilation

When I shook my patient's hand in farewell, I now regularly received an electric shock, sometimes accompanied by a loud crackling noise, often actively painful. I referred to this phenomenon on the next occasion and drew a parallel with our relationship. After the following dream the incident never recurred:

> I'm lying in a hospital bed. John has brought me here, saying: "You've got to get through this on your own." I was to be operated on. I was given an anaesthetic, could no longer speak, then a woman, she was a doctor, made an incision here [points to the throat]. She cut through the oesophagus. The oesophagus was to be washed out with some kind of meal. I asked whether it was necessary. Then another woman asked the same question, going on to say: "It all has a psychosomatic context, why are you letting this happen? You know it's mental. Just think of what might have happened!"

With this dream Ms S was able to refer to our imminent separation. Speechlessness in the dream resolves itself almost casually: "I could no longer speak ... I asked whether it was necessary." At the same time, her spontaneous ideas indicated how difficult it was to see me as an evil or pursuing mother. As if to insist on the good sides to our relationship, she emphasised that I was not the one who cut her throat open, etc. But she could not avoid engaging with these destructive introjections.

> At the last session before the summer vacation, she said: "I'm so angry I could knock your house down. You don't know what forces there are inside me ... [pause] ... Aren't you afraid?" Suddenly I remembered the image of an old woman whose death throes I had witnessed some years earlier when I was keeping her company while she was dying. I was surprised and alarmed to see how much strength there can be in a frail and sick old body. The patient had triggered anxiety in me. Was it hers or mine? I wanted to give her support so that she could get through the vacation period unharmed. I said: "You're dreadfully angry with me because this is the last session before the holidays, I am leaving you and that sets off organismic panic in you, a physical tension that feels like it could explode. Probably you felt that kind of panic as a child when they took you to the crèche. Nothing could reassure you."

Ms S got through the vacation period without too much difficulty. One thing that helped her was a dream in which she defended my house and was pursued by a lesbian woman. After a few weeks she was able to revert to the four-session format. The transference relationship deepened and the electric shocks returned. I was the sadistic surgeon and drew parallels with her traumatisation. I found it difficult to imagine that I was the trigger for so much aggression.

When the electric shocks reappeared in our new four-session arrangement—they stayed with us for the next nine months—it caused me apprehension and disquiet. I developed fantasies about neurobiological processes and asked myself whether her infant trauma might be manifesting itself through this physical tension, whether there was some body memory at work here to which we are exposed whenever we go through separation. After consulting a dermatologist, I concluded that we were both exposed to an electro-physical phenomenon that could not be fully explained but performed some kind of function in our relationship. One possibility would be not to shake hands with her any more, but here I sensed a potential danger. If I did not give her my hand on leaving, this would be tantamount to a re-traumatisation, I would be withdrawing from the direct relationship with her and saying: "You're so dangerous, I'm not going to touch you any more than your mother touched you." As an excellent conductor, the skin produced the connection between us. After each session—and for whatever reason—we were awoken as if by an alarm and exchanged intensive body charges to extricate ourselves from the fusion.

"Not feeling" as trauma and defence

"Not feeling" appeared to be the real trauma. One night, Ms S could not sleep. Looking at her cat, she thought: "In some way she's mad as well." After that, she had a dream that she felt had something to do with us.

> A client comes into my office and starts crawling around on the floor in search of something. I think to myself, he must be mad. Then the cat is sitting there, the man draws a gun (a Colt) and shoots the cat.

This dream was to preoccupy us for some time. First, a number of associations from the patient.

> P: I imagine everything's packed away safely and then it shoots out of me, like that business with the tooth. I ought to have known that I can't just stop here from one day to the next, but no, I have to try first. When I go out of here, I'm forced to get a grip on myself, that's no bad thing. There are things inside you that come out then. When I think what I'm capable of, not just reducing your house to rubble, I can sense it. I mean, it's psychotic, isn't it? That little beast inside you, if it suddenly took over, if it were to get the upper hand, I wouldn't be able to live.
> A: That's why it has to be killed. [Patient goes on talking]
> P: I get all tensed up when I sense it crawling my way. What helps is if I tell myself what you sometimes say: There's plenty of time.
> She says that her relationship with her older child is a part of all this.
> P: On the one hand, everything went perfectly, but then this *not feeling*. It scares me.
> She engages with her anxieties, the splitting processes, and repetitions of "not feeling".
> P: But I'm more open than I was, I have disputes with you. I don't want to destroy what I've got. When I leave, there's so much anger coming to the surface, so much destruction, it's very hard to find a middle course. When I say goodbye to you, there's always this tension between anger and love.
> A: Where there's tension, there's electricity.

P: On the one hand I like looking at you, that's the positive side, but I also have to go, and that's negative. There are these two poles. But things do explode between us. In the session I never feel so destructive about you, it would never occur to me, I just couldn't.

The experience with the cat in the night shows the patient projecting her psychotic fears on to the cat and suspecting that such projections might take place between the two of us as well. In the dream this affective movement is borne out. When she comes to me with the traumatised parts of her personality as a crawling child (= time in the six-day crèche), something dangerous shoots out of her, she is capable of drawing a Colt, the cat represents the uncanny part of her that makes itself felt between the two of us, I think (as she did in her dream): "She really is mad." She draws the revolver and shoots the animal. Vice versa, I too can turn into a murderous object.

Ms S engages with insanity: "It's all packed up and then it shoots out of me." She senses that her defence is brittle, but she may also be describing something that has to do with encapsulated traumatisations or psychotic fears cracking their shells. She refers to her somatisations as an example, the postoperative toothache that disappeared after the interpretation of her separation anxiety and her fury with me. Once again she describes her aggression potential and reminds me that she could demolish my house (= demolish me as a primary object).

With the verdict "That's psychotic", Ms S gains distance from herself and then describes the (psychotic) beast within. She is fully preoccupied with this, and I have the impression that my interpretation of her dream and the killing of the cat fails to register with her. With the sentence "There's plenty of time", she shows me that she has internalised something from me that can reassure her. At this moment I have a sense of relaxation as I listen.

Ms S has recognised something crucial: "Not feeling scares me." Not feeling means being insane, means there is no emotional cathexis with the mother, an experience that her mother, she herself, and her older daughter have all been through.

Incipient object-finding

Before moving on to the further course of therapy, I should like to compare the two dreams and reflect on their significance for the analytic process. In the operation dream, the separation trauma figures as a sadistic physical assault. The part of the body in question is the oesophagus, the link between food intake and the digestive organs of one's own body. I am the one who "operated" her bulimia "away". Another point at issue is the early traumatic experiences in the oral phase. She was confronted with experiences she could not "swallow". Probably the traumatic changes led to intrusions and dissociations, thus laying the foundations for the many instances of somatisation we were confronted with in therapy. My words are "meal" that is forced down her gullet. In this way I purge her poisoned inner world.

When in her dream Ms S refers to the role played by the "psychic" or "psychosomatic" context, this means she is starting to think about psychic reality. I see this as more evidence of progress. After an enactment, Ms S was able to acknowledge psychic reality in her unconscious thinking, a precondition for accepting the reintegration of split-off traumatic experiences (Henningsen, 1990; Chapter Seven).

In traumatic processes, the fate of hatred and aggression plays a special role. In Ms S's case it was essential for the "meal", her anger, or "not feeling" to gain contours. The fear of going insane in the process becomes manifest and is represented by the cat dream. Ms S needs to know by experience that she and I can deal with this cat. In this way she discovers me as her vis-à-vis, someone with both good and evil parts, a process that we will need to engage with in the time to come. Love and hate, life and death, plus and minus, power and powerlessness trigger an existential tension in both of us, a tension that needs to be acknowledged and borne.

In analysis we are concerned with the handing-over of the child in her. Probably the handing-over process from mother to crèche and from crèche to mother was the traumatising factor. Leave-taking is patently over-determined and represents the handing-over process in its various facets. Ms S discovers the *uniqueness* of our relationship. One evening she fell asleep with the following image in her mind:

My mother took me to the crèche for the *first* time and said: This is *my* daughter. Take good care of her!

This fantasy installed a good image of the early mother, but of course the request was addressed in the first place to me. Separation, leave-taking, the end of analysis had started to become a topic. Collapse was always imminent—relapse into increased alcohol and cigarette consumption, weekend headaches—or manic defence. Ms S contemplated getting pregnant again, it was the only thing she was good for, she said, then she wouldn't be alone, she could hold out for five years without me and then come back.

At this point, I had to "take care" to prevent Ms S from reactivating old defence patterns and circumventing the genuine individuation and separation process by way of projective identification or the reinstitution of old fusion cores. I realigned my interpretive activity accordingly. Once she had recognised the defence function of her desire for pregnancy, she recalled other circumstances that had led to a marital crisis eleven years before. Her mother had won a cruise for two people in a competition. Her father couldn't go (for job reasons), so her mother invited Ms S to take his place. Ms S immediately agreed, abruptly stopped breastfeeding her daughter, and on the boat shared a cabin with her mother, which entailed sleeping in a double bed with her. She had never been so physically close to her mother in her life; at the same time she entered into a brief lesbian relationship with another passenger. We had often spoken about the role of a homoerotic relationship as an expression of her insatiable arousal when her mother or I (in transference) gave her physical (sensual) reassurance. We had often drawn parallels between the electric shocks and erotic tension. The new element was that Ms S had suddenly stopped giving her daughter the breast. At the very moment that her mother called to her, she repeated her own trauma by passing it on to her daughter in order to quite literally slip in between the sheets with her mother. This appears to be a transgenerational repetition of a fusion with the motherless mother. Probably this motherless, non-feeling contact had established itself at the beginning of our relationship when my patient turned up for her appointment and I was not there.

> When we discuss separation in our sessions, Ms S is now able to verbalise unbearable body fantasies and feelings: "It feels like a knife in my guts." The development and the sensual experience of her body fantasies during the analytic sessions provide her with a notion of the traumatisation of what Gaddini (1998) refers to as "basic psychic organisation". With the aid of these body fantasies she finds out that she *feels* separated from me but not abandoned by me. This opens up new avenues for working on her addictive tendencies, which are designed to avoid the separation

experience, and for thinking about the conclusion of analysis. Recently she came to one of our sessions with a photo of her at the crèche when she was about ten months old. We stood there looking at the picture: a little girl sitting on a chair staring into an inner void with a terrifyingly absent gaze. I was greatly moved. This picture was a verification of our work, we agreed. Ms S lay down on the couch and said: "It was very hard for me to bring you this picture." "Yes," I said, "looking at those eyes one feels very strongly how abandoned you were at the time. But if we both look at this little girl, she is no longer abandoned."

Conclusion

One of the essential features of this analysis is the fact that at the outset analyst and analysand were confronted with an objectless anxiety that could neither be named nor recognised. In joint fusional defence (I was absent when the patient came for her first appointment) the avoidance of this anxiety was represented in a concrete form. (I too had, as it were, fled from the scene of the accident). Fear of nothingness later manifested itself in analysis as a fear of "not feeling" and could be deciphered as such in small stages. In my countertransference I repeatedly generated images stemming from comparable experiences, for example, the "wobblers' room", children suffering from coprophagy, newspaper clippings of potty scenes from East German crèches, etc. In this way, I filled in the gaps with my knowledge of developmental psychology and external reality.

The task of the analysis was gradually to change objectless anxiety into objectal anxiety. Looking at the transference, we can see this transformation process as a gradual emergence from fusion (Henningsen, 2008). Enactments, facets of trauma, and quotations from earlier stages of development figure in this process. Separation and the interruption of fusions lead to envy and guilt feelings. Here hatred and destruction are central affective states triggering physical reactions and preparing the ground for incipient symbolisation. Object precursors and bodily reactions typical of development adumbrate the structure of the fusion. For example, Ms S experienced the extraction of her wisdom teeth and various other somatisations as ways in which she produced a physical pain to stand in for separation pain. With the electric shocks we were probably conniving to create a field where, in the leave-taking scene, an essential aspect of the trauma was represented and took on a more well-defined form in terms of our relationship. Here I too ran the risk of indulging in concretistic fantasies about the significance of the electric shocks.

All told, Ms S's analysis took six and a half years (one year once a week in a sitting position, later four sessions a week and towards the end three hours a week in a recumbent position). After the conclusion of treatment, Ms S occasionally and at long intervals asked for an appointment to achieve greater security in dealing with a difficult situation connected with the children or her husband.

CHAPTER SIX

"Everyone knows my mother. Everyone except me." Concretistic fusion and denial of object loss

Ms F

Ms F was thirty-six. Two years previously she had discontinued psychoanalytic treatment with another analyst after fifty-five sessions: "He kept on asking me: 'What did your mother have to say about that?' although I had told him that she died when I was two. He just couldn't get it into his head. He wasn't listening properly!" She said that she felt so awful, she just couldn't carry on any longer and was desperately in search of treatment. Her symptoms had got worse over the past few months. Ms F is an unusually slight young woman dressed in casual clothes. She came in with her crash-helmet under her arm, which made her look (to me) as if she were "armed for the fray". Her tan suggested that she was fond of nature, her facial expression was a mixture of toughness and resignation, which contrasted with her mournful blue eyes and a supplicating quality in her gaze. This discrepancy aroused my curiosity. Her distress was patent, and inwardly I was soon able to relate to her.

Symptoms

Ms F has suffered from bouts of depression since she was five years old. When they strike, she cries for a number of days on end, cannot eat, and feels hopelessly dejected. She is regularly affected by stomach cramps, gastritis, menstrual difficulties, and severe attacks of migraine. One major factor prompting her to embark on her first course of treatment was the onset of a state of "masculinisation" accompanied by guzzling, an "explosive increase in weight", and dizziness. Ms F detected male hair growth on her body. At one point, examinations revealed an increased level of testosterone, but later tests did not confirm this, so she did not undergo hormone treatment. Ms F repeatedly takes up with cold-hearted and rough-mannered men and suffers from anorgasmia. "I'm afraid of dreadful diseases," she tells me. "My brain can't cope with it, there's something jamming up the works. When there's a reason for me to be sad, I don't cry, I start bleeding. Then I think: 'My guts are crying.'"

Trauma history

Ms F's mother died of the after-effects of meningitis when she was two: "Everyone knows my mother. Everyone except me." Her mother was a singer and a pianist who made a number of LP recordings. She had been universally popular and when Ms F was a child, people would often remark on the resemblance between them: "You're the spitting image of Traudi."

Though very authoritarian in his attitudes, her father (born in 1912) looked after her and her sister (six years older) after the mother's death. Her sister had taken the mother's place in their parents' bed, while she slept in a bed of her own at the foot of it. Ms F felt that the father favoured her sister and she envied her accordingly. Her sister was the one he spoiled, she got everything she wanted. The father also took the two girls with him on little pleasure-trips.

Completely without warning, Ms F's father remarried when she was five. "This is your mother now," he told his daughters. That same day, the girls were "packed off" to the attic and their stepmother moved into the bedroom. This event welded the two children together. They stuck together at all times; as Ms F was quicker on the uptake, she was the one who supported her sister in situations requiring some kind of joint reaction. Ms F was better at school and also appeared to have inherited her mother's musical gifts. She too played the piano and had a fine singing voice.

The stepmother, herself a strict and authoritarian schoolteacher, "sided" with the father against the two girls. When Ms F lay in bed crying, the father would beat her "so that at least she knew what she was crying about." The girls were hardly ever allowed to do what they wanted, they were frequently accused of being up to no good, and were given regular beatings, particularly when they brought home poor grades from school. "I tried really hard," my patient tells me, "but it was a complete and utter flop. My stepmother put her arms around me twice a year at the most." Ms F lapsed into bouts of depression or attempted to defend herself with defiant protests. On one occasion, when her father made to lay about her again, she screamed in his face: "Why not beat me to death while you're at it, then at least they'll put you in jail!" Because of her poor grades, the parents took her out of school for a while "so she could see what it was like not to go to school." When she was sixteen, Ms F ran away from home and only had herself to depend on. "At one point I decided to kill myself, but something went wrong." The parents threatened to get the police to look for her. Ultimately her stepmother agreed to give her some financial support. After school, Ms F felt the urge to "save the world" and joined a left-wing youth group supporting the establishment of an electoral alliance between various non-mainstream political parties. She set up a printing shop, more or less taught herself the printer's trade, and passed the final apprentice examination with flying colours. But customers were scarce and she lost a lot of money, so she had no alternative but to work for another printer. After the fall of the Wall she went to Berlin to look for a job as a printer in the capital.

After leaving home, Ms F entered into a series of uninhibited, purely sexual relationships, none of which lasted. Usually she was intellectually superior, her partners gradually lost interest in her sexually, she felt unloved, her men friends found her heartless, she became more and more passive until her partners finally walked out on her. Later she learned how to "throw men out" herself. At the age of twenty, Ms F had her first abortion, the second shortly before her first analytic treatment two years before. A psychoanalytically oriented consultation eight years earlier had helped her a lot, which was why she was now so keen to tackle her problems with the aid of analysis.

After the first session I confronted my patient with the possibility that the discontinuation of her first analytic treatment could be seen in terms of the death of a relationship, a demise that was to some extent a repetition of her mother's early death. I also said that her first analyst had obviously been just as inattentive as her father, who had no inkling of what it meant for the two sisters to be banished to the attic from one day to the next. I suggested she should approach her earlier analyst and sort out this whole process with him as something had obviously happened that had not been properly understood. But Ms F insisted on attempting a "new start" with me, saying she had been so severely disappointed by her analyst that she could no longer persuade herself to trust him.

Diagnostic considerations

At our first contact I probably very quickly mutated into one of those friendly aunts or neighbours who were only too happy to be nice to Ms F. In a profounder sense, Ms F had very quickly activated in me the representation of the ideal dead mother. Her mother's illness and death must have had a traumatic effect on her. My hypothesis was that after her mother's death an ego-splitting may have taken place that paved the way for further pathogenesis. In one half of her self she is identical to her mother. Her physical resemblance and her gift for music, itself almost certainly the result of identification, further supported this process. In this part of her, the depression caused by the loss of her mother is warded off by self-substitution: I *am* my mother so I don't miss her. But in this position the patient has always been a surrogate object for others. People looked at her and were reminded of the mother; people were nice to her and in their minds this connected them with the mother. Her father probably also laid into her because memories of his late wife surfaced in his mind when he saw his daughter crying. This is the only way we can understand his statement: "Then at least you'll know what you're crying about."

In psychodynamic terms, my conjecture is a fusion between my patient and the ideal dead mother (cf. Ms O, Chapter Eleven). The father's near-incestuous bedroom arrangement may well have been both reassuring and disquieting for the children. In the framework of the denial of the mother's death referred to above, it seems fair to assume that massive oedipal fantasies had taken hold, forming the basis for later sexualisations. In another part of her self, Ms F was the abandoned little girl ousted by her older sister and seeking consolation from her father, her aunts, and the neighbours. In the process she developed gifts enabling her to please others, become more and more like her mother, and act wisely and prudently. In this respect she was sometimes able to outdo her sister.

The second major trauma was the incursion of her stepmother and the attendant expulsion from the bedroom. Narcissistic rage and identification with the aggressor put paid to all prospects of loving object relations. Defiance, flight, and being a boy rather than a girl were the survival strategies serving to ward off profound depression.

I saw the discontinuation of her first analytic treatment as a major enactment. I suspected an instance of collusion between analyst and analysand in which the patient's traumatic relationship constellation had been re-enacted without being subsequently understood. We agreed on four sessions of psychoanalysis a week. The patient paid for the fourth session herself. The conditions imposed on her by her health insurance fund limited the course of treatment to 300 sessions minus the fifty-five hours she had had with her earlier analyst. The treatment took just under two years.

Initial dream

After a few weeks the patient reports her first dream:

> I am in a village. In front of me is a man in a wheelchair, an old soldier. He draws his gun and makes to shoot me. There is a woman next to him, probably the one who pushes the wheelchair. I am sitting on the steps in front of a house, I move to one side, then a woman comes towards me to protect me. We both escape into the house and up the stairs. Then there's a chase that I can't remember so well. Later we're up at the top of the house and the old soldier and his companion throw stones at us. The village is at war. Soon the woman has gone and I'm alone on the street. I stop a Fiat and ask them if they can take me with them. But then I see that they too are armed, so I arm myself as well. I pull up a post with a reflector on it at the side of the road and carry it in front of me.

This dream confirmed my psychodynamic considerations and gave a number of indications pertaining to the programme for this analysis.

At the beginning of analysis, the patient's father was a vigorous man of eighty-one who had been through both World Wars. The patient's wish makes him a weak man in a wheelchair, but projected guilt feelings have him "reaching for his gun". The woman pushing the man in the wheelchair resembles an accomplice and definitely represents the stepmother, who "always had my father at her beck and call". With the village setting, Ms F is also introducing me to the world of her childhood in which the frequent sadistic incursions took place. Ms F tells me that though she often dreams about war and gunfire, this was the first time she herself had reached for a weapon. I remembered her crash-helmet at our first interview and conjectured that this part of the dream might already be a result of my interventions in which I had drawn her notice to the many belligerent repetitions and the losses that may also have manifested themselves in the discontinuation of analysis. I had occasionally interpreted her identifications with the aggressor and thus probably opened the door for this part of the dream.

The protective woman coming to her aid is an initial transference offer to me that may have its origins in the sister and the many helpful aunts in the village. The stairs are a reference to my practice; to get to my office one "goes into the house and up the stairs". The subsequent chase can be regarded as an image for the initial phase of analysis in which the various assaults and paranoid tendencies of her internal sadomasochistic world were topics for discussion. In the dream they resolve themselves on the one hand into an (ideal?) union—"later *we* are *somewhere* higher up"—and on the other into the split-off paranoid world out there in which evil objects continue to figure as persecutors ("the old people throw stones at us"). But obviously the splitting is not enough: "The village is at war." A new round in the conflict situation is ushered in, the patient is alone, the woman has disappeared. In the dream, the patient thinks through her solitude as if suspecting that withdrawal with the protective person can only be a temporary refuge. An explanation for this may be her biography: though the patient had many helpful aunts who were fond of her, she was ultimately always "passed on", profound and secure attachments never materialised. At the same time there are clear indications of her premonition that analysis will expose her to her anxieties and aggressions. She would also need a "weapon" against me.

I very soon informed Ms F that in her dream she reminded me of Pippi Longstocking. I could hardly imagine how anyone could tear a warning post from its moorings and use it as a weapon; that was the kind of thing Pippi Longstocking could do. Pippi had also thrown policemen out and like herself worsted the Establishment with her superhuman powers. But it took a while before Ms F was able to discover behind her physical feats the lost little girl in search of a constant and loving relationship.

In the first phase of analysis, Ms F stretched our relationship to the limits with her promiscuous behaviour. She took up with and cast aside men at a speed that made any kind of analytic understanding impossible. I couldn't even recall their names. She told me in a tone of despair, but not without pride, that there had been between eighty and ninety men in her life so far. My comment: "You're continuing with your dangerous life, you want to scare me out of my wits." Or: "This way you can triumph over other women, your stepmother, your sister, me. Hardly anyone can tot up that many men." Or: "You're making sure that you get handed on, like in your childhood, but there's never any trusting relationship."

On several occasions, Ms F jeopardised herself, either with potential sexually transmitted diseases or extremely hazardous motorbike outings. She needed the men to discharge her arousals and was regularly disappointed. Gradually she began to sense that in analysis with me she was experiencing a form of pacification that did her good and prompted her to start thinking about things. Here the large number of sessions was beneficial. Ms F called her own behaviour into question and said she could only do one thing at a time, either analysis or a relationship with a man. She opted in favour of analysis. Although in itself such an alternative is of course nonsensical, it made a great deal of sense for Ms F. In transference I had become more and more a reliable object that she learned to adjust to inwardly and that helped her forgo sexualisation. In many recollections we drew parallels between the lack of constancy in her present relationships and the lack of constancy in her earlier relationships in childhood. The arousing quality of the sexualisations was a pendant to her futile infant attempts to stimulate attention in others so that *she* could be seen (and not the dead mother). With her previous analyst the dead mother had resurfaced time and again; she had understood his questions about her to mean that he was denying her death. Her mother had died at an age at which Ms F was fully geared to receiving support from her mother for affect regulation. She could walk and say a few words but it was still her mother's lap that she turned to for security and warmth.

> In this phase of analysis, Ms F recalled more episodes with the previous analyst that for her signified a repetition of what she had experienced with her father. Sitting in the waiting room, she heard through the unpadded door a patient crying bitterly while talking to the therapist. Subsequently she opened her own session with the words: "That man must really be having a bad time." The analyst's reply was: "Yes, he's always wailing about something." This response made her wince, for her it was proof that the analyst—just like her father—was not inwardly prepared to empathise with another person's unhappiness. When Ms F arrived late at another session because she had had an accident on her motorcycle and her knee was so swollen she could hardly walk, he had not once asked how she was feeling.

For Ms F this man was nothing other than the strict teacher-father intent on sticking to the rules and never showing any emotion. The little girl's desire to be perceived and accepted by the father had been reawakened by these scenes. It may also have been evoked by the accident and again by her early arrival and the attendant possibility of overhearing what was going on behind the office door. But the wish was not recognised and thus could not be subjected to interpretation and incorporated into their analytic work.

Ms F began to look at herself critically. She said she must previously have been very naive and had entered into all those relationships with men much too quickly. It was no wonder that none of them lasted. She engaged more profoundly with analysis and sensed her unending longing for appreciation and love, repeatedly related to the transference and the early loss of her mother. Behind her tomboy exterior she increasingly stood revealed as a slight and needy little girl, albeit one with a strong will.

I was able to show her that in her unconscious she had upheld an internal equation in which she was identical with her mother and had thus attempted to deny her mother's death. But as she approached her thirty-fourth birthday, the age at which her mother died, this fusion could no longer be sustained: if she had been physically identical to her mother, she too would have had to die at thirty-four. Probably her body had intervened and produced a distinction between her and her mother so that the body would not have to die. After this interpretation, the male hair and the bouts of depression disappeared. The patient became more secure in her female identity, she began to take an interest in a more durable relationship with a man, and in analysis she discussed many conflicts at her workplace. In transference I increasingly became a female figure harbouring feelings of solidarity for her but also someone who was different from her. As the period paid for her by her insurance scheme came to end, she also felt ready to terminate therapy.

After a short period in which the patient came to see me once a week and herself paid for the additional sessions, analysis was terminated. I have always mistrusted this therapeutic success a little, asking myself whether today there might still be conversion symptoms of the kind described by Freud and later Alexander (1950). Nor was I sure whether one can deal with such a severe fate as Ms F's in such a short time. But the patient saw no reason to carry on with therapy. She was satisfied with the work we had done, and neither she nor I had ever thought that the masculine hair would disappear without trace. It was indeed something of a miracle.

Catamnesis

Fifteen years after termination of treatment, Ms F called me on the phone. "Things are bad," she said. "You got me back on my feet once, can I come and talk to you?"

What had happened? Slightly more than six months before, her stepmother, who had survived her father by a number of years, had died and left everything she owned to Ms F's sister and herself. If, as they intended, the parents' house were sold, both daughters would inherit a very sizeable sum. Though she should of course be glad about this, she found it impossible to exult. She had no idea what to do with all that money. She was permanently depressed, at her wits' end and unfair to her partner. She had started to mistrust him, had groundless attacks of jealousy and could not desist from spying on him. She risked ruining the relationship altogether. Also she was mad at her sister because once again she had to play mother and deal with all the formalities connected with the inheritance.

Ms F was now fifty-four years old and displayed no psychosomatic complaints connected with menopause. The "masculinisation" she had gone through had never recurred. She was suffering from a pathological mourning reaction that we were able to get to the bottom of and work on in the framework of a brief course of therapy. During the previous years, Ms F had contrived to achieve a good working balance. After therapy she had entered into a relationship that had lasted some time. Her present relationship had held up for eight years. She had quit her old job and was embarking on a new position. In the last few years she had been a voluntary official in a sports club, where she was greatly esteemed.

It quickly became apparent that the patient had achieved and maintained mental balance by having her stepmother personify everything evil, thus enabling her to lead a relatively altruistic life. Her stepmother served as a projection screen for everything nasty in the world. Now she was completely unable to understand why this woman had left everything to her sister and herself. Obviously she had been mistaken in her, which set off unconscious guilt feelings. Suddenly she had to learn to deal differently with all the pent-up rage she felt on account of the things in life that she had been forced to forgo. She could no longer blame it all on her stepmother or her sister. She had to understand her own destiny for what it was and come to terms with it. After she had recognised the collapse of her guilt defences and her own dubious idealisations, she bought a piano and started playing again, thus fulfilling a desire that was closely connected to her biological mother. This not only enabled her to accept the inheritance left her by her father and her stepmother but also to shoulder the highly individual personal legacy that had come down to her from her biological mother. She saved the rest of the money so that she had resources to fall back on in her old age, an aspect she had hitherto neglected in her life-plan.

Discussion

The separation trauma struck when Ms F was at an age in which she had already internalised the mother as a primary object for two years. Presumably she was in the rapprochement phase (Mahler, 1968), that is, she was still attached symbiotically to the mother but was also "practising" separation from the object to acquire inner object constancy. This stage of her development was brutally interrupted by the death of the mother. My conjecture is that the mother's sudden disappearance brought about a splitting between parts of the body-self, which was still fully attuned to affect regulation by the mother, and mental processes addressed and encouraged by consoling substitutes. In a split-off fusion core the patient remained physically attached to the mother in her unconscious mind. After the mother's death, the mirroring so indispensable for the child could no longer be authentic. The consoling objects that kept on seeing the mother in the child, and thus concerned themselves via the little girl with the grief they felt for the mother, were not genuinely able to help the child. In the father this process is unmistakable. The patient was never really *meant*—another reason to develop a false self and uphold the splittings. In an unmentalized fusion core, the patient remained linked with the mother and had thus warded off the traumatic loss. Because the fusion is physical, it is once again appropriate to refer to it with the term "concretistic". Finally, in a part of her personality that was still fully attuned to psychosomatic union with the mother, the patient entered into a fusion with part of her own self. This had remained fused with the mother in order to pretend the loss had never happened, to preserve something that the world around her could not give her. This fusional defence collapsed as the patient reached the age at which her mother had died. Later, in the case of Ms O, I shall have occasion to describe a different variation of a similar fusion with the dead mother (cf. Chapter Eleven).

The oedipal conflict constellation became an insuperable task further exacerbated by the stepmother moving into the house. It was impossible for her to enter into mature sexual attachments because to do that she would have had to break free of the mother-body. It was this dilemma that gave rise to her extreme promiscuity. Arousal made her feel alive, promised to dispel all the depression, but satisfactory relaxation was impossible because that would have called for a release of the functions of bodily affect regulation that were welded into the fusion with the early maternal introject. This integration process could only succeed in the course of analysis. The more reliable the transference relationship became, the better Ms F was able to internalise the reassurance that analysis gave her.

The fact that Ms F was able to free herself of her symptoms and develop structural changes within a relatively short space of time was also due to the earlier treatment she had undergone. Since the depth-psychological therapy years before, she had preoccupied herself with her inner life. Her previous analyst had overlooked important signals emanating from the patient in connection with her trauma. From what the patient reported, it appears very much as if the analyst had heedlessly acted out his countertransference (in relation both to the mother and the father). Ms F had discontinued the analysis in troubled confusion, with anxieties, dizzy spells, and bouts of guzzling. Only the growth of male hair was curbed.

Internally, extended enactment and the attendant discontinuation of the first course of therapy had "staged" her problems in a graphic way. When Ms F came to me, the concretistic fusion was already ruptured. The patient began to emerge from the fusion when she reached the age at which her mother had died. The psychosomatic union was disrupted via "masculinisation". In Part One I have discussed emergence from fusion and the hazards involved in transference (cf. Ms R and Mr V, Chapter Two). On the one hand, the termination of analysis contains a repetition of the traumatic relational entanglement, on the other—and seen as enactment—it also contains something that craved understanding. The patient must have sensed this, otherwise she would not have embarked on a second course of analysis.

The superego conflicts bound up with the traumas could not be exhaustively addressed in the brief course of therapy at our disposal. The despair caused by the real experience of wrong was simply too severe. Reconciliation between patient and parents was unthinkable. Initial progress in this direction was only conceivable fifteen years later when the patient approached me once again after her parents' death.

When the patient had read the manuscript and returned for a follow-up exchange, she told me that she had never felt better. She described how everything had come back to life as she read about it, a number of things she could hardly remember. But two things had occurred to her that she badly wanted to tell me about. When she announced her intention of terminating her first analytic treatment, her sister had tried to dissuade her, casting doubt on her complaints about her analyst, declaring that it was exactly the same as with her father and asking "whether it might not all have to do with transference".

What she found even more important was the fact that to this day, her sister, who remembered her mother very well because she was considerably older, repeatedly confronted her with requests and demands that deep down she was probably addressing to her mother. She recalled the situation when her father died. Shortly before his death, he awoke briefly, stared at her with shining eyes and addressed her as "Traudi" (her mother's forename) before closing his eyes for the last time. Her sister had stood next to her without understanding what it all meant.

CHAPTER SEVEN

"The greatest danger comes from myself": destruction and guilt*

With this clinical example I would like to show how, in an analytical relationship, aspects of the trauma can be recognised in small steps as "quotations" (Lipin, 1955; Henningsen, 1990, pp. 223–224) and gradually transformed into symbolic language. Split-off aggression, and the feelings of guilt gradually resulting from them, become accessible to interpretation through projective identification in the transference and in other ancillary transferences. Mr G said at the end of the treatment that the most important insight of his analysis was that he himself was the source of the greatest dangers he could fall into. In the course of the analysis he had recognised his various identifications with unconscious feelings of guilt (Bohleber, 1997), some of which were of transgenerational origin. He was able to cope better with his aggression because he had understood the structure of his traumas.

---

*Entitled "Destruction and guilt: Splitting and reintegration in the analysis of a traumatised patient" this chapter was published in 2005 in the *International Journal of Psychoanalysis*, 86: 353–373. Slightly modified, reprinted with permission of the *International Journal*.

Mr G

In the beginning I took almost twice as many notes on Mr G (Henningsen, 2000, 2005 a) as with my other patients. While reflecting on my countertransference reaction, a remark made by the patient after one year of analysis occurred to me: "You know, I don't have any structure—I'm like a little child and that is why I need you." By writing things down, I was obviously trying to retain something that he had been unable to retain, that is, to give the analysis a structure. I saw my behaviour as a counterpart to his tendency to project split feelings and then act in a very concretistic manner (Grubrich-Simitis, 1981) in "action symptoms" (McDougall, 1982, p. 4). My note-taking was a countertransference reaction at the level of a concretistic fusion. I also thought about his nicotine addiction and the chronic diarrhoea from which he had suffered since his childhood; he had only mentioned the latter because he did not think of it as a psychosomatic symptom. He often said that he found my office so pleasantly warm that when he left a session he felt very cold and had to light up a cigarette immediately.

Interview phase

Mr G was in panic the day he rang for the first time. It was of great importance, he said, to arrange his analytic sessions. When he arrived, I saw a very tall man in his late twenties, very pale, with a childish expression, who gave me the impression of being stressed and agitated. His appearance suggested an upper-middle-class background, yet there was something about him that did not quite fit. His clothes seemed a bit too large for him, and he had the look of somebody who was wearing his older brother's confirmation suit.

He had had a breakdown abroad. His flying and travel phobia had made him incapable of working, and it was only by having someone to accompany him that had he been able to return to Germany. He reported his symptoms in a telegrammic style so that I could get an "objective picture": his failed marriage, which he had "started" almost eight years ago; as long as he could remember he had suffered from anxiety, diarrhoea, and sleeping disorders, all connected to his mother, as a psychiatrist had explained to him when he was nineteen years old.

His mother had suffered from depressions and had taken her own life. "At the time, I was eight years old. As luck would have it, I was the one who discovered her, although there is a lot I cannot remember. I cannot visualise the scene; all I know is that she hanged herself in the cellar; that night I heard footsteps on the stairs. I was lying awake in bed and found her when I opened the cellar door for our cleaning lady to get in because my mother had locked the door. It was morning time. My brother had left already, my father was still asleep." What I heard shocked me—the account of a suicide told in short telegram-like sentences. Without pausing for breath, the patient continued his report. Emotions, aggressions, and feelings of guilt would have probably overwhelmed him had he stopped for a moment, although by interrupting him a number of times I had invited him to do so. Without pausing, he went on to talk about his second mother (this is what the patient called her), who had "taken him over" while he was already suffering from sleeping disorders. She had built "a proper nest" for him. His father had married her a year after his mother's death. From what people have told him, he "used to hang on to her apron strings". He had become increasingly shy with other children in the years before and after his mother's death.

Although there are photos of his natural mother, Mr G has never been able to picture her in his mind or imagine what she might have been like. Before her death, he had been told to keep an eye on her. His mother took a lot of tablets, was very moody, had a cancer phobia, and threatened almost daily to take her life. She used to take a nap every afternoon and he was never certain whether she would wake up again. He seldom dared to leave the house; there was, however, a hole in the garden hedge and that gave him the occasional opportunity to leave his parents' home to play on the neighbouring football pitch.

Mr G came to see me three times. On each occasion, we spoke at length about his separation problems. Each time, I listened supportively in the hope that he could get through to the next session, as he was greatly burdened by his unconscious feelings of guilt. The "false starts" of his marriage and his problem with aeroplanes seemed to me to be hapless attempts to ward off a deep depression at a phallic level.

After a long break, he arrived at our next appointment as white as chalk. I was shocked by the deterioration in his condition and wondered why he had not telephoned me. It soon became clear that he had not been able to do so. He had come to tell me that he would not be going ahead with the analysis. He had felt so ill that he had gone to a psychiatrist, who had prescribed tablets to be taken daily; he had also been to the psychiatrist two or three times a week for a thirty-minute conversation. He said that he liked coming to see me because he felt more at ease talking to me but felt that I would not want to see him anymore.

> I replied: "I offered you analysis sessions and the offer still stands. Of course, it is your decision whether you wish to go ahead. Nevertheless, I would like to tell you how I see the situation. I think that with these difficulties you are pointing at something that is really essential, something that perhaps you are unable to bear. You once lay in bed, awake, and heard your mother going downstairs. Your father was asleep and a catastrophe occurred in the cellar. Now you have to wait for me; you are at the mercy of the situation, and perhaps you are afraid that a catastrophe could strike once again. You've been going to a male psychiatrist—as if you wished to shake your father out of his sleep. You want him to help you to stop your mother from committing suicide."

The patient accepted this interpretation with some relief. I promised to keep a place for him. He could take his time to think about it and also speak to the psychiatrist. We agreed that he would continue to receive psychiatric care until he moved to another flat. I regarded this attack on our relationship as something constructive. By acting in this way, the patient had brought his split-off trauma directly into our relationship. At a stroke, I was confronted with all the feelings he was not supposed to have. It was presumably an unconscious test: Would I survive a murder situation, in this case the murder of our relationship? At the same time, my extended interpretation seemed to have provided a structure and also given the scene a name. In this way, he had been able, additionally, to find for himself both a father (the psychiatrist) and a mother (me).

Biography

Mr G was born in 1963, the second son of a well-to-do family. His depressive mother had reacted to the death of her father (in 1966) with a severe decompensation that continued until her death, coupled with a fear of cancer; her mental condition required psychiatric treatment. During the period of his mother's depression, the patient—a young child—hardly left the house because he felt it was his duty to keep an eye on her. Her moods made her unpredictable; she constantly threatened to take her own life and did her utmost to prove that she was suffering from cancer. The patient's elder brother also suffered from the situation but he protested loudly: he was aggressive and openly directed his anger towards his mother, whereas Mr G lived in total subjugation, in "a black hole", as he later said. By using this metaphor, which is also common in psychoanalysis (Cohen, 1980; Cournut, 1988), Mr G was pointing to what for him was the unfathomable and inescapable situation in which he was bound to his primary love object.

His father was totally preoccupied with building up his business and earned a great deal of money. He engaged a large number of doctors, psychiatrists, and sanatoriums for his wife. Doctors repeatedly warned him that at some point she would manage to kill herself.

"To spare the children's feelings", the patient and his brother were not taken to their mother's funeral; only later did the patient see the grave shared by his mother and grandfather. He had no opportunity to mourn her death; instead, he told what had happened to everybody in the street, at school, in the shops, everywhere, as though he were under some kind of compulsion to confess. To this day Mr G is fidgety, concentrates poorly, and suffers recurrently from severe amnesia. He was never a good pupil; while at school, however, he took an intelligence test that showed he had an above-average IQ, a result that gave both teachers and parents much to think about. In a subsequent psychological examination, the psychologist explained to his parents that the boy was in need of "a lot of love". It was his second mother who took this to heart: she had close physical contact with him and allowed him to sit on her lap until he was seventeen years old.

At school, Mr G was unpopular and tried to gain attention by clowning around, mostly without success. At the age of seventeen, he was still the smallest in his class and was not liked at all. It was the same with football. The pitch was next to his parents' garden—all he needed to do was to go through the hole in the hedge—so he could also return quickly. He was often teased, sent off, or transferred to the B team. At university, he found his course extremely difficult, as his impaired powers of concentration and memory were a permanent burden. Only after his initial consultations did he manage to take his degree, achieving high marks, and start to work.

He met his first wife eight years ago; she was determined to marry him, and he agreed to do so. At first he felt proud and excited: this was his first sexual relationship, although it was never satisfying. His wife soon turned to other men, something he denied for a long time. Again, he felt this to be his failure.

Analysis

I have divided my account of the analysis into two parts. In the first, I would like to show how this patient with his split-off destructiveness entered very quickly into a relationship with me by means of actions, accidents, and symptoms. The triad of thinking, feeling, and acting did not occur synchronically in him. He was able to express his feelings through action but could not think them, and in my countertransference at the beginning of the therapy—for example, when taking notes—I was entangled with him on the action level (Klüwer, 1983, 1995). This concretistic fusion between the patient and the analyst served as a kind of putty that integrated the aggressive action symptoms in our relationship. Only later (the second part of my account) was it possible for this pattern of interaction to be transformed into a transference relationship in which his traumatic constellation came alive. The intrusively experienced destruction that had been split off and linked to symptoms was now able to enter the psychic space and became alive in the transference: the trauma became a conflict. Working through this psychotic transference immediately transformed the conflict into a trauma, which had to be contained (Henningsen, 1990). The account of the analytic process will be substantiated by a number of dreams which, in my view, verified the course of events in line with Quinodoz (1999).

Words are semolina: concrete re-enactments

> He regularly arrived at my office in a hurry. He left his coat, jacket, and everything else lying around the room or hung them on the chair at my desk. When I pointed out that there was a coat-stand in the hall, he replied, "Oh, thank you so much, but I don't need it." Or on another day: "I'm not going to look at your desk, you know that." It was important for him to have everything in the room, his jacket included. The transition from his car to the couch had to be seamless. It was obvious that he had to dominate me and my room in an intrusive manner and that this was not going to be a topic of conversation.
>
> He often began the sessions with the words "Today I'm completely in the cellar again" ("*im Keller*" is a German metaphor meaning "to be down in the dumps"). When I replied by observing, "In the cellar, that's where

you found your mother," he asked, "What did I just say?" Or later, "Did I say *"im Keller"* again?" This metaphor revealed the extent to which he was down in the cellar, although he was unable to connect it with himself. It was only after several years of analysis that we actually got down into the cellar.

Once a week, he arranged to play football on a pitch directly opposite my house.

A: That means that you're quite near me and you can always drop in if anything happens, just as you used to go through the hole in the hedge.
P: To be honest, I had already thought of that.

I felt that I was analysing a highly intelligent but small child who, because of his identity disorder, needed to experience his relationship with me on a concretistic level before it was possible for any interpretation to bring about changes. He had a concrete need to be in me. The symbolic level—me as psychic reality for him—was not accessible.

He was very fearful of making mistakes at the office. He was hectic, never stopped speaking, and for the next six months he continued taking his tablets. It was as if I had a hunted dog or an immersion heater lying on the couch. Every time I managed to make a comment or offer an interpretation, he answered briefly, "What you say is quite correct," and continued in his characteristic style. Unconsciously, he was speaking with his dead mother. He devoured my words without digesting them as though they were semolina pudding, which he greatly enjoyed. Even today he still often cooks it for himself, although he always suffers from diarrhoea as a result: this milk pudding brought him pleasant memories of his mother, which he then had to destroy or expel just as he did with my attempts to understand him.

At the same time he had several accidents (traffic and sport) that showed me how much he was at risk, even if he was not clearly to blame for the situations. It was all too evident that, wherever he was, catastrophes could easily occur. To me he seemed a little careless, as though he wanted me, like his father or second mother, to lay a protective hand on him.

"Total fusion" with Claudia: the beginning of split transference

He reacted to our first holiday interruption by re-enacting his relationship to his mother: he fell in love with a young woman. The two of them "merged totally"; she suffered from severe bulimia, unpredictable depressions, and had suicidal thoughts. It all had to do with his experience from his preverbal days: between him and his mother, as between him and Claudia, his girlfriend, there was a destructive but indissoluble bond.

His life was now organised along the following lines: he had sessions from Monday to Friday and afterwards would drive 500 km to visit Claudia and then come back again for the Monday session. Separation was difficult for both: he had panic attacks and she would phone him every hour; any sign of a real separation would make him react with diarrhoea and her with depression. He was devoured by her and then spat out again. On a psychosomatic level, these dynamics found expression in his diarrhoea. If she threatened to break off the relationship, he thought of suicide and went through severe depressions.

> A: It is as if I had two people here on the couch.
> P: Yes, when I talk about Claudia, I'm also talking about myself.

Whenever I had a chance, I interpreted every detail of this relationship, including the instances of psychosomatic interaction. Just as he was unable to recall anything about Claudia, so he could not remember a thing about me from the previous session. There were, however, differences between Claudia and me that showed that the work of interpretation was gradually bearing fruit.

> P: You are always calm and friendly. When I deposit my destruction in Claudia, she hits back twice as strong ... Claudia is even sicker than I am ... I am conscious that I am contributing to my own downfall in the relationship with her but I can't escape from it ... Claudia is destroying herself and me with her.
> A: Yes, I think this situation helps us to see and feel something similar to what you experienced with your mother, but at that time you were probably unable to feel it.
>
> There was considerable trouble when, during a short break in the analysis, he accepted Claudia's plans to marry him and move elsewhere only because he wanted to be in agreement with her.
>
> A: You are creating facts with which the analysis can hardly keep up.
> P: I have sold myself to Claudia.

In my countertransference I felt the need to act, which I did through interpretations: I was his dead mother whom he wanted to bring back to life or his passive father who wanted to make him see reason. I was supposed to act and stop the unstoppable. It was possible to show a wealth of parallels between the present situation and the past situation with his mother. Although he was able to remember some things and had some insights, he could not say "no" to Claudia.

A: "No" means separation and separation means death.
P: You know, I don't have any structure, any form. I don't know what I want. I'm a child, and that's why I need you.

His mother's face, an organiser in transference (the beginning of reintegration)

The death of the patient's maternal grandmother provided him with an opportunity to hold several conversations with his father and also to visit his mother's grave again. It was important for him to look at his mother's grave, and for that reason he returned there alone on one more occasion before departing. Tears came into his eyes. A: "Going alone did you good."—P: "Yes, you know, this improves my standing with my mother." I was surprised by the answer. My hope that he would now be able to mourn somewhat seemed to be premature. In line with his narcissism and his masochistic ties to his mother it was important for him to be "in her good graces". Implicit in his magic idea of his mother sitting in heaven looking at him was an unconscious guilt that he shared with her: each of them had left the other; victim and non-victim had fused permanently with each other (Cournut, 1988; Oliner, 1996).

For the first time during a session he saw his mother's face. It expressed a degree of contentment. By describing the scene, he allowed me to participate and we were both able to look at his sleeping mother. Only then did he develop the idea that perhaps he would be able to take leave of her. During this session, the atmosphere was calm and meditative. In a flash, I had a series of ideas: if there is such a thing as an organiser of psychic development, then it had just emerged in the patient (Spitz, 1965). And if by means of free association the face of his mother appeared for the first time, then this was perhaps because there is also an organiser involved in the transference. It seemed as if a reintegration of the split-off mother introject was about to take place.

However, my hope that his mother would now appear in his dreams was initially disappointed.

He managed to end his relationship with Claudia, who once again made him go through hell. He was shaken and depressed and was afraid she might really kill herself. I interpreted these events to enable him to find in his inner being what he was experiencing. At issue now was how to deal with his destructive mother introject and with separation.

"Fear of total loss": the first dream with his mother

His grandmother died in an old people's home. She was mostly interested in furs and jewellery and in the "good old days". His grandfather, a factory director, had an honourable reputation. The family went to South America after the war.

A: So what made your grandparents go to South America in 1949?
P: As ethnic Germans from the Sudetenland, they were stateless at the time. Nobody wanted to have them.
A: Really? But didn't the refugees from the Sudetenland receive loans to help them get started again?

I flushed. We remained silent. Naturally, I was wondering whether his grandparents had been Nazis. I said nothing, realising that I was in danger of adopting the accusing tone of a prosecutor. My silence had obviously triggered something in him. In our next session, he reflected on whether his mother's depression might have had something to do with his grandfather's depression. He had taken the opportunity to ask his father about his grandparents' past and learned some frightening facts. The grandfather, a Nazi party member, had been the manager of an armaments factory that used slave workers. An uncle (his mother's brother) was an SS man who died shortly after the war. Grandfather was "in love" with his daughter, Mr G's mother. Mr G wondered whether his mother felt the same way. The grandparents had had a difficult marriage and for the rest of her life, the grandmother remained caught up in the Nazi world of her past, and never gave any support to her daughter.

During the sessions, the patient engaged with the trauma of his father, which the latter could never come to terms with. As a sixteen-year-old anti-aircraft gunner's assistant ("flak helper") in the last days of the war, he had barely survived a Russian assault; nearly all his comrades had been hit and disembowelled. After the end of the war, the patient's paternal grandfather had been taken to a concentration camp and executed by the Russians although he was completely innocent.

Fear of enormous destructive potential led the patient to engage with his "yes-man side", both in his work and in analysis. He recognised that, by merely agreeing with the person he was dealing with, he was switching off his own judgement and ending up in dilemmas.

During one of the following weekends, he suffered "from a fear of total loss" and blood appeared in his stools. He feared that his new girlfriend, Dagmar, might leave him and that he might use the analysis as some kind of alibi while, in fact, nothing would change. I said, "I can imagine that your body has to find some way of expressing itself here when we are dealing with so much unimaginable destruction. There is an injury inside you and perhaps there is something you want to separate from. And, if you are afraid that the analysis could become an alibi, then the issue would seem to be whether both of us feel able to face the truth."

Mr G went to see an internist, but none of the tests showed any problem. What was presumably manifested in this instance was destruction at a psychosomatic level that signalled the onset of the dissolution of a pathological fusion and made symbolisations possible (Trimborn, 1999): after this episode came the first dream in which his mother appeared. This dream sheds light on the complicated transference situation.

> The dream was made of pieces that didn't quite fit together. But I saw her face; I can vaguely remember that. My mother had given me some job to do. I went off to do it but couldn't manage. I tried to do it in many different ways and it didn't work. The pressure became stronger and stronger. I started to feel afraid that I would have to go back to my mother and say: "Sorry, but I can't manage, I'm not able to do it."

Mr G reacted to the dream with severe diarrhoea. Once again, the physical retention of what he had recognised was not possible: on the one hand, it was a matter of a "feeling of pressure" which arose because he always believed he would not manage to keep his mother in a good mood: "I always had to be vigilant and do whatever my mother wanted." At the same time, this was also connected to the two of us in my office: was I making too many demands on him with this analysis, did I want something from him? The position I had adopted had caused him to turn to his grandparents' roles as perpetrators and victims, something he had unconsciously prompted me to do. There was a danger that the "yes-man" in him was pursuing the issue so as to be a good analysand. In addition, his grandparents were further away than his own trauma—he could ward off the present with the past. On the other hand, engaging with his grandparents gave him an opportunity to observe his identifications and, with me, to work out a basic pattern for dealing with destruction (Oliner, 1996).

> P: Other people have illnesses you can see ... that is actually simpler. My father left me on my own then, even though he liked me. What could he have done? He was probably afraid of putting my mother in a clinic. Then everything would have cracked up much earlier. What he actually did was to delegate something to me. As long as I was there, she would not kill herself.
> A: And now you don't want to do this job any more—you can't manage it.
> P: No, but I haven't got that far yet. I'm just beginning to stop play-acting. That is possible with Dagmar and with you, though I still feel quite unsure of myself. Elsewhere I cannot do it yet.

During this time, there were a lot of dreams and memories related to his mother's death. His mother had been hanging with her back towards him when he discovered her. His father had taken her down, carried her upstairs, and laid her on the sofa. The police were called.

By now he was often able to carry the "warmth" he experienced during the sessions for the rest of the day. He said to me, "I can get on with you better" or "You have become more open." Here, of course, he was speaking about himself. Gradually, he was also able to remember a previous session.

A child of perpetrators and victims: first steps to an engagement with guilt feelings

He made many mistakes in the office and he mentioned them to everybody, just as he had told everyone about his mother's suicide. Once, he wanted to pay my monthly fee with two one-thousand-mark notes, and suggested that the considerable surplus could be offset against the next monthly fee. Here we were able to recognise the enormous pressure of guilt under which he stood and how much he wished me—like his father, who paid most of the analysis fee—to share that guilt with him. At least for a month, I would owe him something. (In German, "guilt" (*Schuld*) and "owe" (*schulden*) have the same etymology.)

Mr G had watched *Schindler's List* on video with his girlfriend. Both of them had cried. "Did Schindler really exist?" he asked me. He told me about a dream in which, like Schindler, he had rescued factory workers. His desire for reparation became clear. But then the session took quite a different direction:

A: In your dream when you are Schindler, you express a desire for reparation.
P: Yes, but I don't believe I would be able to do that in reality. I believe I am a coward. And I also don't know how I would have acted if I'd been a soldier in the East German army. If I had been a guard at Auschwitz who had to shoot at others, I believe I would have shot myself ... Why am I so addicted to television programmes on the liberation of Auschwitz? ... I used to wish I had lived at that time; what do you think the reason is?
A: For you it was a time of many uncertainties, and it was also linked to the most unimaginable atrocities. And your family has been affected more than once as perpetrators and as victims. Perhaps you want to clarify or understand something.
P: It was shameful, I feel the guilt. There are so many sides to the whole thing.

This was followed by several weeks of intensive work during which his identification with his parents was at issue. His father's role as a victim helped him to focus on the perpetrator within himself. In a dream, he was a soldier and strangled another young soldier. He saw himself as a potential murderer and again he went through the stages leading to the discovery of his mother. From the footsteps on the staircase, he had realised that it was his mother who had gone downstairs and, as it wasn't Christmas, there was no reason to lock the door to the cellar. He had sensed that something awful could happen if he stayed in bed. He could have prevented his mother's suicide. "And another thing, though it is perhaps rather a strange thing to say, Dagmar enjoys it when I run my fingers along her throat. And yesterday an idea flashed into my mind: I could grab her neck and keep it in a stranglehold, but I would never do it. I like Dagmar; I'm getting fonder of her all the time. I'd never do that. But this feeling that I could do something that would throw me off track, bring about a catastrophe, came back in an instant, and I have this fear again and again, at work, too."

His realisation that he could at any time become a murderer by way of an impulsive action seemed to me to show that the treatment was making progress: the omnipotent destructiveness that I sensed in his actions, which invariably expressed itself on a psychosomatic level, was now becoming clear in an ancillary transference.

The liability case: re-enactment in transference

In the meantime, my countertransference had changed. It was no longer necessary for me to write down so much. The dimension of the patient's problems of guilt and aggression made me feel particularly alarmed. A catastrophe could easily strike, and I was very careful lest I should bring guilt upon myself. I often felt depressed, pessimistic, and stretched to the limits of my abilities. This was because in the transference with me he could establish contact with the suicidal and depressive elements that kept him in contact with his dead mother, which, again and again, he had to split off and project.

To prevent possible catastrophes, he did not leave his workplace before midnight. Nevertheless, he soon made a major mistake. Immediately after a session with me, he achieved undeserved success by ignoring an important piece of information. For this reason he saw himself as a criminal and feared dreadful consequences. Again, he expressed his "fear of going mad". At home, he constantly felt the impulse to run through his living room onto the roof terrace and throw himself off. During the day, more than ever before he lived "as if under a veil".

"I live on two tracks," he said, in order to explain this split. He had not linked the facts with each other, just as he had not done when he heard his mother's footsteps on the staircase. In fact, he had called out to her ... His grandparents had also practised the same kind of juxtaposition: his grandfather had been a respected chemist and had Jewish friends, and at the same time he was the director of this armaments factory. His grandmother enjoyed playing on the tennis court next to the factory in which slave labourers suffered. "My grandmother lied to herself—she did not give tuppence for the truth. I do not want this inheritance!"

Because he could not feel, he could not make connections. Fear made him flee. He began thinking seriously about suicide and developed extreme diarrhoea and vomiting. Over the next five months, with some fluctuation, this condition continued. The analysis acquired a new quality. He became extremely serious: there were no more signs of his play-acting. Not-feeling, the missing connections that accompanied everything he did, now became evident in the relationship between us.

He was not just suffering from psychological or inherited guilt but had also, through his behaviour, taken objective guilt on himself. He recounted the following dream:

> A cleaning woman leads me to the toilet, opens the door, and sitting on the toilet bowl I see a dead child of about twelve years old. Then she opens the next door. The bowl is disgusting, filled to the brim with excrement, nauseating. The cleaning woman puts her finger in it and stirs the shit as if she wanted to show me something. Awful.

With the cleaning woman he had discovered his dead mother … back then part of him had died. He is the dead boy in the dream. I am the cleaning woman, who is showing him all the shit. But the cleaning woman in the dream acted "in a completely routine way", in other words, between us there was a spark of security, which had grown during the treatment.

His condition became increasingly desolate. He repeatedly played with the idea of throwing himself out of the window. He was not sure of himself; he felt he could not control himself. "I cannot use my capacity for logical thought … I cannot retain what happens in the session." Everything had to be "shat away" immediately afterwards. His fears had a psychotic quality; in the office he was incapable of working and could not leave his desk; I recommended him, in vain, to take sick leave. However, he gladly accepted my suggestion that, for a time, he should come five times a week. I gave him an appointment for 6 p.m. so, on that day at least, he was forced to leave the office before 11 p.m.

Although the risk of negative consequences in external reality was soon overcome, Mr G was unable to calm down. Every day he believed he had made some error, that he had done something for which he would be liable. He needed this guilt in order to punish himself. I said, "The office is your suicidal mother whom you have to look after. Just as you think only of the office twenty-four hours a day, so you used to think about your mother around the clock. If you miss out a comma, it is the same as misinterpreting your mother's footsteps on the stairs."

> Gradually, he began to formulate his hatred of his mother. "You know, I've never been so near my mother as I am now and I can't get any nearer. I want to be comforted." He informed his employer that he was undergoing analysis and that he considered himself to be a "risk factor" for the company, whereupon he was no longer permitted to sign documents. He wanted to suffer from a disease, preferably leukaemia. I said, "You want to have leukaemia, just as your mother wanted to have cancer."
>
> With some disappointment he told me he that he had had a medical check and that all the results were good. His diarrhoea and vomiting were diagnosed as psychosomatic. Now he only weighed seventy kilograms. His thoughts of suicide became extreme. I said, "You're often afraid of having to accept liability. You were once supposed to keep an eye on your mother as though you, as a child, could accept liability for your mother. And now you want me to feel how much that oppresses you. Will I be liable if you kill yourself?" He was only able to feel a threat if I felt it and held it.

The analysis made him furious. I had brought all this upon him. As a sadistic attacker I had become a (potentially) traumatising object, and this could quickly be reversed by suicide. The introjection and projection of hatred and violent fantasies alternated. He felt his "total breakdown": his condition was worse than ever. At the same time, he realised he could not get away from me. If he gave up either the therapy or his job, he would kill something and, if he stayed, he would be killed. "You are furious with me and at the same time you feel that you need me. I believe you were in quite a similar situation when you were a child. On the one hand, you were dependent on your mother and, at the same time, you felt this enormous hatred." In this connection I again mentioned the strangulation fantasy of last summer. He got the idea that this impulse, which had shot through him at that time, was a "severed hatred" such as he had had towards his mother without ever realising it. That was why he had not gone any further after he heard the footsteps on the stairs.

Destruction and omnipotence: the perversion

With many variations, we worked both on his tendency to take on blame and on his hatred of me. He was to blame when he went round in circles during the analysis, and I was to blame that he hadn't made more progress. He was a failure in his profession and, with this analysis, so was I. "You experience us both as failures. And in this way the link with your mother is maintained." Now he took on the role of his mother, and I took on his role. He wanted me to feel the way he had felt at the time: he was destroying himself and needed to see the horror in my face. He wanted to destroy me, just as his mother had once destroyed him. Mr G sensed that, despite all this destructiveness, we both held fast to each other. At this time he was probably able to nourish the hope that, after all, he would be able to leave his suicidal mother behind. This made it possible for him to confess his perversion to me. For him, destruction held something fascinating on account of its omnipotent quality. He told me about his "masochistic sexual fantasies" as his "last secret".

> P: This is also something you need to know. I imagine strong, sadistic women in leather skirts and boots. I am totally at their mercy or crawl in front of them on all fours; that guarantees me an orgasm. I often think of that when I masturbate. That relaxes me; I can leave things behind me, a bit. I also think of that kind of thing when I sleep with Dagmar.
> A: This is the way in which you establish contact with your mother.
>
> He told me how cold and strict his mother had been, how she had threatened him with punishment, and how his father had carried out the beating in the evening. "The worst thing was the humiliation and having to wait till evening to be punished."

Gradually I began to feel he would not kill himself. Both he and the course of transference acquired clearer contours. The sadistic elements were bound up with the leather woman. When he engaged with the traumatic constellation of his relationship, I became the leather woman.

He remembered how he had been sexually excited when his second mother wore shiny trousers. "When I was around thirteen or fourteen I used to pull shiny things over my head, wore my second mother's clothes, and forced my feet into her shoes. I then crawled into a big clothes bag and masturbated. To be on the safe side, I always took a knife with me so that in an emergency I would be able to cut the bag open. I often used to wear my hockey helmet as well. That's sure to be some kind of transvestite behaviour. After all, my mother wanted me to be a girl. As a child, I sometimes used to stick my mother's stockings up my shirt so as to have breasts. It's easier for girls: they don't have to be so strong."

His first wife could only sleep with him if she humiliated him in the process. After this "confession", he told me about a dream.

> I find this embarrassing. This is the first time that I have dreamed of you. I'm lying here on the sofa. However, the door isn't back there; it's here at the front on the right. The door opens, you come in and you're naked. Behind you, there's another woman. She's wearing black leather clothes. You are very natural and have a very attractive body. In my dream I think that this is a therapeutic measure. Somehow, the idea is that you want to drive the leather woman out of me through a confrontation. You had very large breasts. That is important for the child in me.

The leather woman—a collated internal object (Khan, 1979)—is an aggregation of the patient's natural mother, his stepmother, and his grandmother. She is the female edition of the SS man whom his grandmother was always crazy about. His mother's psychiatrist had once explained to his father her close ties with the grandfather: "You know, when your wife sleeps with you she is really sleeping with your father-in-law." Mr G's sexual fantasies, so he thought, were subject to a similar mechanism. I said, "And perhaps this is also about how it is here. When you have real contact with me, the leather woman is lurking. P: And what if you desire her?"

We were able to gain a new understanding of his fear of flying, which asserted itself again during this phase. He sits in aeroplanes, as in the clothes bag but without a knife. When he crawled into that plastic receptacle, he was crawling into his mother's body. It was a game between life and death, and the knife gave him omnipotence and sexual excitement. He was the master of his own fate, and in the case of danger he could slit his mother open. The panic he has is fear of committing murder. At the beginning of the analysis, on the level of action, he had crawled into me by means of the many things he acted out. My special caution in my interpretation work now became clearer to me: unconsciously, he had always ascribed to me the role of the leather woman, a role that I was neither willing nor able to play.

Fighting the leather woman: working through

He started fighting: with the leather woman, with his suicidal mother, with his office, with me. His goal was to be assertive without committing murder. He gave up his job, and nobody died. He was now unemployed and still came for five sessions a week. Again, he wondered whether he was at all capable of loving his wife and of feeling anything about me. At issue was his inner autonomy. Could he find out what he wanted without being under any obligation to someone else? He was now on his own, without external obligations, and was able to experience this as an opportunity. Despite his desolate condition, he carried out his plan to get married. His future wife had stood by him all the time (as I had done), and he was able to show his gratitude to her (and to me).

He got through the fourteen-hour honeymoon flight without any problems. "Ms H, I can think again, the veil is gone," he told me beaming with joy. He took up his job again part time and did well, not just in the office but also in analysis. He became more independent in dealing with his dreams. With great enthusiasm he described the firm consistency of his stool. He had now had eight good days in a row (no fear, no diarrhoea, sound sleep). This was something that he had never experienced, as far back as he could remember. And then one day in his office he was overcome by an attack of fear: he was able to interpret it as his fear of the end of the analysis and his tendency to punish himself. He no longer needed the fifth session. He gradually put on weight and was soon able to work full time.

His tendency to crawl on all fours before others was not just related to his sexuality. The leather woman, "my inner mother is like a black ghost, like a monster inside me, even when I can't see it. I've seen it a lot in the last six months sometimes through the anger I felt towards the analysis; when, in fact, I noticed how much I need you. I'll be afraid again and again in the future, but I won't jump straight out of the window."

He had a serious discussion with his parents during which his father admitted that he had not realised at the time how great a burden the mother's situation had been for the children. His father had immersed himself in his work so much, because this gave him the chance to atone for the injustice his own father had suffered, which had led to his death in a concentration camp. While trying to atone for one guilt, he had himself become guilty in relation to his children. Once again, Mr G was confronted with the concurrence of the roles of perpetrator and victim. He felt a sense of identification with his father on a new level and increasingly developed the desire to fend for himself, to bear responsibility for himself. He insisted that his father should deduct my fees from his inheritance and was determined to pay for analysis out of his own pocket as soon as he had a salary increase.

With reference to a dream, he said, "I was in a cage, caught in my mother's spider's web and she, herself, was caught in *her* mother's web. But now I defend myself. I can feel contours. Perhaps I will get a personality after all." I found this formulation very moving. People get children, but do they get a personality? With the words he used, Mr G expressed something that, depending on our theoretical approach, we would describe as an integrated or coherent self. Everything—split off and projected—was outside him, ran through him, only to trigger fear and a sense of being pursued. The more he recognised and felt that these forces were part of his own person, the more he was able to contain them and feel himself to be a structured person, just as he could now produce a firm stool and had to act out less. If he regards the analysis as the search for his personality, then for the transference this also means that he is looking for his real mother and through her he can find himself.

After initial indecision, he and his wife decided to start a family. After she became pregnant, it was once again important to work on his fears in a concrete way. In his fantasy, he could no longer associate the leather woman with his wife. It was important to be able to immerse himself without drawing the knife and re-emerge without destruction as a clearly delineated individual. This applied to his wife, the sessions with me, and his work.

In the meantime, Mr G has become a proud father and got through the birth of his son without any problems.

End of analysis

After the birth of his son, Mr G decided to end the analysis. He terminated his treatment a year later. At first he projected his massive fear of separation on-to his wife and his child, the baby cried on his behalf, and breastfeeding was at risk. After I had commented on this event with the words: "That is certainly strange. Your wife has succeeded so often in calming you down, and that is much more difficult than calming down a baby", he was able to give up his projection on-to the mother–child dyad and work on his fears in the transference with me. It was a matter of weaning and breaking habits, which became clear to him through his cigarette consumption. He decided to desist and left the analysis, deeply grateful, as a non-smoker. One point on which I cannot go into detail here but would like to emphasise is how his relationship with his son helped him to consolidate and integrate what had been achieved. When he started the therapy, Mr G had indeed lost his recollection of the first good object, as outlined by Money-Kyrle (1971); only through the symptoms of his actions had it been possible to imagine it in the form of mnemonic traces. And now it was alive again. The following episode may serve to illustrate this process. Mr G asked me one day, "Can you actually picture my son?" I replied, "I think so." "You know, I never carry a photo of him with me, and yet I always have a picture of him inside me," Mr G said with a certain pride. He remembered how, earlier, he had not been able to picture his mother, and he found it immensely encouraging that he could carry his son in his imagination, that he had developed a psychic representation of him.

Of course, I often wondered how stable these achievements were and, again and again, I entertained the following fantasy: Mr G will come back for analysis when his father dies. This countertransference reaction made me sit up and take note. It was not just a matter of "weaning" in the maternal sense: it was also a matter of relinquishing paternal protection. Financing the analysis himself was part, of his development towards autonomy but by no means the whole story. In transference, his entire professional development had always had a paternal aspect. For him, leaving this protected sphere always involved great inner risks that, in turn, had a genetic point of reference: his identification bond with his father—which also became clear through the fact that both of them, as young adults, had developed a fear of flying—had prevented him from entering puberty at the normal age. His father had been forced to enter the war as an anti-aircraft gunner's assistant, suffered severe traumatisation, and had lost his own father immediately after the war. Only at the age of seventeen—the age at which his father had survived his traumas—had the patient been able to enter puberty. This side of his development only became clear just before our actual separation at the end of the analysis.

Conclusion

The perspectives of developmental psychology still seem to be essential to the understanding of traumatic processes (Greenacre, 1967). In treating this case they helped me to recognise the layers of transference.

Diverse quotations of the traumatic constellations became manifest concretistically, and it was possible to transform them into symbolic thought patterns by working on them in the transference. Four different phases of and forms of traumatisation are discernible. In each phase it is possible to observe the interaction of trauma and drive development on the one hand (Grubrich-Simitis, 1988) and individual and transgenerational identification processes on the other (Gampel, 1994). Here is a brief outline of the four phases:

Up to the age of three: from the very beginning his mother's depression is likely to have had a cumulative traumatising effect. Emotionally absent and bound first and foremost to her father, whose feelings of guilt she carried with her unconsciously, his mother laid in her child the foundation stone for the development of a false self. The pre-concept of the good breast could not become a concept as described by Money-Kyrle (1971) and Meltzer (1966, 1990). The anus became a falsified substitute for the breast. Conversely, the patient's inability to grasp the container function of the analysis and use it to his own benefit can be seen in his persistence in taking tablets at the beginning of the therapy.

In his earliest childhood Mr G became "an involuntary bearer or unconscious borrower" of parental feelings of guilt (Cournut, 1988, p. 76) as described by Freud:

> One has a special opportunity for influencing it when this Ucs sense of guilt is a "borrowed" one—when it is the product of identification with some other person who was once the object of an erotic cathexis. A sense of guilt that has been adopted in this way is often the sole remaining trace of the abandoned love-relation and not at all easy to recognize as such. (1923b, p. 50)

From the age of three to the age of eight: in the inner being of the patient, the "secret vault", which through the death of his grandfather irrevocably united mother and child, became the determining principle of his further development. The real task of preventing his mother from taking her own life led to a permanent destruction of integration, coherence, and autonomy. The impulsive and psychosomatic correlation can be seen in his chronic diarrhoea and in his difficulties in going to sleep. The ties with his mother could only lead to splitting processes in several respects, in this case—in line with the child's development—on an anal level. The diarrhoea can be understood as a split between the material and the immaterial and expresses the introjected assaults of the container on the content (stool = self and/or self-object), a path laid down in the patient's early years by a mother–child relationship that was primarily material, lacking in emotional care (Bion, 1962, p. 10 et seq.). If the mother kills herself, he will also be killed; and the same happens if he kills his mother. The excrement can be seen as the murderous partial object that connects both of them. When he ejects the excrement and has blood in his stool, he is ejecting the murderous introject. At the same time, we see here the expression of pathological omnipotence, for he rules over life and death. Feelings and ideas have been split off. Everything happens on the material-physical level. The same dynamics can be assumed in the case of the sleeping disorders. As long as he is awake, he watches over life and death, over the split-off and projected introject, which again begins to pursue him as soon as he is not attentive.

In his eighth year: a radicalisation of the splitting processes occurred through his mother's real suicide. His hatred of his mother became a reality. All aggressions and feelings of guilt had to be ejected and the picture of his mother obliterated. The constant threat through projected guilt had led him to a chronic dissociation. In this way—as Khan (1979) describes with great clarity—it is not possible for the child to internalise a whole object. It is only possible to receive parts of the object that are assembled to form a collated internal object permitting a (perverse) form of satisfaction (Henningsen, 1993). The leather woman is such a construction: she holds the patient in the masochistic position while the sadistic elements are projected on-to her. There are also features of her identity that in turn suggest a transgenerational genesis: his grandfather, his grandmother, the SS man, his first and second mothers, his first wife. In her thoughts about collective perverse introjections, Chasseguet-Smirgel makes use of Nazism metaphors that are identical to the features of the leather woman and confirm the necessity of fusion in order to bind destructivity:

> All apocalyptic ghosts are held by imagining that a magic recreation and reparation is preceded by destruction and that such recreation emerges from a destruction … This fusion with mother constitutes a marriage that lasts a thousand years … then all obstacles erected against this union will be swept aside by warriors who spot the emblem of the dangerous mother: black uniforms, whips, boots; all phallic symbols of virility in disguise, products of an anal-sadistic regression, i.e. that exist outside the genital universe of the father. (1988, pp. xvi–xvii)

The stagnation of his physical development, his clowning around at school, his concentration problems, and the special attachment to his stepmother, like his masturbation fantasies in a clothes bag, show that it was hardly possible to keep his trauma latent, even though the child may perhaps have made a "pseudo-normal" impression in the outside world (Lorenzer, 1965). By creating a "nest", the patient's stepmother had probably served to support acts of adjustment in line with the needs of the false self. Stroking him and allowing him to sit on her lap calmed him superficially. However, the child with his inner destructive objects was not really reached by anybody.

In his seventeenth year: after Mr G left his mother's lap at the age of seventeen, he began to grow. The symptoms of fear, however, became worse, with the result that, at the age of nineteen, he had to consult a psychiatrist for the first time. Probably we can see here a further transgenerational identification process: Mr G could only grow after he had passed the critical age at which his father had been traumatised. At the same time, however, he remained at the mercy of his father's transmitted trauma and developed phobias and a condition of panic.

The unconscious test during the probatory sessions and the beginning of the relationship with his first wife caused the onset of the compulsive repetition that repeatedly called for attention in analysis. Via acting-out, Mr G approached the traumatic relational constellation, a process culminating in a phase of psychotic transference. Despite all the shocks and complications this involved, he experienced me as a "stable ally" and was able to mentalize and integrate parts of his trauma.

The analysis lasted five and a half years, with four sessions a week throughout. Mr G became a very successful businessman. He came to see me thirteen years later. "You wrote to me saying that I would turn to you for help when my father died," he said. "My parents are now very old and frequently require my assistance, but I can handle that all right. The thing is that my wife wants to leave me, our children are in puberty, it's a challenge for me as a father. I don't want to leave them on their own the way my father did. That's why I need your help." In the subsequent two and a half years, Mr G came to me once a week, towards the end once every two weeks in a face-to-face setting, to cope with the separation from his wife and gain greater security and authenticity in his role as a father. During this time he took his children to the Czech Republic for them to see where his grandfather had worked and to visit his mother's grave.

CHAPTER EIGHT

Acting out and compulsive repetition

In the analytic process, the human inclination to re-enact traumatic situations is an invaluable asset. It takes a resuscitation of relational trauma in transference to open up paths leading us to improved understanding and also to emotionally corrective experience.

> Patients repeat all of these situations and painful emotions in the transference and revive them with the greatest ingenuity. They seek to bring about the interruption of the treatment when it is still incomplete; they contrive once more to feel themselves scorned, to oblige the physician to speak severely to them and treat them coldly; they discover appropriate objects for their jealousy; instead of the passionately desired baby of their childhood, they produce a plan or promise of some grand present—which turns out as a rule to be no less unreal. None of these things can have produced pleasure in the past. (Freud, 1920g, p. 21)

The significance and the cause of compulsive repetition have been judged variously in the history of psychoanalytic theory. Freud's explanation for our strivings to repeat an unpleasurable situation was the efficacy of the death drive, a conception that remained speculative in theoretical terms and found few adherents. It is, however, an idea of immense heuristic value.

Phyllis Greenacre describes how traumatic events taking place at a particular stage of development can leave memory traces, fantasies, and fixations in the mind of the child. She argues that it is the task of psychoanalysis to reconstruct the specific relations with the parents, including identifications stemming from the oedipal and pre-oedipal stages.

> I have already stressed the fact that severe trauma tends to leave an organized imprint on the young child and, absorbing and modifying the underlying fantasy, it may induce a greater need for repetition, usually in some acted-out form, than is the case with the fantasy alone. The need for repetition of the trauma formed the basis of Freud's original conclusion that the traumatic experience was itself the cause of neurosis. (Greenacre, 1967, p. 287)

I should like to take up this approach and extend its implications. The patients we have discussed so far all suffered from the restrictive consequences that an early trauma had for their lives as a whole. Simultaneous psychosomatic processes were partly destroyed, producing split-off fusional cores that were brought back to life with the help of analysis and partly mentalized, symbolised, and reintegrated. Neuroscientific research provides increasing confirmation of psychoanalytic theories on experiences in infancy and their detrimental influence on physical and mental development (Carhat-Harris & Friston, 2010; Schore, 2003). The unconscious memory traces described by Freud correspond to the implicit procedural memory (cf. Chapter Four). The traumatic *relationship* triggers in the infant a psychobiological form of hyperarousal that culminates in dissociation. To avoid pain, feelings are numbed, affects restricted, and the cortisol level rises (Schore, 2003, p. 67 et seq.). This defence strategy can cause durable structures to form in the right hemisphere of the brain. While these can neither be verbalised nor symbolised, they announce their presence in actions, physical symptoms, and ego-restrictions, and trigger certain kinds of interaction and subjective experience determined by the unconscious. This is where my theory of concretistic fusion sets in. I have described unconscious projective identifications in transference and in the relations of the patients to their significant objects that were genuinely connected with the respective trauma history. In defence, the unintegrable, dissociated affect is fused with the primary object or—in analysis—with the transference object. In the transference relationship the fusion had to be recognised and understood before it became susceptible of integration at a symbolic level.

Fonagy, Gergely, Jurist, and Target (2002) have shown in great detail how infant traumas can restrict or damage the capacity for mentalization. They see in this a precondition for the origins of borderline states, explaining the inclination to repeat as a product of the defective representation of thoughts and feelings.

> There is a mutual developmental relationship between trauma and mentalizing that may undermine the child's willingness to play with feelings and ideas (felt as too real) in relation to external events, but, at the same time, the lack of a full mentalizing mode of internal organization will create a propensity for the continuous repetition of the trauma, in the absence of the modulation that a representational view of psychic reality would bring. (Ibid., p. 384)

Masud R. Khan has coined the term "cumulative trauma" to refer to a relational trauma frequently encountered in early infancy. Grave recurring disorders in the early mother–child relationship are chronic in their effect and lead to "ego distortions". "Cumulative trauma is the result of the breaches in the mother's role as a protective shield over the whole course of the child's development, from infancy to adolescence" (Khan, 1974, p. 46). In his thoughts on the reconstruction of the cumulative trauma in analysis, Khan points out that in certain phases of analysis such patients do not perceive the analyst as a "whole object". Instead, they make use of the analytic situation in "regressive states of archaic affectivity and primary dependence on the object" to ensure that with the help of interpretation and reconstruction the essential aspects of infant ego distortions and the nature of the mother–child relationship can be discerned: "The patient repeats with acute finesse and in minute detail all the elements of the primary infantile situation. This indeed is repetition in the concrete, as it were" (ibid., p. 66).

Khan makes the following admonition in connection with working on the trauma in transference:

> The analyst's task is not to *be* or *become* the mother. We cannot, even if we try […]. What we do provide are some of the functions of

the mother as a protective shield and auxiliary ego. (Ibid., p. 67, original emphasis)

Müller-Pozzi (1982) has described in detail the propensity of the analysand to identify with the traumatising mother. In transference the analyst then becomes the defenceless traumatised child. Earlier, such a constellation might have triggered discontinuation of analysis. But with their knowledge of projective identification and counter-identification, today's analysts are in a position to understand these therapy crises better and use them productively for the work of interpretation. In all the cases presented so far, and in those yet to come, crises and complications of this nature between analysand and analyst are ubiquitous. Under certain circumstances they may indeed spell premature termination of treatment, but they can also be a major opportunity for deeper understanding and the creation of a new plane of symbolisation.

For example, Ms F's withdrawal from her first analytic treatment (Chapter Six) can certainly be understood as a repetition of the relational trauma that beset her in infancy. The "demise" of the analytic relationship corresponds to the termination of the mother–child relationship caused by the mother's sudden death. The patient understood the original analyst's inquiries as indications that he had forgotten or was denying her mother's death. This mode of interaction must have come about via the effect of the patient on the analyst's unconscious. It matched the experiences of the patient in infancy. Her presence reminded everyone of her mother. For the child's unconscious, an exclamation such as: "Why, you're the spitting image of Traudi" sounded like: "When I'm there, Mummy is there too." The analyst behaved as if the mother had been alive at the time, which was entirely in line with the patient's unconscious defence. Analyst and patient had become entangled and could no longer find a way of understanding the situation. "It's not true, my mother is dead", was the patient's conclusion, and this was sufficient reason to break off therapy. Obviously a death in the figurative sense of the word had to happen for the events to be felt and experienced. It was this enactment that opened up a path to understanding and a resolution of the psychosomatic symptoms.

In the case of Ms S (Chapter Five), the error I made in connection with her appointment can also be understood as an enactment. I had offered her a date I could not keep to. With this initial contact I had become the mother who is alive but not present, who neither feels, nor mirrors, nor imagines. During analysis "not feeling" was identified as the central traumatic affliction. Ms S had to repeat her relational trauma in many different variations before she could see it for what it was, for example, when she left a jar of jam with me, an apparently unimportant action the covert drama of which only became discernible at a later stage. She had left the jam with me in the same way as her mother had left her at the crèche. It required these insights for us to gradually get nearer the pain, the shame, the anger. At a later stage of analysis, Ms S had two teeth extracted after she had decided to reduce therapy from four to two sessions a week. Again, it was only afterwards that she was able to see the significance of her action. She required physical pain to feel and mentalize the psychic pain of separation.

Implicit procedural memory clamours for the acting out of unconscious affects when trigger situations invite such a response. The analytic situation is especially conducive to recognising and investigating these transferences that Freud refers to as compulsive repetitions. In the ideal case, the patient's ongoing regression during treatment will lead to a re-enactment of the infantile trauma. In the course of therapy we repeatedly experience the way in which patients gravitate towards their individual traumatic situation. The question however remains why individuals tend to repeat the trauma (albeit in a modified form and in a different context) despite the fact that this will normally inflict renewed suffering on them.

This tendency becomes understandable if we regard not only the compulsive repetition and the attendant regressions to traumatic situations but extend our purview to those regression processes in which the analysand falls back on successful adjustment processes occurring in childhood. Winnicott refers to the difference between "going back to an early failure situation" and going back to "an early success situation" (1955, p. 19), suggesting that the former leads to the organisation of personal defence structures while the latter triggers the memory of dependence on the environmental situation in the favourable sense of the term. In my experience, this aspect is mobilised in every analysis and is present (albeit sometimes in a very rudimentary fashion) in every analytic transference relationship. The analytic setting, reliability, commitment to veracity, abstinence, free-floating attention, and the essentially benevolent attitude of the analyst are all contributory factors. Regression to dependence favours what Kinston and Cohen (1986) refer to as the "primary relatedness" between analysand and analyst. In patients with infant traumas this relatedness is very seriously disturbed. It is necessary to expend the greatest care on establishing a trusting relationship at the beginning of therapy, and initially one should actively go in search of good experiences with the primary objects. The basis for the success of adaptation efforts is the experience of being understood in the mother–child relationship (or corresponding primary relations). These successful efforts are the experiential foundation from which resilience factors develop that are not inherent and that have major significance for diagnosis and indication. In assessing the role of compulsive repetition in the course taken by traumas, it makes good sense not to leave the positive memories and experiences out of account. Both regression lines leave their imprint on transference, and it is precisely the interplay between these transference processes that facilitates a deepening of the relationship and stepwise progress in getting at the trauma.

The analysis of Mr G (Chapter Seven) also makes it apparent that normally the repetitions an analysand enacts in analysis are not exclusively destructive but may contain a hopeful aspect best understood with the aid of Winnicott's concept of regression to dependence (Henningsen, 1990). This became clear to me in connection with Mr G's first attempt to discontinue analysis. Deep inside he hoped to obtain from me some kind of response to what he was doing, otherwise he would have cancelled by phone or simply not turned up. Similarly, the first woman friend figuring in the analysis is not exclusively his mother. But with this friend, who with frightening precision embodied the murderous and fusing aspects of the mother, he constellated a splitting in transference that enabled him to experience me as an idealised object (cf. "warmth") and to garner experiences in analysis that proved their worth much later. A similar process is discernible in the appearance of the mother's face. Only *after* he had once again symbolically consigned his mother to the grave in my presence (during the session) and experienced me as a "stable ally" could he imagine his mother's face and then dream of her.

Mr G neared the traumatic situation gradually. The psychotic transference in which the trauma turned into conflict and the conflict into trauma took place in the job context. At this point, his relationship with me was extremely tense and very much at risk. But there was one tie that held, and—I believe—it had to do with the hopeful part of our relationship that obviously could not be entirely destroyed.

Cohen (1980) emphasises the effect of infant development on compulsive repetition. He contends that compulsive repetition is a structure-forming function of the psyche. It should be conceived of as part of the id and of the primary process and correlates with a species of somatic drive organisation characterised by the absence of memory traces in the mind. In terms of developmental psychology, the structuring of affects and drives manifesting itself in compulsive repetition takes place at a lower level than in wish fulfilment. An essential feature of compulsive repetition in the reproduction of traumatic situations is, in his view, the repetition of an event that because of its traumatic effect is not psychically represented in the same way as an annoying but tolerable frustration/conflict that the individual is able to repress.

> Such experiences, because they were overwhelming and disorganizing to the child's capacity to perceive, represent, and form memory traces, are not only unrecallable in the ordinary sense that repressed memories are. Rather, they are unavailable for recall because *they do not employ adequate mental representations*, even in the unconscious. (Cohen, 1980, p. 422, original emphasis)

At present, notions like these are being confirmed by neuroscientific research. Schore, for example, refers expressly to the nonverbal representation of traumatic experiences in infancy and emphasises the difficulties of perceiving them in countertransference and using them for the therapeutic process "because the experience of traumatic pain is stored in bodily based implicit-procedural memory in the right brain [...], and therefore communicated at a nonverbal, psychophysiological level, not in the verbal articulation of discrete subjective states" (Schore, 2003, p. 84).

It is for this reason that these events are frequently revived in analysis via acting out or physical symptoms. The analysand delivers "replicas" (Lipin, quoted from Cohen, 1980, p. 422) of the trauma that capture the attention of analysand and analyst. Under the influence of the analytic situation, these quotations of the trauma, figuring, as it were, in disguise, gain increasing significance and favour psychic structure formation.

> During this process, before interpretation in the classical sense is applicable (to material in any given memory sequence), the analyst helps translate and render comprehensible the content and mental

organization of each living-through phase, including his role as transference object. (Cohen, 1980, p. 424)

These examples show how in the analytic relationship aspects of the trauma could gradually be identified as "quotations" figuring in a different context and translated into a symbolic language via transference. Split-off affects and the feelings resulting from them gradually become susceptible of interpretation through projective identifications in transference. The primary relatedness between analysand and analyst permits regression to dependence and keeps the hope of being understood alive. Generally, little is said about this hope in analysis, but it is there as long as the patient keeps returning. Ms F (Chapter Six) had to act out the death of the relationship and her profound despair and hopelessness, but very soon she was making another attempt to find understanding via analysis.

PART III

EXPERIENCES OF VIOLENCE AND ABUSE IN CHILDHOOD

PART II

CHAPTER NINE

A helper in search of help: splitting and psychic reality

The next two case histories (Ms A, this chapter, and Mr E, Chapter Ten) discuss individuals with childhood traumas dating from the Second World War who embarked on analysis in middle age. In the case of Ms A, the role that the war had played in her life only became apparent in the course of analysis. Her traumatic experiences gradually acquired emotional significance for her and thus ultimately achieved the status of psychic reality.

Ms A

At the beginning of analysis, Ms A, (Henningsen, 1990) was forty-five years old. She had a university degree, was unmarried, and earned her living as a committed and successful social worker. After being "hassled" on the phone by her immediate superior (a woman with an alcohol problem), she had had a "breakdown". The phone call had made it suddenly and startlingly clear to her that for this woman she played a similar role to the one she had assumed vis-à-vis her mother and her sister, both of whom were addicted to tablets and alcohol. The symptoms reported by the patient were bouts of depression, insomnia, occasional diarrhoea, and outbreaks of excessive perspiration. It was only at a later stage that I learned of her rheumatic disorder. At the first interview, I was struck by the stiffness with which she behaved and moved. She had an athletic physique and wore trousers, which gave her a very casual, sporting air. At the same time she pushed herself into the room as if she were a cupboard. Her bright blue eyes exuded sincerity and warmth so that I took to her immediately.

When I suggested psychoanalysis with four sessions a week, this gave her "a sinking feeling in the pit of her stomach". In psychodynamic terms, the woman sitting opposite me displayed a marked helper syndrome. So far she had been able to contain her rage at her own helplessness by asserting her superiority to evil, helpless, and outwardly projected objects through the help she gave them. (This defence system based on projective identifications had broken down during the said phone call). What would happen if as an analysand she were to agree to accept interpretations? Was that at all possible? Ms A appeared to be constantly fleeing from this world without sensing her own loneliness. Despite her many professional activities she had few friends (most of whom lived far away) and no intimate relationship(s), a situation that she found perfectly satisfactory.

I intend to describe her biography and the first three years of analysis on the basis of two dreams that we worked on at regular intervals. In my view it was characteristic of the transference and countertransference processes involved that although the two dreams occurring at the beginning of therapy revolved around similar subjects, they were located on different planes and provided indications of covert splitting processes. To some degree, the second dream is a defence against the first, which is the initial dream in the proper sense of the term.

After the preliminary interviews, the patient had the following dream, which she reported four months later at the fourth session of analysis proper:

> I have been asked to look after two little girls, one about two years old, the other just under eight. The children are playing near my chair. I have a rather unclear memory of the older girl. Sometimes the smaller girl comes over to where I am. I take her on my lap and cuddle her.
>
> Then the two of them go away at the behest of the older girl. The older girl wants to be a ballerina, something she can only learn in East Germany. Accordingly, the two girls leave for East Germany. I am very unhappy to see them go. Then I learn that they both want to come back but are not

allowed to do so. Next I am in a lawyer's office, standing diagonally behind the lawyer and dictating a document the purpose of which is to bring the two girls back home.

One striking thing about this dream is its secondary process function. The events are complex, feelings are verbalised in an ordered, formal manner. At about this time, Ms A demonstrated that she was capable of writing a much more precise application to her health insurance institution (cf. "document") than I was. The dream also contains biographical details that were to preoccupy us in the sessions to come.

Ms A was born in a small town in Silesia (now Poland) in 1938 as the youngest of three children. Her father had set up as a notary there; the family lived in a big house of their own, parts of which were rented out. The house had a large garden. When she was small, she ran out of the garden on various occasions to look for her father in the town. She was fond of roaming, a child one had to "keep an eye on". When she was two, her father was conscripted. In 1945, when she was almost eight, "the house was seized by the Russians and the family driven out". Her escape to Berlin with her mother, her aunt, and her siblings was dramatic. The family arrived there in the summer of 1945; they lived in a little summer house consisting of one single room. In 1949, when the patient was eleven, her father returned home from captivity.

The two little girls in the dream are quite definitely Ms A herself. Their ages correspond to those at which Ms A experienced distressful separations, from her father (at age two) and from her home (escape at age eight). If one further considers the dream in terms of internal objects and biographical matches, we find the operative defence mechanisms to be transformation into the opposite and switch from passive to active. Whereas in reality the father left his daughter behind to go off to war and the patient later (at age eight) experienced expulsion from her home, in the dream it is the children that "cross the border" and can then no longer return. Ms A described her mother as moody and unreliable. On the one hand she frequently beat her children, on the other she needed their help. In the dream, the patient assumes the mother's position, has the two of them (two aspects of her self) romp and play around her and try their hand at rapprochement. As a child, the patient had an idealised image of her father; during the war she probably dreamt of him enfolding her in a protective embrace. After his return home, this image was brutally discredited by his sternness and rigidity. For example, it was only against almost implacable resistance on his part that she managed to get out of the house wearing a petticoat and go dancing in Berlin (cf. "ballet" and "East Germany"). She was never allowed to take part in school outings as this was "not necessary for girls". In general, the father's opinion was that while girls have long hair, they are short on intelligence. She had always been fond of physical activity but had been seriously restricted by her father in this respect. Only her brother was given a bicycle and allowed to play rough games on the street. Today she is still fond of being out and about but is greatly hampered by her rheumatism.

The patient had crossed many borders in her life. The question was whether the dream was also alluding to problems associated with (self-)demarcation on the one hand and the removal from West to East (female to male) on the other. Just as the patient had hoped to receive help and consolation from her father (the lawyer), now she hoped for liberation via analysis. Another important detail was that in both parts of the dream she was the one in charge (superiority). She looked after the two girls and cuddled them, and she dictated the exeat document (application for health insurance support) to the lawyer. Her impotence and neediness are transformed into omnipotence and helpfulness. In this way a narcissistic defence structure took shape, the purpose of which was to protect Ms A from further shame.

Talking to the stone

Shortly after the beginning of analysis, Ms A reported a second dream she had had the night before. It cast further light on her defence structure.

> **A large rock lies in the sun. It is warm and it glitters. Suddenly it turns into a tiled stove. I sit on top of the stove.**

This second dream needs to be understood in narcissistic terms. I see it as the expression of those split-off traumatic experiences that were central concerns for us in the first years of analysis. At the same time, and in a condensed form, the dream cast light on the transference/countertransference situation that we found ourselves in and that needs to be outlined at this point. At the outset it was almost impossible to enter into a dialogue with Ms A. My impression of a cupboard pushing itself into the room and the striking warmth I discovered in the patient's eyes can probably be understood as what Green (1975, p. 11) calls an "analogue" to the image of a tiled stove. Presumably, my countertransference feelings corresponded with the patient's pre-conscious. The communication of the images of the rock and the tiled stove were instrumental in constituting a transitional space (Winnicott, 1953).

Ms A herself *was* the rock and the stove. Though she had "fires within", the walls of the stove were so thick that no one could get at them. In the Berlin flat the family later moved to, a tiled stove once exploded. This story was a demonstration of how dangerous it would be for me to try and "get at" her. A perennial topic was whether one vent of the stove should be opened so that I could at least catch a glimpse of the fire. Vice versa, none of her friends and no one at her workplace suspected how serious her problems were, how she shut herself away inside herself and kept her *self* out of everything. In our sessions she spoke very impersonally about her relations. She would also frequently toss me an astute diagnosis of herself to keep me occupied. Just as she had dictated the document to the lawyer in her first dream, she now wanted to dictate her own analysis to me and thus preclude any emotional exchange between us. At the same time, this displayed how helpful she was, how generously she took my part, as she did with everyone else, relieving me of the work involved.

Initially, the aggressive component of this behaviour was fully denied. She was the one who, like the stove, exuded warmth. On the rare occasions when she was not dispensing warmth and energy for others, she was the rock that soaks up warmth. Here only an either-or was possible; either she was on top and I was underneath or vice versa. The dream also displayed experiential modes of the dual union. The qualities at issue were coldness and warmth. Ms A sat on the stove because she was cold, as cold as she was on her mother's lap. Here the relationship became amorphous, stony and undifferentiated in the presentation, and I attempted to translate these phenomena into her actual experiences with the primary objects and with me. As I have said, in atmospheric terms the initial phase took place primarily at this level. I frequently had the fantasy that today the rock or the stove was coming for an appointment. This countertransference reaction made me uneasy. I asked myself whether here I had fallen foul of the defence mechanism of isolation or whether the patient had set in train a splitting process in me that corresponded to her own object-splitting. Both possibilities seemed plausible. At all events, it was essential to include the warded-off phenomenon in the treatment, so I spoke to the stone, the stove. At this stage our communication frequently resembled child analysis. It was a treatment phase characterised by timelessness and inertia.

When analysis had to be interrupted temporarily, Ms A quickly developed a specific technique of denial. If I told her I would not be available for a certain time, she would lie down apparently nonchalantly on the couch and then tell me where *she* was going in the period in question. Her plans always sounded as if they had been laid weeks before. Because of her separation traumas, Ms A was forced to deny the significance I had for her. She reversed the dependence relation and turned me into the abandoned victim.

She came to me both to "fill the tank" (Mahler, 1968) and to display her own grandeur. Interpretations and communication made the walls of the stove increasingly thin, tears gradually softened the stone. Here too we can restrict ourselves to a few significant stages. Men, the father, or any third persons, hardly existed. The patient rediscovered her own (hi)story in the process of filling the tank. Like theatre props representing a play undergoing performance, she found Polish words in her dreams, objects in my vicinity and in my office that enabled her to remember.

An antimacassar on the back of the couch with a tree on it was the big apple-tree in her parents' garden with a bench underneath it. Her mother beat the children frequently. To avoid her bouts of rage they would run out into the garden and remain invisible for the rest of the day. If I approached the patient emotionally, she would frequently do her best to escape. She fell silent and immersed herself in the image of the tree she had become so fond of. From a strictly analytic viewpoint, Ms A abandoned all dialogue with me and switched to the action plane. The scene from childhood was repeated. I soon realised that on the one hand the tree was performing the function of a transitional phenomenon and that on the other it was to be understood as the precursor of the third person. For a long time, the tree as a place of refuge and trust functioned as play material for our exchanges. Ms A adhered to it very concretely when she warned me about the risks of setting up a practice elsewhere: "Take the tree with you, whatever you do!" I complied with her wish. The tree stood for the lost paradise in Silesia; at the same time it was a substitute for the father. Who knows whether she might not have fled to her father if only he had been there! But at this stage, these thoughts remained very much on an intellectual plane, they were not genuinely felt. The reason was probably the following: for fear of renewed traumatisation, Ms A avoided direct emotional exchange with me and assumed an omnipotent attitude in which she could control me (like her bad mother). A triangular situation would have greatly weakened this position, so the tree as a place to flee to (firmly rooted in the earth) was a good compromise because it could not establish any kind of relationship with me.

> In another dream, the patient came to me by tram and underground train with a sewing machine in her luggage. She remembered a nanny from the Ukraine that the father brought home as a domestic servant during the war. This woman made dresses for her dolls on the sewing machine. I realised how in transference I would gravitate to the vicinity of this woman if the patient began to enter into the spirit of analysis. She started to internalise me as a good object. At the same time, she attended a Russian course, planning to go to the Ukraine for her next vacation.

Her mother's addiction to alcohol and tablets manifested itself during the war. Together with the appalling events going on around her, it was one of the sources for Ms A's multiple traumatisation. Both topics remained taboo in the family. Her mother hardly figured at all as an intermediary between the child and the horrors of warfare or as an object providing warmth and consolation. Accordingly, the patient was exposed directly and cumulatively to these traumas, one essential reason for the establishment of a strikingly rigid defence structure in which splitting processes were of decisive significance.

On many occasions, compulsive repetition (frequently in the form of identification with the aggressor) manifested itself in little episodes between us, when, for example, Ms A sometimes wanted to close her eyes in the given session, much as her mother would mutely draw down the blinds when outside the house people were being deported to the labour camps. Frequently Ms A would leave me in the dark about what was concerning her in precisely the same way she had experienced with her mother, who would lie in bed in a drunken stupor, her breath so shallow that it was impossible for her daughter to decide whether she was still breathing or not. Everyone had to come to terms with their panic and their helplessness all on their own. Here I frequently assumed the role of a translator. In the course of time, it became possible to reconstruct historical reality and regard and feel the horrors of war, the terrors of expulsion, and the mother's appalling self-destruction. At this stage I asked quite a lot of questions. The patient sensed my readiness to contemplate the horrors of that period with her and was able to identify with this attitude (cf. Grubrich-Simitis, 1981 on this subject). Up till then, the real traumas had been taboo and denied. This was the first time she had been able to tell another person about these experiences.

A journey home

After two years of analysis, Ms A bought herself a car, procured a visa, and set out on a journey home alone. The journey was a riveting experience, both for her and for me. The memories acquired under analysis were confirmed. The swimming pool in the woods was still there, the school had been given a new door, her parents' house still stood, but the tree had been cut down.

> "Thank heavens, the fence is no longer there." "What fence?" I asked. "Soldiers would often come and threaten us with their rifles. Our mother would always call to us to come out and stand in front of her and protect her from the soldiers. She said that soldiers wouldn't shoot at children. One time when she called us, I was standing near the fence and couldn't get to her because a soldier held me back. He pointed his gun at my mother and the other children. It was dreadful."

The mother wanted her children to protect her from two things: rape and murder. But this was never made explicit. At this stage of analysis, other historical details were cleared up as well. Memories resurfaced: bombardments, expulsion, anyone too weak to go on was shot, a forced march along the banks of a river in which swollen corpses floated. The difficult beginnings in the Berlin garden house came alive again. During the Berlin blockade (1948) Ms A was with her sister in West Germany. Throughout that time, neither of them ever said that they missed the others. Back in the present, the idea that she might think of me when she was away on one of her further-education courses and that I might think of her made Ms A "sick to her stomach". She felt mercilessly exposed and completely ravaged by her mistrust of me. Her nausea felt like a very bad hangover, as if her head might split. "Your mother probably tried to drown her sorrows in alcohol," I said to her. "Do you often try—without the help of alcohol—to blot out your feelings so as not to show me how angry you are?" After that she felt "sober" again and was able to talk about her relationship with me during a hiatus in the analysis. She felt dependent on me, more dependent than she wanted to be. She also told me about a colleague of hers, Mr X, who in her presence had enthused about his professional contacts with me. "I don't know who he thinks he is," she said. "Anyway, I didn't tell him I was coming to you for analysis."

The experiences of her journey home soon found expression in the transference relationship. Arriving for one of our sessions, she confessed: "Today I'm coming home." Greatly frightened by what she had said, she immediately backed down and said: "A *little bit* of a relationship with you would surely be enough!" A long silence ensued.

At one of the subsequent sessions she told me about a dream she had had:

> I want to talk to the janitor. I know he's down in the basement of our house where the central heating is, and I go down there. I see that he is repairing the furnace. It has broken down. He wants me to go away, I want to stay and watch. I see him open the door of the furnace and poke around in the hot coal. Then he shouts at me: "You're in the way, you have no business to be here!" He throws a piece of burning coal at me. Luckily I woke up after that. The coal fell to the floor right next to me. I remember thinking how I was going to get out of there.
>
> "It reminds me of the tiled stove," she says, "the warmth and my desire for security. This is all about repairing my emotional life, the difficulties I have in admitting my feelings, demonstrating them, and the difficulties I have here with you." I said: "Recently you said it was like coming home when you come here. But then the fire went out." She said: "Yes. I'm afraid to look at it."

Subsequently Ms A interpreted her dream from a subjective viewpoint, saying she was exorcising her interest in observing things. At one and the same time she was the janitor, the person who wanted to watch, and the furnace itself. Her commentary was as follows:

> "It's odd, today one has oil-fuelled central heating, there's no coal and no red-hot embers to poke around in. I couldn't really see the janitor but I presume it was the man who looks after the house where I lived. He is quite tall, in his mid-fifties, and he really does have a workroom of his own down

in the basement. The way he bawled at me in the dream really made me afraid, and I couldn't get away! The way out of the room was in the direction of where he was making to throw something at me." I added: "Earlier on you said very convincingly how you, the janitor, and the furnace all stood for you yourself, and I believe the same is true of me. Perhaps you want to say: Don't get too close to me! You're in the way, you have no business to be here with me." Ms A: "I said a short time ago that I prefer to look and see before I get any closer. And when I know what's what, I still want to think over whether and how much of it I want to disclose. Then I'm the janitor." "Yes," I reply, "and there's something else. Our difficulties here started with the feeling you had of *coming home*. Your father came home at a time when people heated their homes with coal. We now know that the image of the tiled stove that you're sitting on also has to do with wanting to sit on your mother's lap and be warmed by her. What does it mean when the father appears on the scene? You used to sleep in the gap between the two mattresses on your parents' bed. What did your father do with your mother? Was he poking around inside her like the janitor in the embers? And what about me, when you come here? Does Mr X. say to you: You have no business to be here?" "It's true," she says. "In the time after the war when my father was home again, my mother often said to him: It would be better if you had never come back."

After this session Ms A had back pains. "Exactly the same pains I had lying in the gap between the mattresses when my father came home. I can't remember much else, but now I do know more, I can remember exactly what the room looked like where we slept."

Ms A reacted to this session not only with pains in her limbs but also with an inflammation of the jaw. The dentist removed what he called "an old encapsulated inflammation source" that must have formed twenty years earlier when she had had a wisdom tooth extracted. Subsequently the rheumatic pains disappeared.

The session we have been discussing can be regarded as paradigmatic for this stage of analysis. In transference terms it is a harbinger of a switch from dual union to triangulation. Concrete memories of her father's return home and her situation in the gap between the mattresses in her parents' marital bed led to a confrontation with the primal scene and to renewed physical pain. This process also resulted in an extension of psychic space; both the psychic trauma and psychic reality became more tangible.

Incipient triangulation

Little by little, Ms A succeeded in internalising me as a good object and relinquishing her mistrust. At the transference level there was initially no place for a third person although the latent presence of a third person was undeniable, as the initial dream and the role of the tree during therapy indicate. In my view, the prime concern initially was avoidance of a triangular relationship, as this implied a profound and highly unsettling confrontation with Ms A's own self. We first had to devise a symbolic language; transference was at the same time "creative illusion" (Milner, 1952, p. 183). The rock, the stove, the room, the East German border, and much more were the media expressing the patient's unconscious conflict situation.

We can obtain a better understanding of the analytic process by comparing the "stove dream" with the "janitor dream". With the images of the rock and the tiled stove, the dreamer had introduced a "personal metaphor" or "metonymy" (Sharpe, 1937) into the proceedings that frequently preoccupied our attention and made initial steps towards symbolisation possible. It was a way of communicating the uncommunicable. In retrospect we can list the experiences addressed in a condensed form with these images:

- at the level of the body self: the patient's immobility and rigidity
- at the level of object relations: partial object relations; absorbing or giving warmth, a symbiotic theme; splitting of the objectal relationship
- at the level of drives: aggressive impulses, the stove may explode; throwing red-hot pieces of coal. Expulsion from the basement (= home, primal scene)
- at the level of conflict: the theme of dead (= rock) and alive (= fire) was addressed at an elementary level: oedipal conflict, confrontation with primal scene
- at the level of memories: fire in the war, the stove in Berlin, absence of closeness to the mother, absence of the father, furnaces of mass destruction (as it transpired later, p.)

The parameters belonging to the "stove dream"—onset of analysis, initial dream—suggest that concealed behind this dream was a topic from the negative Oedipus complex that the "official ego" (Loch, 1985, p. 158) could not yet perceive. The janitor was a challenge to the uniqueness of her position vis-à-vis the mother. In her associations, she put her own thoughts in her mother's mouth: "... it would be better if he had never come (back)." In the "janitor dream" the furnace/stove (= the mother) figured in a triangular relation with the janitor (= the father) and Ms A. Whereas the dream of the rock contains two static images, the other dream expresses a goal and motion towards that goal ("I want to talk", "I go down"). Watching was the point at issue ("I wanted to stay and watch.") The key to the work of interpretation was certainly the quotation in direct speech: "You're in the way. You have no business here." We can safely assume that the direct speech in the dream had its source in what Ms A had heard in her waking life (Freud, 1900a, p. 190; cf. also ibid., p. 401 et seq.).

A second important stage is the translation of the metaphor back from stove to mother. The important thing here was that this should take place at a juncture when the dreamer could already *feel* how extensive the implications of this process were. Only then did the psychic reality become concrete.

Finally, a reference to the psychosomatic plane. The dentist had spoken of an "encapsulated *source* [German *Herd*] of inflammation". In German *Herd* is one of the words for stove. In view of the theory of psychosomatic simultaneity (Mitscherlich, 1966/67) the question arose whether this "encapsulated source of inflammation" had been identified at the same time as the "encapsulated source of conflict" had been identified in analysis.

How are we to understand this "encapsulated source of conflict"? The word "encapsulated" can be seen as synonymous with "split-off". Probably the early separation from the father and the events of war were the most traumatic experiences for Ms A. As a small child, her love for her father had been unusually intense, as we can see from the way in which she ran away into the town to look for him. Probably she initially denied his absence by introjecting him; later she will probably have idealised him and partly identified with him. This is the origin of the omnipotence with which she attempted to control her mother and me (in transference). Her father's immortality, and hence the immortality of her own person, were safeguarded, as it were, by the idealised introject. The object-splitting attendant upon this process (cf. M. Klein, 1946, p. 101 et seq.) served the vitally important defence structure required to cope with the traumatic situations. The point at issue was relinquishing or challenging this omnipotence. Though at the session before, Ms A had assured me she would not let a third person (such as Mr X.) get near me, her unconscious thinking in the dream (Meltzer, 1984) showed that she had progressed further and was confronting us with the dramatic nature of the constellation. Trauma turned into conflict, conflict into trauma.

Parallel to this change in metaphorical thinking, the relationship also changed from dual union (in which the analyst on the one hand embodied aspects of the split-off (negative) self but on the other was already auxiliary ego, function, and identification object) to triangulation. Gradually the relationship between analysand and analyst was consolidated. A feeling of "primary relatedness" (Kinston & Cohen, 1986) that had grown during analysis is likely to have been the precondition for dreaming and interpreting a triangular constellation. The triangulation was still rather rudimentary, the mother was seen as an inanimate object (stove). And it was a matter of life or death.

The stone starts moving

Parallel to the onset of a triangulation process as described above, the defence against object-splitting also started loosening. It is conceivable that the disappearance of the psychosomatic symptoms may have stood in some comprehensible relation to this, although it can certainly only be explained in part. It is a well-known medical fact that there is a connection between rheumatism and dental disorders. But Ms A and I were about to face an extremely stressful situation. Death entered into our relationship. Despite all the difficulties encountered at this stage, I felt confident that we had a common "wavelength" that would withstand even immense pressure. The dream and the subsequent interpretation released part of the hitherto split-off paranoid position, a part that could now manifest itself in transference.

> In her dreams, Ms A equipped herself with a penis. She talked about her envy of men and let me feel her hatred and anger. The atmosphere became threatening. Ms A dissociated and expressed the feeling that she had of sliding backwards on the couch into a void. "I'm still here!" I answered spontaneously. Ms A: "I had this appalling vision of you. I saw you as if in a distorting mirror, your face all twisted."

Here and in the subsequent sessions we understood that Ms A feared that she might disintegrate in my presence. She wanted to kill me, to "poke around" inside me like the janitor in the dream. She wanted to threaten me like the soldiers who pointed their guns at her mother. She contemplated discontinuing the analysis, which would have been tantamount to the death of our relationship. In her mind, things she could not control had to be destroyed.

As a child she had often wished she were dead. She recalled an abortion many years ago. At the time, there were no two ways about it, she did not want a child, it would have interfered with her professional ambitions. She said she always thought of her mother who gave birth to a stillborn child at the age of forty-five. Despite various attempts at abortion, it had been fully developed.

> "I hated my mother and often wished she were dead … When she died, it was a relief." When her mother was dying, she had "nasty thoughts": "I bet she'll go and die precisely when I'm in the middle of an exam and mess up my degree prospects." At the beginning of this stage, Ms A was "as if petrified". Later she wept a great deal, notably during the weekend hiatuses of analysis from Friday to Monday. She said she could not remember having wept much as a child; at her mother's graveside she had not shed one single tear. She said she was appalled at herself for never having feelings of guilt when she wished her mother dead. Now she often wished she were dead herself, "then it would all be over". She wept at the "artificial time" with me during which she was "so shut off" and wanted to discontinue analysis. "I'm ashamed because the façade is deceptive. It's so smooth, no scratches on it … I think I'm most ashamed when I'm helpless."

I have distinct memories of how threatening I felt this stage to be. Ms A was in despair, I felt pushed to the limits and totally worn out. The death wishes became real in her relationship with me. Ms A wanted to die, she wanted me to die, she wanted the analysis to die. Later, mourning and shame became possible, followed by the onset of integrative processes.

In this period, Ms A bewailed and mourned the abortion of her child, which would now have been adult. Twenty years before, when she had had her wisdom teeth extracted, she terminated her relationship with a man and decided never to marry: "It looks like I'm incapable of sustaining a relationship." In analysis, this issue was equally central. Was she capable of sustaining a relationship with me, was I capable of sustaining a relationship with her?

Shortly afterwards, Ms A entered into a love relationship with a man her age. Courageously she squared up to the extreme emotional ambivalence of the situation. Her division of men into "male men" (to sleep with) and "other men" (suitable for platonic friendship) gradually began to disintegrate. Her new friend did not appear to fit into these categories.

On the one hand, this gratifying development was fully in line with the oedipal constellation and announced a structural change. On the other, I asked myself why Ms A had entered into a relationship with a man precisely at this juncture. Was it to ward off the homoerotic transference relationship with me? Were things between us getting too murderous, too heated? I also asked myself why at this point it suddenly occurred to me to write an article about triangulation processes. In one respect, the motivation was the curiosity and enthusiasm sparked off in me by the course the therapy had taken. At the same time, I had sensed the dangers of the situation, I wanted to understand my anxiety, and probably needed a degree of supervision that I procured for myself by deciding to write about it.

In the subsequent years of analysis we were increasingly successful in working on the ambivalences. Despite the many problems, Ms A managed to establish a credible relationship. The man she had met also remained faithful to her. In this relationship she experienced a degree of sexual fulfilment that she had never experienced before. Earlier she had thought sex to be a "pleasurable gymnastic activity". Now she was able to experience it as a dialogue enhancing her relatedness to her partner.

In the fourth year of analysis, Ms A suffered a minor rheumatic relapse when she had to work through an event that she found extremely shaming. But there was no recurrence of the dramatic developments described earlier. Her newly acquired capacity for dealing with conflicts was put to a severe test. We succeeded in confining the murderous threat to the psychic space so that the rheumatic symptoms disappeared relatively quickly and never returned. This episode gave us an opportunity to recall and once again work through the situation described earlier when the trauma gained psychic reality in transference. Only in the last few years of therapy did we achieve access to her rigid defence structure that repeatedly caused conflicts with her partner and also made itself felt in transference.

Reciprocal effects between trauma and conflict

Right at the outset of analysis, Ms A was able to recall the essential stages in her trauma history.

> Two years: Her father was conscripted. Her mother lived alone with the children. Polish and Russian soldiers turned up out of nowhere. There was a German labour camp in the vicinity of the house. The father seldom came home.
> Eight years: Expulsion, onset of her mother's addiction (alcohol and tablets).
> Eleven years: Father returns from captivity.

However, Ms A was unable to relate these events to herself and her life situation, let alone sense the degree of traumatisation involved. In contrast to the course taken by "classical" neurosis, the trauma was known at the beginning of therapy. But its *emotional* significance was split off. The main task of analysis was to reintegrate the split-off affects and to bring to life in the transference relationship what Ms A had experienced so that it could be mentalized and symbolised and thus achieve psychic reality.

Lorenzer and Thomä (1965) have investigated and described an abundance of traumatic processes similar to the case we are looking at here. One or more traumatic events are followed by a "mute phase" of "pseudo-normality". The traumatic event disappears in latency, only to resurface as a result of some banal event and trigger a psychic breakdown (Lorenzer, 1965, p. 694). Lorenzer indicates that this apparently compulsive defence in trauma patients may conceal psychotic phenomena, which is why today we refer to such defence structures as splitting processes.

In the course of analysis, the patient's rigidity and inertia (the rock) gradually became fluid; the relinquishment of splitting in many small stages was always bound up with a conflict, either the rivalry between omnipotence and imminent helplessness or the progressive contradiction between the idealised oedipal relationship with her absent father and the bitterness of reality. As soon as we entered the psychic space, everything hurt. The painful points had to be named and retained within the relationship to the analyst.

Ms A's analysis lasted seven years. The terminal phase took two years and was marked not only by the usual separation issues but also by a general consolidation of the internal conflict processes. Much was once again transposed to the social and professional plane and could be worked on from there. It was at this stage that Ms A realised that the stove/furnace also stood for the many furnaces of mass destruction situated near her home and along the roads on which she escaped.

Two years after termination of therapy, Ms A asked for an appointment so that she could express her gratitude and take her leave of me. Ms A had decided to pack her bags and move to another town to be with the man friend she had met during analysis. A promising new job held out prospects of a successful career in her new surroundings. Her rheumatism had never returned.

CHAPTER TEN

"I want no part of this hell": en route to perversion

Mr E

The following is an account of the analysis of a homosexual man (four sessions a week, five years six months) whose life became increasingly difficult to cope with as he grew older (Henningsen, 1993, 2011c). When he came to me for help, he was on the "threshold" of manifest perversion (sadism and paedophilia). Perversion structures, be they latent or manifest, impose major restrictions on an individual's capacity for love (cf. Reiche, 1990). Relational traumas in infancy can lay the foundations for a progression to perversion. Morgenthaler speaks of the "sealing function" of perversion, which closes a deep narcissistic wound from early infancy (1974). Masud Khan (1979) points to pathological introjection processes that gel into a "collated internal object" evolving out of the dissociated primary objects.

The scene in the interview situation

The man's voice on the phone requesting an initial interview sounded youthful. Mr E introduced himself with his full name, the impression he made was a little too effusive for the circumstances. I assumed that this was due to the youth I had ascribed to him. After we had agreed on an appointment, Mr E gave me three telephone numbers: his private number, his office number, and his secretaries' number "so that you can contact me if anything should crop up". This made me feel like a secretary myself, someone constantly under surveillance, sensing that there was no escape. I imagined that the man was a manager with Siemens or BMW and no longer believed that he really wanted analysis. At the same time I was curious, his voice sounded intelligent and sympathetic.

The man who turned up at my office was just under fifty. He was extremely tense, he was slim and good-looking, his movements and his choice of words were controlled, almost mannered. Mr E was at the end of his tether, he was doing his best to contain the dangerous rage he felt. He wore a dark suit, which he referred to as his "working clothes" because he was a clergyman. If he had changed before coming, he would not have got here on time, he explained apologetically.

Mr E sat down, gave me several piercing stares that I responded to with calm and friendly gestures. Then he told me why he had come.

"The main reason I want analysis is that I am homosexual and I am increasingly afraid of the difficulties that this might cause me. Inwardly I'm under intense pressure, outwardly I fear for my professional status. If word gets around, it could put me in a very difficult position. My problems stem from a development I can trace back to my grandmother. She had wanted my mother to be a boy. In her childhood, she would often stand my mother on a chair and tell her that girls were no use in themselves, that as a girl she was like the moon, consigned to the dark and needing to be lit up by the sun. My mother was very ambitious about me, I was always on my best behaviour, never got dirty and never established a strong attachment to her. That's what I want to work on. That's why I need a reliable partner ... I'm expressing myself cogently to you, but I have very chaotic sides when I vent my feelings. It's like falling into a void ... And I drink too much when I can't stand things anymore ... There's a screaming child inside me, kicking and punching, too hard to handle." I remarked: "If you want me to analyse you, the essential thing will be for us both to love that child a little so that it can develop." In response, the patient relaxes visibly, his eyes soften. Perhaps I have been able to give Mr E to understand that I am prepared to accept and face up to his enormous tensions, maybe we can deal with them, and neither he nor I will necessarily be badly injured as a result. He tells me that one reason why the situation is so acute is that the man with whom he has a homoerotic relationship and who is only half his age has started querying his own sexuality. This friend now believes that he is not genuinely homosexual and was only seeking a father figure when he took up with Mr E. Mr E feels spurned and disparaged. He is still on friendly terms with the young man, who however refuses to have anything to do with him sexually, which for Mr E is an unbearable insult. I say: "You feel pushed off into the sidelines like the moon that is dependent on the sun, as your grandmother said." Mr E responded favourably to this interpretation and was able to talk a little about his fears of the dependency he found himself in and his sexual needs.

What was this "overture" announcing? Both on the phone and at our first meeting Mr E kept close control of the situation, as if he were on his guard against some potential attack. His voice had given me the impression of a youngish adult, perhaps "the child in him" had already struck a chord in me. In the course of the interview, his tense, controlling attitude receded when I spoke of the child in him that we both needed to love. The next thing he brought up was a narcissistic problem. He felt offended, spurned, and rejected, first by his mother, now by his friend. Was he trying to keep his helplessness and vulnerability at bay by means of identification with the assailant and narcissistic omnipotence? Had this defence strategy now broken down or been so seriously undermined as to give rise to the "chaotic" incidents he referred to and to symptomatic actions of a destructively narcissistic nature (Rosenfeld, 1987)?

Biography

Mr E was born in Silesia in 1936 as the only son of his parents. During the war, his father, a craftsman, was hardly ever at home, only returning from captivity in 1948, when the mother had already been living in the West for some years with her children. During her pregnancy, Mr E's mother had not been happy, suspecting that she had chosen the wrong husband because he was not "refined" enough for her. She contemplated an abortion. In early infancy the patient had cried a lot. Mr E was a narcissistic part of the mother compensating for all the deficits she experienced. Accordingly, he had order, cleanliness, and punctuality "drummed into him" from earliest childhood. When his father had to go back to the front after a period of home leave, the parents kept this from the boy because he would definitely have thrown a tantrum if he found out. When he was told to go shopping as a small boy, he had to recite all the prices for the goods to his mother by heart. If he was unable to do so, he was given a thrashing with a whip that hung there specifically for the purpose in the jamb of the kitchen door. When he went for a walk with his mother, she made him hold on to her hand. If he failed to "keep pace" (walking too slowly or daydreaming) she would bore a sharp fingernail into the palm of his hand. His mother loved his long eyelashes and boyish curls and for that reason never let him have his hair cut. When he was about six, she put her wedding dress on him and had a photograph taken of him. This picture of the "sweet" little boy was then shown to all the relatives. When on one occasion at the age of three the patient's fingers got jammed in the toilet door, causing him to scream with pain, his mother told him she would only open the door if he stopped crying for long enough. This she then did.

These patently sadistic and sexualised actions on the mother's part will probably have hindered the development of an integrated self in the child. In an overview on the subject of perversion and sadism, Kernberg (1991) shows how the experience of physical pain can lead to disintegration and sadism. The sadistic and perverted assaults of the mother on the child had a cumulative traumatising effect. The absence of the father meant that there was no helping third person in the vicinity to mitigate this effect. Identification with the aggressor and precocious ego-development helped compensate for his deep-seated fears of helplessness and abandonment and probably created a "collated internal object" (Khan, 1979, p. 139 et seq.) as a counter-image to the mother, who so frequently made his life a misery in dissociated states (cf. Greenacre, 1971; Grunberger, 1979; Reiche, 1990).

The older he got, the more completely he subjected himself to his mother's reign. As a child he suffered from intestinal pains, diarrhoea, and enuresis. "If this doesn't stop, we'll have to cut that off!" his mother threatened. Weakened by the war, his father became disillusioned and despite a loan from the bank proved incapable of setting himself up in business in his new surroundings. The parents quarrelled continually and then separated. Mr E adopted his mother's viewpoint and condemned his father just as she did. Later this made him feel profoundly guilty. Alongside all the humiliating scenes, he remembers his father as a friend and a nature-lover who was usually kind to him.

His upbringing was strictly pietist, designed to turn him into a "good Christian". In church he often thought: "I hope Jesus of Nazareth is a boy and looks like me under his loincloth." In his distress, these desires were certainly addressed to God as a strong, protective father. Probably the child's longing for the absent father was rerouted towards God and lived out in religious faith as a means of sublimation. The mother demanded "grooming" and "refined behaviour" from her son. This was where Mr E discovered a niche for himself. Because for the mother Mr E on horseback was "like a prince", this gave him a fair amount of scope. He kept company with coachmen, hung around in stables, and later looked after the horses of well-to-do families, where his excellent manners stood him in good stead. As a young man he once suffered testicular contusion while riding.

Between sixteen and eighteen he fell ill with a variety of psychosomatic complaints. During a sojourn at a sanatorium, he met an older, paternal man who advised him to study theology. After completing his studies, he married a woman three years older than himself in the hope of overcoming his homosexuality. In the first seven years of marriage he slept with his wife fairly regularly but invariably felt alienated. Subsequently he would go to the bathroom and pray to God, asking: "Lord, how much longer do I have to keep this up?"

After the birth of his second child, he confessed his homosexuality to his wife, entered into various homosexual relationships, and frequented the corresponding establishments. His marriage and the family life built up on it remained (outwardly) unaffected. The church never got wind of his proclivities. He became an excellent preacher, a particularly empathic clergyman, and a respected superior, who could, however, at times lose his temper both with colleagues and staff.

His preferred homosexual partners were young men on the verge of adulthood. In these relationships he entertained fantasies of himself as a twelve-year-old girl "who wants to be taken". In the last few years he has observed in himself an increasing urge to approach even younger boys, a development he finds alarming because he fears that at some point he might sexually abuse a child.

Transference splitting at the onset of therapy

Once we had agreed on analysis, Mr E went to his superior and asked permission to undergo treatment during his working hours. He also asked to be relieved of confirmation classes. At first, I was surprised and annoyed by his behaviour, because I dislike having my name publicly connected with an analysand. I also thought his superior probably suspected that he was homosexual and that negative consequences might ensue. I soon realised, however, that in his own way the patient was constellating a sound outer framework designed to protect the analysis. Without the confirmation classes, he was far less likely to succumb to the temptation of interfering with a child. Coming to me during his working hours was a source of reassurance and enabled him to escape the many tensions church work involved for him (cf. Khan, 1979 on this point).

Mr E told me about these events in the first sessions. He had never confided in anyone before; he felt relieved, but at the same time was alarmed by his extreme aggressiveness. He felt like a serious criminal. This shocked me and caused me to ask myself how a person can put up with so much. Once he confessed: "If I'd been born a few years earlier, I would definitely have become an SS man." I asked him: "Are you trying to frighten me?" This was the first time he sensed that he shouldn't go any further and also that I was feeling and imagining what he told me. His murderous aggression became tangible in our relationship. He frequently came back to this scene in later sessions; it played a major role in resuscitating and working on his aggressive fantasies. As a homosexual in the Nazi era he would very probably have ended up in a concentration camp; his sadistic traits would not have saved him. Later, in analysis, he made the acquaintance of the "Hitler inside" or the "Saddam Hussein inside" and after working on these features sensed the qualitative difference between a potentially conceivable murderous act and the genuine article. My response at the time was very spontaneous. I suddenly remembered the interview in which Mr E told me that he needed a "reliable partner" to work on his aggression with. Of myself I knew that I could never accept an SS man for analysis; I probably wanted to indicate to him how far he could go with me.

The language Mr E used with me was highly organised, his sentences were well-constructed, indeed almost immaculate, his thoughts were complex, and descriptions of his feelings were by no means absent. I sensed his gift for rhetoric, he was well-versed in the discussion of psychological processes, perhaps as a result of his pastoral duties. But the statements he delivered were very largely monologues, as if he wanted to convince me with his intelligent, carefully worded disquisitions that

I had a genius or a famous personality lying there on the couch. These countertransference feelings put an increasing strain on me, his compulsive need to be special was a restrictive thing getting in the way of a relationship based on give and take. When Mr E sporadically became aware of the tension inside him or the monological nature of his remarks, I would occasionally say something like: "Perhaps you'd just like me to analyse you." Interventions like these took some of the pressure away and we were able to communicate more easily and directly.

In the first (lengthy) vacation period, Mr E bought himself a "magnificent" dressage horse, an Arabian pedigree mare that cost him 15,000 deutschmarks. He regarded this decision as a positive consequence of the first stage of analysis, which had given him enough courage and confidence to try and link up with a good part of his childhood. For me, this event had more to do with resistance. Mr E was investing lots of time and money in an expensive and time-consuming hobby. Who was to say whether it would leave him enough time to come for analysis alongside his professional duties? His way of coping with the feelings of helplessness exacerbated by the interruption of therapy was to effect a narcissistic elevation of his own self in the framework of acting out. These thoughts gave me grounds for concern, but at the same time I felt an alleviation of the strain involved in my countertransference. Perhaps in future Mr E would crack the whip to impress his horse and spare me his sadistic impulses. When he bought the horse, the breeder warned him: "Don't cut the mane off whatever you do!" The horse was a strawberry roan with a "long reddish mane" that he found almost "identical" with my hair. For Mr E, quoting the breeder's words was probably a way of talking about his castration anxieties. In the patient's unconscious, the horse's mane, like his own "boyish curls" and my long hair, represented a penis substitute (cf. Freud, 1927e). As long as I was equipped with a penis, his was not in danger. In his unconscious I was the mare. As long as he rode me, controlled me, put me through my paces, reined me in, he had power over the (castrating) object. For Mr E, riding was a substitute for sexual gratification and played a major role in the first three years of analysis. It was dealt with like a dream or unconscious thinking (cf. Kinston & Cohen, 1986; Meltzer, 1984) and interpreted in the transference relationship. A minor "relational mishap" in the session was regularly followed by a dangerous situation on horseback. The horse reared, Mr E took the whip to it, the horse was seriously injured. Mr E was full of anger, fear, and despair.

With reference to these scenes we were gradually able to recognise and work on his transference splitting of me into angelic analyst and diabolical mare. This splitting into angel and devil also indicates the narcissistic side of the transference. Both love (or the enormous need for love) and hatred were very archaic and rough-hewn, so they had to be ascribed to extra-terrestrial beings. His childlike identification with Jesus (see above) and his theological studies will probably have supported defence formation. Angel/devil and love/hatred were not understood here as rival forces but as important emotions standing for the relationship between the analysand, the world, his biography, and me. The point was to recognise and accept them as psychic reality (cf. Bion, 1962, 1970; Meltzer, 1990). The animal involved made it possible to live through the archaic experiences of love and hatred and to put them into words. Accordingly, the horse also performed the function of a transitional object throughout (cf. Winnicott, 1953).

The ongoing interpretation of these processes made it possible for Mr E to deepen his relationship with me. He exchanged his horse for one that was less capricious. His desire was to indulge in riding as a congenial, unproblematic sport, but he was (initially) unsuccessful in this endeavour. He sold the second horse as well, and after approximately 300 hours of analysis came to me "without a horse".

Re-enacting the traumatic relational constellation

In his spare time, Mr E went riding at a "therapeutic horse clinic" to support the owner of the establishment: "She does with horses what you do with me." At these stables, valuable dressage horses that had been mishandled by sadistic and over-ambitious owners were ridden in anew and put on a special diet. Mr E had now become a "therapeutic rider". His identification with me was patently obvious, riding was relatively unproblematic and satisfactory for him. This was the point at which Mr E began to discover my "earthiness". His relationship with me became more direct and more concrete, which was a source of gratification for both of us. At the same time, the transference relationship became more intense, split-off traumatic and aggressive topics manifested themselves in transference, and this led to a re-enactment of the patient's relational trauma (cf. Henningsen, 1990). Mr E was beset by increasing tension, he thought about killing himself, terminating the analysis. The impression he made on me was one of extreme jeopardy.

His psychic condition was comparable to that of primal repression (Cohen, 1989).

The following is a brief outline of the most significant stages in this process. We still had sixty sessions (out of a total of 360) before Mr E's health insurance scheme would discontinue payment. My expectation that he would pay for further analysis himself put him into something of a fix, and he contemplated the termination of treatment. When he was a child, his piano teacher had given him lessons for nothing because he was so gifted. And here was I asking for money! Unconsciously he feared that if money changed hands between us in such a banal manner, I might overlook his uniqueness and fail to realise how special these encounters were for both of us. He quickly sensed that our relationship could not be defined in terms of money alone. He wept because he feared that he could not do justice to my "capacity for love" and had nothing to give me himself.

This awakened memories of the first interview, when he had described himself as a screaming child and had felt "held" by me. He came closer to me by asking himself whether I sometimes had a midday nap on this couch or saying something nice about my clothing: "In that pullover you always look so cuddly." He was aware of me as a "flesh and blood" figure. This insight gave him a brief moment of happiness, which almost immediately turned into dreadful panic. He quickly withdrew into homoerotic fantasies. One evening, he ran into a schoolboy in town and persuaded him to go for a walk in the woods. Intimacies were exchanged. Mr E was "head over heels in love", there was no holding back. Some days later he caused a road accident, driving into a hearse that had right of way. His car was a complete wreck. He lived way out in the country and could not get into town in time for our next session. His condition appeared to me to be very serious, and I did not intend to play the role his mother had played when she only opened the toilet door after he had stopped screaming. Accordingly, I agreed to let him phone me at the time the next session would have taken place. Mr E was appalled and shaken by the accident. There had been no coffin in the hearse, and luckily for him he had only sustained a few bruises.

> After he had given me a tearful account of how the accident had happened and told me about his fears and his exhaustion, he took a deep breath and started telling me what it was like in the room where he was sitting and what he could see from the window. "Why do I feel the need to tell you all

this?" he asked. I said: "I think it's very important that I can see exactly what you see, so that I can imagine where you are and we can both look in the same direction." As I said this, I actually felt as if I had the screaming child on my lap and was holding it.

My willingness to conduct an analytic session on the telephone in these circumstances and the intervention I have just described are probably best understood as "reconstruction proper". "Reconstruction proper is the specialised intervention required to repair the disorganisation characteristic of primal repression" (Cohen, 1989, p. 25). Closeness to me in transference had seriously reduced Mr E's capacity for symbolic thinking and sustaining emotional tensions. This was why he resuscitated a traumatic experience. In this situation, reconstructive interpretations were impossible, in fact they would probably have been actively counterproductive. In the subsequent weeks and years we repeatedly referred back to this event. In so doing, we realised that Mr E had experienced something that encompassed his traumatisations in a condensed form. At the place where one could "cuddle to one's heart's desire", where love is possible, something murderous lurks. This link manifested itself in transference; my murder was acted out in the accident. This constellation permeated Mr E's life with frightening consistency, as we found out in the years to come. Here is a brief listing of significant episodes:

- His mother had tried on various occasions to lose the baby when she was pregnant. The newborn baby almost starved to death because the mother did not give him enough to eat. He also suffered from pylorospasms (see the terminal phase of analysis). Whenever he cried as a baby, his mother would sit him up straight on the nursery table and lay into him (verbally).
- When the patient was about two years old, his mother threw "little Johnny", the child's transitional object, into the fire because it was "so dirty". The patient reacted with high fever, no other doll could console him. In his relationship with me, the question recurred constantly whether, like "little Johnny", he would be consigned to the flames if he confided in me, relinquished control, gave himself up to his fantasies, and played with me.
- The father went off to war with an Alsatian dog (German shepherd dog) that he had promised to give to his son. Mr E loved this animal more than anything else and had the feeling that through this dog he

was with his father. The dog was shot. Later Mr E had many Alsatians of his own; all of them died in accidents that happened while he was away. In analysis, the riding hazards and the purchase of the various horses were seen in connection with Mr E's experiences with the dogs. In the same way as earlier he had been unable to keep a dog, Mr E now saw himself in analysis as a "liability for any horse" and in connection with the car accident as a "liability for other people on the roads". In his thoughts about terminating analysis a prominent topic was whether he could "hold" me and I him because he was "a liability for any analyst".

– During the war and afterwards, the patient shared the marital bed with his mother. The mother regularly embraced and kissed him and sucked his penis. When we talked about this in analysis, Mr E felt as if he had been deprived of something substantial. He had never felt as if his body, let alone the male member, had belonged to him. We established that by "not feeling" he had attempted to protect himself from his mother's abuse. The mother had robbed him of his penis and of "little Johnny". He believed that this was why in his homoerotic relationships he fantasised himself as a girl so that "nothing nasty can happen to me anymore". Mr E developed a longing to be able to feel himself to be a man without giving up his homosexuality. On horseback and in analysis there were scenes in which he felt physically present with the blood coursing through his veins. Neither the horse nor I represented any obstacle to this, so in line with the urge for compulsive repetition he had to ensure that he felt cold and lifeless by constellating a dangerous situation, for example, an accident (cf. Ehlert & Lorke, 1988).

– In the post-war period his mother frequently threatened to end her own life, planning to take an overdose of tablets or cut her wrists with nail scissors. This regularly struck panic fear into the boy, who did his best to thwart her plans by emptying the medicine cupboard and keeping a close eye on the nail scissors. In analysis there were times when he would enter the room and check the contents of my desk with a questing glance, focusing particularly on a small pillbox that I kept there. Later we were able to identify this behaviour as the questing glances of his childhood.

The patient found it exhausting and draining to work through these topics. He was desperate and sometimes cried out so loudly that I feared that though my children were a long way away in the other rooms of the house, they might still hear him and wonder what was going on in my office. He believed that he was nothing, that his existence had been snuffed out by the burning of "little Johnny", the cutting-off of his effeminate locks, the sucking of his penis, the shooting of the dog. "Little Johnny", the penis, the hair, the dogs, the horses were attributes safeguarding his identity on the concrete plane. This was vitally necessary because he did not have enough stable internalisations at his disposal. In constellations of this kind Masud Khan sees the causes for the genesis of a relationship to a fetishist object:

> It is possible to postulate here that in this type of patient the earliest relation to the mother has not been internalized. It is available only in terms of identifications and not as a stable internal representation of the good mother. Hence, when the patient was not operative in such identificatory manner his sense of his self was one of bleak and morbid vacuity. (Khan, 1979, pp. 148–149)

At this juncture, Mr E realised that his outstanding gift for pastoral care was largely based on his capacity for fleeting identifications. Another part of it was his ability to get inside another person's skin in the same way as he insinuated himself into the mother to prevent assaults or identified himself as a girl waiting to be "taken". In this sense, both Mr E's homophile fantasies and his sadomasochistic tendencies probably functioned as a kind of shield protecting him against nothingness. These insights helped him to experience his professional activity as less stressful; he required less effort to separate himself off from his vis-à-vis.

Working through depression and castration anxieties

In the two years after we had worked on the murderous relational constellation in transference, Mr E developed a lasting depressive mood that was accompanied by massive castration anxieties, notably when riding. He became an increasingly skilful rider, and towards the end of treatment, riding had become a sport that afforded him considerable gratification. He bought several horses and finally found a more staid animal in line with his wishes and his equestrian skills. In phases of major destabilisation and uncertainty he suffered massive anxiety states when riding and these were then transferred to the horse itself. At times he even lacked the courage to mount his own horse. Parallels with the transference situation manifested themselves repeatedly. In the first years of analysis the point at issue had been life or death in an archaic sense. Now his masculinity was the central topic. Riding was a confirmation for him. If the morning ride was successful, the rest of the day was much less of a problem.

At the same time, his homosexual fantasies began to change. In these fantasies he no longer saw himself as a girl but as a man and longed to have a man as a partner. He succeeded in finding a married homosexual, but Mr E was unable to establish a partnership of equals with this man, so the relationship never progressed beyond an exchange of intimacies and the decision to remain on friendly terms and not take the matter any further.

He now frequently came to me invigorated after a successful ride, like the prince his mother had fantasised about. Both in analysis and in his job he no longer felt the need to "crack the whip"; many people told him that he had become much more balanced. His voice, which had always been one of his assets, gained new resonance and assurance, a fact that struck others beside myself. I recalled the youthful sound of his voice when he first contacted me and asked myself whether the child in him had matured.

The final stages of Mr E's analysis turned out to be especially gruelling. The patient was determined to bring his therapy to an end, but at the same time he feared what would happen. He allowed himself almost a year to take his leave of me. It was the first time in his life that he had to handle an intentional separation and face up to the pain involved. In all other cases he had "upped and gone" from one moment to the next. The same was true of the way he got rid of his animals. His mood and the atmosphere in the sessions were frequently marked by severe depression and regression. He fell ill, suffering from gastritis and pylorospasms, and reported sick. He was ashamed of reacting "like a baby". He required my care; in identification with the film of the same name he fantasised himself as the "last emperor", twelve years old, with myself as his wet nurse breast-feeding him. There were many parallels between himself and the boy emperor who, although isolated and weighed down with narcissistic expectations, was destined to achieve greatness. He enjoyed being able to express these fantasies without fear, but then immediately remembered that in the film the nurse had to leave the emperor and that his analysis was also coming to a close. Perhaps at a psychosomatic level Mr E was once again living through his disastrous start in life with his mother; after all he had nearly starved and had suffered from pylorospasms. The twelve-year-old emperor reminded us of the twelve-year-old girl he had turned himself into in his sexual fantasies at the beginning of therapy. He was twelve years old when his father returned from the war broken and disillusioned and drove him out of the marital bed. In retrospect, we were able to recognise that as the twelve-year-old girl he had constituted a "collated internal object" that sustained the perverted attachment to his mother. Perhaps identification with the mother was designed to assure him of the love of his father, but if so, the attempt was a failure.

At this time, I bought Eugen Drewermann's book *Kleriker. Psychogramm eines Ideals* ("The Cleric: A Psychoanalytic Study of Clergymen and Religious Orders") (1990). As I read it, I realised that I was not only satisfying my curiosity about the psychoanalytic issues posed by the life of the clergy. In fact, I was seeking to temper the immense loneliness I was experiencing with this patient by reading my way through a host of similar cases discussed in the book.

The patient's mother had Parkinson's disease and had spent the last three years being cared for in her son's house. She now became acutely psychotic and had to be entrusted to a nursing home. In psychosis, the mother validated once more the psychodynamics of her relationship with her son, embodying, as it were, the insights that Mr E had achieved in the course of analysis. He was shaken and astonished by the truth content of her "insanity". For example, she would lie down in his wife's bed and call for her bridal gown or utter the firm conviction that there were children starving in her bed (like the patient just after birth!). Her cries of "Lord God, have mercy on us!" echoed through the house, and Mr E identified them as the cries she had uttered after the war. "Probably my mother was always a latent psychotic," he said, "and I probably have a psychotic core that will always remain." When his mother lived out her sadism in her fantasies, he invariably related this to a real event he had experienced with her. The mother reported that in her dealings with evil people she would slit open the skin behind their ears with a razorblade. Here Mr E drew a parallel with the walks on which she had rammed her pointed fingernail into the palm of his hand: "My mother lives in a kind of hell! It is her own hell, I cannot share it with her and I have no desire to. I want nothing of it!"

His separation from me and from his mother ran parallel. His mother withdrew into psychosis, the doctors diagnosed schizophrenia. Inwardly, Mr E took leave of his mother by going for a last walk with her before she was admitted to the nursing home. He engaged with his mourning and his helplessness. The question then arose where I would go when he left me. He was increasingly aware of his loneliness, the psychosomatic symptoms disappeared, he once again brought dreams for analysis. In one dream, he was selected for a high ecclesiastical post. When a golden cross was hung round his neck as chain of office, the crowd of spectators withdrew and he was alone "like in Brecht's *Caucasian Chalk Circle* when the ordinary man gets to be the judge." For him, this dream was a "warning", he felt the splendour of the cross to be deceptive. He feared the loneliness in the grandiosity and felt that he was no longer so dependent on the opulent trappings of the church. The allusion to the Chalk Circle extended to his leave-taking from me. Could I let him go as a homosexual? Shouldn't I convert him to heterosexuality? Separation from his biological mother was hell for the mother (= psychosis); would I start pulling at him until he was torn apart? Mr E sensed that I was fully prepared to assist him in getting to the bottom of these questions, while of course not in any way inveigling him into some form of well-adjusted identity formation. This made him feel confirmed in his masculinity as a homosexual and said that the point at issue was "being born again". In masturbation he was able for the first time to experience his penis as a part of himself. In the last long vacation before the end of analysis he took his wife on a trip to Denmark. Neither of them had ever been to Scandinavia. "It's strange," he said. "Everything was as familiar as if I'd been there several times before. I believe you come from Flensburg or Husum. I felt really at home up there, and that's because I have something of you in me." During this vacation he was also able to talk to his wife about his homosexuality; both of them recognised that there would probably never again be any sexual contact between them and allowed themselves to mourn the fact. Despite these difficulties they were both willing to stay married.

In the last few weeks before the termination of analysis, Mr E reflected on the question whether it was his "disposition" that had made him avoid falling in love with me "in the proper sexual sense" despite the intimacy between us. With the help of a dream in which we both lay next to each other without anything happening, we were able to recognise how important it was that, although we were close, I had never thrown myself on him like his mother, who kissed him all over and sucked his penis. Having an intimate relationship without abuse was probably an essential factor. On this point he saw his wife in a very similar light, which, despite all the problems, made him feel confident that his marriage would last. He left analysis in profound gratitude, felt "freed of cracking the whip", and had no qualms about taking confirmation classes again. Mr E knows that he can return to me for further analysis if he should feel the need.

Discussion

The interplay between trauma, homosexuality, perversion, and the creation of a "collated internal object" (Khan, 1979) was a crucial factor in this analysis. Split-off, dis-integrated part-objects bound into a perverted mother–child relationship were worked on in transference. Mr E was gradually able to effect more stable internalisations and to integrate his experiences of alienation and bodily dispossession. His sexual urges over and against children and adolescents disappeared, his sadism lost much of its force. Of course, Mr. E was a theologian with heart and soul, so naturally his profession took up a great deal of our time in analysis. In the sessions he would frequently reflect on the texts for his sermons and also on funerals he had conducted. Work on his individual approach to these topics repeatedly gave him new strength for the conduct of church services. As already mentioned, he frequently indicated to me how important his belief in Easter was for him. Probably his identification with Jesus helped him to bear up under the martyrdom imposed on him by his mother in his father's absence. Though his father had abandoned him, God the Father would not do that, he would call his son to him. In analysis I invariably respected this attitude; we were able to designate and acknowledge his faith. Frequently we asked ourselves whether his homosexuality had to do with his love of God. Massive traumatisations had led to splitting processes and an early development of the ego functions, as described in detail by Masud Khan. Thinking and faith—both of them highly structured psychic functions—here also serve as defences. We were able to work on part of these defences when Mr E discovered me as a "flesh and blood" person; another part will certainly have been coped with when he was able to engage more and more authentically with his son. However, essential parts of the negative Oedipus complex remain bound up with God.

From a psychoanalytic viewpoint, Christian faith or the absent father rediscovered in God can be understood as containers protecting Mr E from disaster. Remarking on his last-mentioned dream with the words "The lustre of the golden cross is deceptive", he is also demonstrating the boundaries of this analysis.

This case contains many indications that (homoerotic) love of the father was a protection against the perverted, dispossessing mother. This is not however to suggest any straightforward causal connections along the lines of "he became homosexual because of his mother". Looking at it the other way round is equally justifiable. For example, we might say that his homosexual disposition was helpful to him in the relationship with his mother, and he developed into a highly structured individual. Mr E himself considers his homosexuality to be largely psychogenic, he gives little credence to predisposition, and feels that he is too old to go into all the ins and outs of the matter, preferring to call a halt right here. The answer he has found to this question is a matter of "more or less" rather than unequivocally clear-cut. It is of course conceivable that in the first years of his life Mr E developed an irreversible core gender identity of the kind proposed by Stoller (1985) and taken up by Künzler (1992, p. 213 et seq.). It was not my job to find an answer to this; the question must remain open.

The genesis of his perversion is easier to discern. In his childhood, the patient was exposed to a perverted mother–child relationship in which sexual and physical abuse engendered cumulative traumatisations. The absence of the father and the wartime circumstances meant that the child had little chance of escaping the mother's intrusive assaults. To survive, the child ego had to remain in the position of the mother's narcissistic object. On the one hand, the mother's perverted and sadistic acts led to bodily dispossession and "not-feeling"; on the other, the patient had to maintain a close attachment in order to stay alive; it was the only way he could respond to potential dangers. Love and hatred could not be reconciled; the twelve-year-old girl of his fantasies was a life-sustaining compromise designed to mitigate the traumatic constellation. At the same time, it established his disposition for a later development towards paedophilia.

In the subsequent years, Mr E maintained a good working balance and in the final stages of his professional life devoted himself to his duties with commitment and determination. He also gave me a token of his appreciation. After he had read this report, he told me how often it had reminded him of the occasions when he came to our sessions with the firm resolve: "Today I'm going to say it", or "Today, I'm going to be more open". But on very many occasions he had failed either partly or completely in the attempt to show more of his feelings. Also, he had never realised how much time I had spent thinking about him and the analysis as a whole and how lonely I had been throughout his treatment.

CHAPTER ELEVEN

"I can look after myself": Destruction and consolation in one and the same object?

Ms O

Ms O is an attractive, casually dressed woman in her late forties. Her clothing is a little more individual than one might expect from a successful businesswoman with a university degree, but her makeup carefully conceals any facial expression of feeling. When I first saw her, I thought: This woman is severely traumatised and suffers from depression, but she's a fighter. She had spared no effort to arrange an appointment with me although I was fully booked up and had told her as much on the phone. "My therapist—she's an analyst too—told me to get in touch with you because you specialise in traumas. There's nothing more she can do for me." Appealing to me as a "trauma specialist" made me sceptical; too often I had experienced how severe the pathologies can be that masquerade as "traumas" in order to achieve greater social acceptance. For three years, Ms O had been to a (female) colleague of mine once a week for face-to-face psychotherapy. There had been no appreciable improvement: "We're very fond of one another, we drink coffee during the sessions." I asked myself what degree of destructiveness was being warded off with this behaviour. I also feared there might be covert rivalry behind the idealisation of my person. This "overture" was a warning.

There must be enormous rage and aggressiveness lurking in the depths that could not be allowed to surface in transference. I interpreted the companionable coffee-drinking as a sign of split-off aggression.

Symptoms

"As far back as I can remember, I've always suffered from depression, I'm full of anxieties and nightmares. Last spring I had a total breakdown after my stepmother had disappointed me once again. I cannot live without psychoactive drugs [200 mg serotonin, sleeping pills], sometimes I drink too much as well. I can't stop this nonsense. I'm also afraid that it might ruin my marriage." Later Ms O confessed that she occasionally visited swinger clubs when she could no longer bear the tension she was under. She and her tyrannical husband quarrelled almost daily, their disputes sometimes culminating in physical violence. Ms O had massive conflicts with her sadistic stepmother, who had now started taking advantage of Ms O's daughter, Carol, to involve her in these conflicts. "She can do that to me, but not to my daughter!" This sentence was uttered with such vehemence that it remained in my mind like a kind of legacy throughout the therapy.

Trauma history

Ms O is her parents' first and only child. Her mother was buried on Ms O's first birthday. A routine operation had led to septicaemia with fatal consequences. The maternal grandmother had died three months previously and the patient's mother had lapsed into depression as a result: "They all said, stop crying and take care of the baby, but she couldn't." Up to the age of four, Ms O was brought up by a great-aunt of whom she has very fond memories.

After that, the patient returned to her father, who had remarried in the meantime. Two half-brothers were born (four and six years younger). Life became a "nightmare" for Ms O, her stepmother beating her almost every day for no apparent reason, breaking a number of wooden cooking spoons and coat-hangers in the process. When Ms O started school, her stepmother gave the teachers written permission to beat her if she disobeyed. The parents also hit each other regularly. On one occasion, the stepmother broke a beer bottle over her drunken husband's head, the place was full of blood, Ms O had to wipe it all up.

Despite all this, Ms O was good at school. She had no trouble passing her school-leaving exams and did well at university. She had divorced her first husband (twelve years older, her daughter's father) ten years before. At the beginning of treatment she had been married to her second husband for eight years. She described her new partner as a violent "macho".

After the initial interview I concluded the following agreement with Ms O: She was to go to her present therapist once a week up to the summer vacation and also regularly visit her psychiatrist. After the holidays she could come to me once a week for face-to-face therapy. As of January the following year I could then accept her for high-frequency analysis (four times a week). I could not offer her an earlier place, but I thought it sensible to have her experience me as a concrete object before analysis in a recumbent position began so as to support a positive transference relationship and avoid too much nascent anxiety and destructiveness. At the same time I was more clearly set off from her, which gave the patient greater security. To "cut down on" the number of sessions the insurance scheme would remunerate her for, she paid for this preliminary treatment herself at the statutory rates.

Two initial dreams

After our first interview, Ms O recounted two dreams that already mapped out the programme for our joint work and strengthened my resolve to accept her as a patient. It was her way of telling me that she too was willing and able to work with me. Initial understanding of these dreams (much as in the case of Mr V, Chapter Two) was extremely helpful, representing as they did a first attempt at symbolisation that gave both the patient and me something to hold on to.

> With my husband I am on my way to the Catholic church in our home community. But it does not look like it does in reality. Leading up to the altar is a long corridor with two swords hanging from the ceiling. I say something to my husband that he doesn't understand, the gist of it is: "I'm the one who has to deal with the swords." On the left-hand side of the church a christening ceremony is taking place, so I keep my voice low when I talk to my husband. I don't want to disturb. My husband walks on and I follow him to the altar, where a woman is arranging something. She welcomes me: "How nice to have you back with us!" Suddenly my parents are standing in front

of me (father and stepmother). My nose is running. I have no handkerchief and wipe my nose with the back of my hand. My father finds this disgusting. My mother pulls her leg back to gain more momentum, she is wearing snakeskin boots and makes to kick me in the stomach. I get hold of the boot and hit my mother with it. I can look after myself.

The second dream from the same night:

> There was a room full of diabolical creatures and lianas. A heart had been dug up in the cemetery. The heart was in a plastic bag hanging down below my husband's jacket. It gave off a dreadful stench. I said: "We've got to get rid of that."

These dreams made a big impression on me. I could see the danger of my patient being overwhelmed by her rage and fears, no longer able to project the aggressiveness on to her husband. I thought the direct speech ("How nice to have you back with us") might be the harbinger of a positive transference relationship because we needed to take a different perspective on the sacrificial altar of her life from the one chosen by her last therapist. The sentence addressed to her husband—"I'm the one who has to deal with the swords"—expresses a premonition on the part of the patient that also tells us something about her attitude to analysis. She is the one who has to "deal with" her severe fate and that is why she needs analysis. The two women in the dream obviously had to be separated: the good one at the altar, the evil one (with "perverted" snakeskin boots?) that she had to defend herself against. "I had no handkerchief" means there is no consolation, no container for my anxieties and my sorrows. I was able to tell her that she was probably hoping to find her biological mother's love by digging up her heart from the grave. I said: "At the moment everything is destructive and repulsive and you are full of rage. But there is perhaps a ray of hope for better times to come, for example, memories of the time before your mother died, the time before your mother lapsed into depression and your grandmother died. 'I can look after myself' sounds like the motto for your whole life."

The two swords remind her and me of the sword of Damocles. But why two swords she has to fight against? Father and mother? Real mother and stepmother? The good and bad breast? Past and present? Primary object and transference object? There were so many "doubles" in her life that probably found expression in this image and are further evidence of the many sadomasochistic repetitions she had to cope with. The fact that Ms O is so quick to symbolise her traumatic experiences in this highly differentiated way makes me optimistic and sceptical at the same time. One the one hand, I ask myself whether this immediate co-operativeness is a sign for a lack of psychic distance. On the other hand, the initial dream reminds me that the time spent with her great-aunt probably opened the door for a number of integrative experiences and offered the child convalescence and opportunities to develop. It was this that enabled her to identify the subsequent experiences at the hands of her father and stepmother as "evil" and to reactivate old splitting processes for her own self-preservation.

In this case, the early mother object is at the same time the traumatic object (due to her depression and sudden death). Children going through such experiences have to split off their affects and frequently withdraw into themselves. In the case of Ms S and her severe separation trauma (Chapter Five) I have described this as concretistic fusion with a part of the self. In Ms O's case the great-aunt probably helped to prevent the worst. But the abrupt confrontation with a stepmother who herself was both young and pregnant tore open an old wound in the patient.

In the preliminary (face-to-face) stage of therapy, our exchanges revolved continuously around the repetitions. The patient recognised how she had re-enacted the relationship to her stepmother with her husband and how her daughter embodied part of her ideal self. In this way, Ms O achieved a cognitive conception of her life, but she could not *feel* what she had learned about herself. She and her husband separated. After he had moved out, she reacted with manic defence strategies. All kinds of rearrangements were made and various things were purchased, for example, two expensive Siamese cats for her daughter and herself. She told me they both needed an animal of their own to console them. This bore in on me the extent to which she was indeed a manager, someone unable to allow herself respite or a place for mourning and quiet.

The first year of analysis: no bridge between the mother and the disaster on Earth

At the age of six, Ms O realised that nothing could change the situation she was in. She vomited frequently, suffered from severe bouts of anxiety, and longed for her biological mother.

One day she went to the cemetery alone and lay down on her mother's grave: "It was cold. Then it was good." This description gave me an initial idea of Ms O's splitting processes into a state of not-feeling ("it was cold") on the one hand and an idealised world with the mother in heaven, which probably had to remain unconscious but helped her survive the many experiences of sadism. I said: "That must have been a trenchant experience for you that marked you for life. You were completely alone in the graveyard, and there was no link between your mother in heaven and your distress on Earth. We need time to understand what happened to you there."

Ms O was probably acting out her split state, as if she were trying to unite with the dead mother, to be close to her, to fuse with her.

The subsequent sessions were replete with reports on dangerous enactments: uncontrolled surfing on the internet, various sexual relationships with highly disturbed and severely traumatised men. She tried to convey to me that she had her life under control and that this evil world had nothing to do with her, the others were the villains. I attempted to create a connection with the world of her internal objects. My interpretation:

> This man's life could have figured in one of your nightmares. [...] The sheer horror of it fits in with your story. [...] Perhaps it is so fascinating for you because he claims to have everything under control. [...] You have the impression that his fate is a good deal worse than yours. [...] The horror is outside, perhaps it is easier to contemplate this man's life than to look inside and see your own life.

Another projection surface in the long period of acting-out was her daughter. Initially Carol had been described to me as the ideal daughter, intelligent, creative, responsible, well-liked at school. At the time her mother's analysis was commencing, she performed a self-written sketch in school in the course of which ghosts came out of their graves to kill people. Ms O was shocked. Her own dreadful experiences had obviously left their mark on her daughter after all. Carol had probably been too frequently exposed to the many marital disputes and her mother's breakdowns and alcoholic excesses. The more clearly Ms O was able to describe her own horrors in analysis, the more the image of the ideal daughter crumbled. Ms O was able to recognise the excessive pressure bearing in on her daughter and to talk to her about it.

Carol embarked on psychotherapy, mother and daughter both went to their "shrink sessions". At this point Carol was fifteen and tried to liberate herself from her mother's projections and her controlling behaviour. At first Ms O was unable to recognise the power she exerted over her daughter. She had to be in charge at all times. Her omnipotent defence began to totter. At this time Ms O missed various important appointments connected with her job, for example, because she overslept. Unconsciously I was supposed to support her, like the idealised dead mother, and give her a few tips on how to sort things out with her daughter. The main areas of conflict were playing truant from school and spending too much money. My interpretation: "The daughter behaves like the mother." Though the parallels were obvious, I had to pluck up courage in countertransference to confront Ms O with this and to unmask the acting-out, the point at issue here being, of course, projected parts of the self. Observing her daughter was for Ms O like looking in a mirror. In analysis, Ms O demonstrated to me without further ado how much energy and potential brute force she was prepared to invest in exercising object control. On no account should the helplessness of the beaten and abandoned child become conscious; the intrusive acts of violence had engendered identifications that were to preoccupy us in analysis for a very long time.

After six months, Ms O reduced the serotonin dosage to 100 mg with her psychiatrist's consent, then after another six months she was able to do without it altogether. I saw this development as a sign of an incipient transference relationship in which dependence was permitted and asked myself whether she would be able to see me as an object receptive to her split-off affects.

The second year of analysis: rage at the idealised object—attempts at omnipotent control

After the patient's divorce went through, new turbulence ensued. Ms O had no choice but to increasingly admit to her own destructiveness. She developed guilt feelings and lapsed into a progressive state of depression.

There was, however, always a counter-movement. She bought herself an expensive dog. The daughter suggested the name the dog was given, a modification of my own name. This was quite patently the creation of a transference object that, unlike myself, Ms O had complete control over and never moved from her side. Reports on sadistic training methods employed by the dog school and descriptions of the dog barking at other people in her stead made it possible to interpret the transference. At work her colleagues protested at the dog's presence, and Ms O had to leave it at home. She was now unprotected and lapsed into depression again. She was bullied at work, no dog and no analyst could bark and bite on her behalf. At the same time, a dispute came to a head with trouble-seeking neighbours on the estate where she lived. It had been smouldering for four years. While the behaviour of these people was certainly eccentric and vindictive, my patient gradually had to admit that she had a special gift for putting their backs up.

I was worried by the way she appeared to have got bogged down in this paranoid world, in her depression and her inability to see things from a slightly more distanced perspective. I tried to interpret her identifications with her destructive internal objects. As her affects were still largely split off, I feared this might turn me into the sadistic stepmother. Another danger was that she identified narcissistically with my interpreting function so as to control me omnipotently. Then her affects were split off once again and her depressive condition got worse. The following session protocol gives an indication of the balancing act that all this involved (the patient came to me on Mondays, Tuesdays, Wednesdays, and Fridays).

Tuesday session:

P: I'm late today. It's because of the chaos inside. When I woke up this morning, I felt fresh and fit. But my colleague at work made one blunder after another. I shouted at her, telling her she had no idea what she was doing, I've never screamed at anyone like that before. By the way, she's the one who made sure I couldn't bring my dog to work anymore. Today she did the dirty on me again. [Ms O describes what happened, then waits] I want peace and quiet. [Waits] Yesterday I was out walking the dog, two women runners came our way. The dog butted one of them with its muzzle, it was next to nothing. But the woman bawled at me with so much aggression! "Keep that dog away from me!" Then an elderly gentleman came past and said: "Wait, let me help you." He managed to pacify the women. [She describes this.]

A: So someone came to your aid.

P: Yes, after that I did some training on the dog, she obeyed immediately, it went really well. The bad vibrations had gone. And then I had a good midday nap. Everything was just fine. In the evening I went out with the dog again to that little park. A neighbour called to me: "Put that dog on a lead, you stupid cow!" I said, "You're so civilised!" I thought, One more remark like that and I'll be scratching his car. I know where he parks it. ... Then I thought, No, I must get out of here. A little further on there was an ambulance taking another neighbour to hospital, a real alcoholic. It's like living in a madhouse! That bloody architect woman ... [She continues with her vitriolic complaints. One crazy story follows the other. I think to myself: the madhouse is in her mind, however "mental" her neighbours may be]

A: [energetically] Look, may I interrupt you for a moment? These attacks affect you as if there were no other alternative than to give as good as you get or become destructive. That's the way children react when they feel threatened. You know that well enough from a childhood spent with your stepmother. There was no protection, nothing that could stop you from turning destructive.

I felt overwhelmed by her arousal and had to put a stop to the proceedings if I didn't want to be swept away by her torrential display of emotion. The intensity of the projective identifications manifesting themselves in a split-off, highly aroused affective state were an invitation to fusion, an invitation I had to resist so as not to become part of her sadomasochistic and paranoid world. I wanted to help her distance herself so that she could contemplate things more justly.

P: I'm developing incredible fantasies of violence, aren't I? [...] [She carries on in the same vein, have I not got through to her? But slowly she calms down] After four years of legal disputes, the judge ought to say, "All right, you lot, enough is enough!"

A: You want the judge to settle the dispute just as the elderly man did this morning, the way your father never intervened when you were fighting with your stepmother. [I sense that my analytic thinking has forsaken me but find no way of expressing this in an interpretation]

P: Yes, and it was the same this morning, I felt totally paralysed. I was really well prepared, I was willing to do the dirty work for the others! And then that woman!

For Ms O the analysis was rapidly turning into sheer torture; in her eyes my interpretations were frequently sadistic assaults, although some of them did produce insights in her. Hatred of me and the ideal mother who had abandoned her became manifest. Whenever I interpreted something, her control edifice collapsed. At the beginning of this period, Ms O said on one or two occasions that she was thinking of buying a horse. She pooh-poohed my injunction to think it over carefully and to ask herself what it would mean for her and our time together. A horse meant investing considerable time and money and that might be detrimental to the analysis. Defiantly, she told me that her horse would soon be arriving, she had purchased a Spanish stallion. This shocked me, I had visions of having to conduct as dangerous an analysis as with Mr E (Chapter Ten). Ms O's transference message was obvious. She was telling me, you can't control me. I anticipated a continuation of the many sadistic enactments.

By buying the horse, Ms O had turned away from me. She felt exhausted, depressive, and aggressive and refused to talk to me about her decision. I felt that she was in extreme danger, she felt that she needed "time out" from the analysis and opted for an interruption. She had booked a week at a training camp for her dog.

A: Ms O, you need help and you should stay here so that we can understand what's going on. ... It's probably not so easy to take advantage of this opportunity. ... What will your daughter do when you're away?
P: She can stay on her own! No problem! [Angrily] I've got to wind down, the only chance of some fresh air is with my dog. [Even more angrily] I'll pay for the sessions I've missed, don't worry!!

During this vacation the dog had a serious accident. For the next school year, her daughter decided to move to her father in the western part of Germany. A woman friend of my patient's had hit on this idea and encouraged the daughter accordingly. Everything had been decided in my patient's absence and without her participation. Her depression worsened. When she went to see her daughter's psychotherapist, the impression he got was that she was an alcoholic. She lapsed into new depths of depression.

A: This interruption didn't do you or your dog any good.
P: [extremely angry] It's none of your business and has nothing to do with the analysis. And I have to pay for the sessions as well! The cheek of it!

Ms O paid for the sessions. At work she started making mistakes. She was tormented by disappointment at her daughter's decision to go and live with her father and by feelings of guilt. The daughter's therapist appeared to tolerate, if not actively support, her "year abroad", which meant termination or interruption of her therapy. Ms O had the feeling that her daughter had been taken away from her; she suffered severe anguish, which reminded us of how infinitely painful the loss of her own mother had been for her. Ms O could no longer feel any hope for herself. Nor did she have the strength to assert herself at work. In one session she developed thoughts of suicide.

> I said to her: "I'm not going to let you go to the cemetery alone!" Ms O felt understood, calmed down a little, and recalled dissociative states in her childhood. She had frequently lain in bed and felt as if her body had swollen up like a balloon. I said: "You felt completely abandoned, no one comforted you. You could not fathom your feelings, either with your body or your senses. And now it's hard to imagine that I can reassure you, even though you are so desperate and angry."

Ms O then recounted how her half-brothers would clamber into the parents' bed on a Sunday morning and have fun with them. Ms O was not allowed to join in. She had to stay on her own, as in the summer vacations when she was sent to her aunt and was excluded from the family holiday. Other traumatic memories followed in the subsequent sessions. As she began to better recognise her sadistic identifications, she would cancel the next session so as to regain control over me and the situation. Again she attempted to combat her depression by acting out.

Third year of analysis: analysis of the zoo—sorrow and pain

When Ms O got her new horse, her daughter bought two mice for herself. Both these events happened in the second year of analysis. The mice went with the daughter to live with the father and returned with her in the middle of the following year. Later the daughter also acquired two geckos that someone gave her as a present. The cats were still doing well, and the apartment had turned into quite a little zoo. Transference still played itself out on a sadomasochist plane; everything that occurred during the sessions was acted out in parallel with the animals. The animals enabled the patient to *feel* what she had experienced. Not without an accusing undertone, she emphasised that she needed her *own* therapy programme, independently of me, and that was what the animals were able to provide: "I need exercise, fresh air, training, nature."

This transference splitting was meant not only to protect her but me as well. In this way she could live out her aggressions and keep me in safety. Outside my office she could play the animal-tamer without injuring me. It was also a way of keeping one feature of the ideal—but dead—mother alive. Most of the aspects of positive transference were bound up with the mother in heaven, but real, perverted, sadistic life took place on earth—in her job and with the animals.

Working on the patient's sadistic identifications now became a viable proposition. I frequently felt shattered, scared, and stressed. I also asked myself whether it might not be dangerous to submit such a patient to analysis. I interpreted how the patient projected her split-off aggressive impulses on to her horse, her daughter, and her colleagues at work in order to fight them. She recognised her identifications with the depressive mother, the sadistic stepmother, and the stern father. She was perpetrator and victim at one and the same time! After a number of dangerous situations with the stallion, the horse had to be castrated. I was relieved and realised once more the extent to which the patient had frightened me with her hobby. In transference, the parallels were played out. She was no longer the fighter she had been before analysis began.

Here is the protocol of a session:

P: I've taken to listening to mantras in the car. It's part of my tranquillising programme. Yesterday we were talking about extremes. There's no sense in that, I shan't be available for that kind of thing. Yesterday I went out riding with my friend, I had no time to put the horse on the long rein beforehand, to make him tired.
[Alarm bells started ringing in me, although she had turned up in a balanced mood and her friend is an experienced rider.]
She describes how they were riding along an avenue when two women came towards them swinging their arms as a loosening-up exercise. She politely asked the women to interrupt the exercise until they had passed but the women turned aggressive and refused to stop. Ms O repeated her request a number of times and explained that they were scaring the horses. The women had no compunction and started bad-mouthing riders in general for churning up the ground underfoot. The two riders reined in their horses and Ms O's friend said: "We're allowed to ride here, and no one's stopping you doing your fitness exercises. Now just calm down." The women then backed down and

everything returned to normal. "Only when they saw how big the horses were did they understand why we had behaved the way we did."

Now for another story. A dishevelled female alcoholic from the neighbourhood had let her two small dogs run loose. They attacked Ms O's (larger) dog, which defended itself. The woman grabbed Ms O's dog, pulled him up by the ears, poked him in the ribs and shouted: "I'll kill you, I will!" The incident culminated in the dog owner reporting Ms O to the police. Later, a policeman declared that all three dogs might have to be examined by the police veterinarian.

P: That's another extreme case that I have to deal with. I have to avoid these situations with those dogs. Maybe that woman has a hard time of it, but I can't help her.
A: I have a question. What's with the obligation to keep dogs on a leash in the park?
[I feel I need to put the patient on a leash; at the same time I think that if I do, I'm abandoning my position as an analyst.]
P: They weren't on a leash, we'll both be fined for that. [She explains the law.] All the dogs there run around free. My dog's a hunting dog, he can't do his business if he's on a leash.

Ms O tells me how well-behaved her dog is in comparison to those of her adversary, but even with the best-trained dog dangerous situations can arise if other people start looking for trouble. Her dog trainer once told her a story about a dog biting a small child to death.

A: Horses can shy and dogs can be unpredictable in situations like that.
P: A dog can get all fixated on such a situation, normally I wade straight in and sort things out, no nonsense. I'm good at that.
A: At the moment you are describing on the animal plane everything that we are experiencing in analysis. You are trying to calm yourself. Maybe you need me as an experienced analyst in the same way you needed your friend to intervene yesterday as an experienced rider. Talking about the episode with the dogs you seem pretty fixated yourself.
P: Yes, I have to be careful.
A: And nothing would have happened if the dogs had been on the leash?
P: No, nothing. But my dog can't do his business when he's on the leash because he's a hunting dog.
A: The same is true of you [an allusion to conflicts in her job and to her analysis]. You think you can't do your business when you're on the leash.

There are so many parallels between you and the animals and you and me. You have a hearing at work, the dog with the police veterinarian.

P: Mmm. [Pause.] The policeman said: "Perhaps, perhaps not." At any rate, I'm not worried, my dog is friendly, he's well-trained and he never bites. But those little white curs, they're like fire-crackers on four legs! I hope they take away at least one of them from her, then it'd be easier to control the situation. As long as she's not right outside my house, I'm going to keep out of her way. I can go on training my dog. [Pause.] Have you noticed how calmly I'm saying all this? I'm not in one of those excitable moods!

A: You were just as calm when you were out riding yesterday. Perhaps that scene in the dream in which you wipe a crumb off your husband's face had the same reassuring influence.

In the subsequent sessions, Ms O was able to recognise that in her unconscious the woman with the two ugly dogs represented the stepmother with the two half-brothers who on Sundays were allowed into father's bed and travelled around with the parents. The dogs were "fire-crackers" because she wanted them out of the way. She was progressively more aware of the way in which she was projecting her aggression(s) on to the animals and gradually became a more sensitive rider. One day she said:

P: You have to observe a horse very closely, you have to relate to it with a high degree of sensitivity, then you can start making progress. You have to be very careful how you deal with it!

A: That's precisely how an analyst needs to deal with a traumatised patient.

She laughed briefly, felt relieved. The following night she had a nightmare, "a horror trip with monsters". In the session she had been able to relax, contemplate her inner world, and feel her identification with me as a reassuring object. But at the same time this gave her inner monsters more leeway. This dynamic can be observed in many patients: the security of the transference relationship gives more scope for profounder engagement with the psychic trauma. The projections are re-introjected, localised in the patient's inner world and thus made more accessible for working on.

A: You experience the same when you're out riding and the horse runs away with you.

Ms O began to feel more secure, she withdrew less into herself, her moods lightened somewhat. This hopeful development was brutally interrupted when her employers threatened to give her notice. She was just the wrong side of fifty—at fifty they could not have thrown her out. For the company this was a financial risk. In addition, she had almost exhausted the resources allowed her for analysis by her health insurance scheme. However, in this crisis she was able to make better use of analysis and draw upon me as a reassuring object, which subsequently enabled her to see things more realistically.

The scene in which she stood before her mother's grave as a six-year-old girl resurfaced in analysis. The heart and the warmth had been dragged down into the grave. But I was with her. In the initial dream the heart had been dug out, it was in a cold plastic bag. What about her own heart? Her mother is dead. Her heart is cold. Something had happened to the little girl when it lay down on the mother's grave. It was essential to understand what it was. As she lay on the grave, she gave up her own heart and turned into a fighter able to look after herself in a cold, hostile world.

Ms O managed to have a constructive exchange with one of her bosses. She was not made redundant, but she earned less. She was able to pay for the ongoing analysis from her own pocket. Her superior said he felt guilty about not having talked to her about these things earlier. She admitted to her psychic problems and said she was undergoing analysis. She explained that in the last few years she had not been feeling well but that she was now recovering. "I told him, I have a wonderful analyst, she's my last chance. He was awfully nice, almost gave me a hug ..."

The riding problems were more obstinate. It turned out that the horse had always been ridden in the wrong way. Ms O had to walk her horse on the rein, without a saddle. In many respects she felt ejected from her saddle, with regard to her earlier life, in her relationship with her daughter and with me. This stage lasted three months and made itself felt in the transference relationship. For some time already, her daughter had moved back in with her, but now she moved out again (plus mice and geckos) to get through her last year at school on her own. This brought it home to Ms O that her daughter was more important than her animals. She now had to put her daughter on the "long rein", much as I had when she took time out for the dog-training course. After a brief idealisation phase, she was able to integrate the good experiences she had had with me. The cathexis of the animals was increasingly displaced to people and direct contact with them. Soon we were both more securely ensconced in the saddle as far as the analysis was concerned.

Ms O began to mourn and I was able to accompany her. Acting out was no longer necessary, at least not with the same vehemence. It was now possible to achieve a different understanding of the sentence referred to at the outset when she said her stepmother could do what she liked with her, "but not with my daughter". Ms O no longer required her daughter as a projection surface for her split-off ideal self. She could acknowledge the ups and downs in her own life and in her daughter's.

After 400 sessions, job-related and financial constraints made it necessary to reduce frequency. Ms O was able to maintain contact and profit from the sessions. We discussed termination of the analysis. "The depression has gone," Ms O asserted, adding that she had achieved what there was to achieve but that she still needed me to consolidate what she had learned about herself. She spent another two years with me in low-frequency analysis, towards the end only once a week, sometimes every two weeks. In this period she reflected on the analytic process and worked on her attitude to her daughter. After an interval of some weeks, Ms O was able to show me how she continued her inner dialogue with me. "You see," she said, "I stay in contact with you even when I'm not here. I need that so much." Here we see the onset of self-analysis, which facilitated the separation process.

Discussion

Ms O was another of my patients who had already tried to deal with her psychic problems by undergoing therapy at an earlier stage. Although it brought no prospects of recovery, this earlier therapy was a preparation for analysis. Perhaps, as with Ms F. (see Chapter Six), an idealising defence had to be acted out before the traumatic relational constellations could manifest themselves in transference and become susceptible of symbolisation. It was important for the patient to be able to calmly take her leave of her earlier analyst, who probably represented the great-aunt who looked after the patient after her mother's death. If the switch to me had been too abrupt, the trauma of the sudden loss of her great-aunt would have repeated itself, and a helpful object would once again have been massively devalued. The therapist had been able to show the patient that she had ended up in collusion with her. Her advice to undergo analysis with a different analyst enabled the patient to embark on the search for her early mother and an understanding of the cumulative sequential traumas. In this way she could potentially overcome her severe depression.

This is another case where one can see the processes of intergenerational transmission at work *in statu nascendi*. Michael Parsons (2011) describes them with reference to the graves that turn up at the beginning of this analysis. The mother became depressive through the death of her own mother; three months later the mother is laid in earth herself. At the age of six the patient lies down on her mother's grave; in the initial dream the mother's heart is disinterred. In a sketch at school, the daughter conjures up the murderous spirits from the graves of the deceased.

For me, the patient's cry: "She can do that with me, but not with my daughter!" was an indication that the patient had a premonition of the extreme stress her problems meant for her daughter. Only in the course of analysis did the patient become painfully aware that she had been projecting idealised parts of her own self onto her daughter, who in this way had assumed part of her mother's trauma defence.

In the school sketch, the daughter "staged" her own inner world, which was also the inner world of the mother. It is entirely possible that the daughter's creativity was released by the fact that her mother had been undergoing analysis for some weeks, had previously been to me for one-session-a-week therapy, and had "made contact". Despite many turbulences that I cannot enlarge upon here, the fact that both of them were subsequently able to go to their "shrink sessions" very probably helped in breaking the chain of repetitions. When the daughter suggested a name for her mother's dog that also contained an allusion to my own name, this was a further unconscious attempt to extricate herself from the sphere of self-object relations and have me take her place.

In this analysis I invariably felt myself in transference to be the traumatising object (the dead mother that lived on in the child or the sadistic stepmother embodying the diffuse destructiveness arising from the daughter's projective identifications). A mother that abandons her child embodies the all but irreconcilable divide between love and hatred. In transference I had to accept and stand up to this irreconcilability and see whether and how consoling, loving parts might gain the upper hand.

Occasionally there was a danger of my forfeiting my analytic stance in the maelstrom of negative affects. My helplessness expresses itself in self-assertive admonitions ("May I interrupt you for a moment?") or references to law and order ("I have a question. What's with the obligation to keep dogs on a leash in the park?"), because of course these too are only understood in transference. But at the same time they show the necessity of imposing limits when the patient is in danger of losing her own limits and disintegrating. In these situations I was definitely trying to engineer a relatively abrupt change of perspective by assuming the role of father, legislator, third person. But the patient was able to respond to these signals and persist in her analytic work. The point was for the patient to create with me a transitional space with greater possibilities, a space in which she could recognise her own perceptions and learn to distinguish them from mine. With her subsidiary transferences (the animals, the daughter, the neighbours) and her acting out, Ms O was trying in her own way to take pressure off the analysis and me. It is here that we see the roots of her capacity for love. Distance was necessary, achieved by way of the animal kingdom. Only then could structural changes take place.

CHAPTER TWELVE

Love and hate

The patients discussed in this part all suffered traumatic experiences in very early childhood which resulted in persistent splitting processes. In their later lives, other experiences of violence or abuse followed, leaving profound imprints on their personalities and leading (amongst other things) to identification(s) with the aggressor. The case history of Mr G (Chapter Seven) reveals many parallels to the cases we are looking at here: for the child, one of the qualities of the mother's suicide was *violent* destructiveness. But the developments undergone by these patients are complex and dissimilar, thus indicating once again the necessity of an approach specifically geared to each individual.

Of all the patients, Ms A (Chapter Nine) is the one whose infancy we know the least about. But she must have emerged from it with a disturbed or at least too weak an attachment to the mother, as this is the only way we can understand her wayward life as a "stray" shortly before the war. The main concern of analysis was to give Ms A access to her psychic reality. The defence configuration quite definitely had its roots in early childhood. The mother's inadequate psychic presence probably led to the experience of insufficiency in the development of the self; the potential for affect regulation failed to develop fully and with the requisite differentiation, thus establishing a response mode involving denial of reality and the formation of psychosomatic reaction patterns. My impression was that Ms A did not display any autistic features, for that to occur the inadequate mirroring in early childhood would probably have had to be more serious still. But her life was shot through with a leitmotif of "being quiet" and "not feeling" that restricted her psychic space. When the war came, her father could no longer function as a helpful object. Fear for the father, the many experiences of violence during the war, the horrors of the escape, and her mother's final psychic breakdown were the central traumas leading to psychosomatic illness with considerable ego restriction. The presence of her alcoholic colleague will probably have recalled her experiences with her mother.

Mr E (Chapter Ten) was born in 1936, which makes him three years younger than Ms A. He too suffered before the war from a pathological mother–child relationship, albeit one that was completely different from the constellation involving Ms A. From the outset, Mr E was cathected as a narcissistic object; he embodied the mother's ideal self and had little opportunity to develop an identity of his own. This stunted identity was unstable from the beginning and was pressed into service to uphold the mother's narcissistic equilibrium. In many of her actions (attempts at abortion, deprivation of food, punishment during nappy changes) the mother projected her negative self-image intrusively on to the child and subjected the baby to physical abuse. Here I again suspect very early splitting processes. The organismic panic aroused in the infant by hunger and violence led on the one hand to rigid stasis, on the other to persistent fusion with the mother. Here we can observe *in statu nascendi* the oscillation between fusion and objectlessness described by Mentzos (see p. 67; Mentzos, 2009, p. 170). We may legitimately assume that this was the time at which the basis was established for Mr E's psychosomatic problems and his core sexual identity. The perverted behaviour patterns continued with sexual abuse. While the father was out on the battlefield, the patient shared the marital bed with his mother and the mother regularly sucked his penis. Sadistic assaults complete the scenario. The mother was incapable of offering the child any kind of protection against the dangers of war and displacement. The opposite was in fact the case. Mr E took immense care to ensure that his mother did not take her own life. He was parentified. At this point the mother was presumably inextricably bound up with her misery, her unreachable ideals, and her rage, so that at a very early stage Mr E attempted to escape into an anally narcissistic world via splitting processes. The father returned late from the war, a broken man unable to initiate any change for the better. What materialised instead was the perpetuation of a perverted structure in which the irresolvable oedipal conflict formed a vitiated alloy with the trauma of sexual abuse.

For Ms O (Chapter Eleven) the fateful course of events in infancy begins with her grandmother's death and the mother's depression associated with it. We may assume that as an eight-month-old baby, Ms O had developed a concept of mother and non-mother in the way René Spitz and others have described. Her mother's depression may have triggered futile search efforts in the baby to reactivate the mother. André Green (2001) has given us an impressive description of the way in which "white mourning" in the children of depressive mothers can lay the foundations for later depression. The mother's death will probably have exacerbated the constellation and contributed to the cementation of the splitting processes. The suddenness of her death will have brought about a rupture in the inner representation of the ideal mother, which in some children is clearly articulated in connection with eight-month separation anxiety. Destructiveness had to be split off and projected, idealisation was upheld in a rudimentary fashion as there was no real contact with the biological mother. Ms O's great-aunt functioned as an idealised surrogate object. Though she certainly assuaged the pain of loss to some extent, she could not replace the true mother. My conjecture is that in Ms O a fusion core had formed that remained bound up with the genuine, ideal mother. She experienced the outside world as destructive and threatening, which led to the constitution of a paranoid object world menacing the existence of ideality. Day in, day out, the struggles with her sadistic stepmother consolidated and confirmed this condition. As I see it, when the patient lay down on her mother's grave, concretistic fusion took place. The patient attempted to stabilise her defence in a concretistic fashion; lying down on her grave was a bid to be at one with her. The split between material and immaterial reality was designed to help her face up to the bitterness of the present. "It was cold. Then it was good" (p. 184. This was her way of accommodating herself to the trouble and strife of earthly life. She became depressive and stayed that way for good. When she had left her parents' home, she entered into a relationship with a much older man, married him, and had a child. The man was unable to fulfil her unconscious expectations of a protective father. Unconsciously, she had chosen him as a repetition and in the hope of a better solution. Up to the beginning of analysis, the daughter played the role of ideal self in the patient's unconscious. The stepmother provided an opportunity to destroy these projections. The onset of puberty was another reason for the daughter to try to separate herself from the mother. The mother's analysis and the daughter's psychotherapy were a chance to break through the chain of transgenerational identifications.

In all these case histories the perpetuation of splitting processes in early infancy plays a crucial role. But the splitting structures themselves are very different. All of the patients had developed some kind of attachment to the early object, and they were able to preserve it. The relationships of Mr E (Chapter Ten) and Mr G (Chapter Seven) to their mothers displayed a perverted structure that also left its mark on their symptomatologies and the development of their personalities. At the love–hate level they were bound up with their internal objects in a sadomasochistic way and had to learn in analysis the difference between love and hate. Accordingly, it was in my eyes a great step forward in therapy when they were able to admit to their aggressiveness. Mr E chose riding for this purpose, selecting a secondary field of transference and at the same time taking some of the pressure off me. This created a transitional space that permitted symbolisation(s) while leaving me in my role as a potentially loving and beloved object.

Due to her experiences with her stepmother in childhood, Ms O was also forced to identify with a perverted aggressor. The processes she underwent invite similar interpretation. Ultimately both of them became therapeutic riders, doing to their horses what I was doing to them and, as a result, developing internally a better balance between love and hate. These two analyses were twenty years apart; possibly Ms O profited from my experience with Mr E. But there is one essential difference between them. Ms O had suffered traumatic object loss in earliest infancy (the mother died when she was twelve months old). The incursive, sadomasochistic relationship with the stepmother began when she was four years old, that is, at a time when she could already speak and symbolisations and memories were possible. In structural terms, distinctions can be drawn that are similar to those between Ms R and Mr V (Chapter Two), though Mr V suffered traumatisation later than Ms R and was able to benefit from analysis more quickly. Due to the early separation trauma in the first few years of her life, Ms O could not satisfactorily integrate splitting processes at the level of exclusively good and exclusively bad objects. Ideality and delusions of omnipotence had helped the four-year-old girl deny her mother's death. This artificial world caved in with the first conflicts between her stepmother and herself. This critical phase of development is similar to the one undergone by Ms F (Chapter Six) who (albeit at the age of six) was torn out of the narcissistic world that she had fashioned for herself after her mother's death by the arrival of the interloper stepmother.

The hatred these patients had developed, and which to some extent they acted out in sadomasochistic relationships and constantly repeated, was invariably relational and in the course of analysis could be traced back to unconscious processes and the original infant traumas plus transgenerational identifications. In the initial interviews I was able to recognise a degree of potential relatedness that prompted me to recommend high-frequency analysis.

In all three analyses in this part (Ms A, Mr E, and Ms O) there were many critical situations in which the trauma constellation broke through and the analytic setting was in jeopardy. For example, at the height of her hatred of me, Ms A developed a dissociation that can be understood as a psychotic experience. She had the feeling that she was slipping down off the couch (p. 155). My spontaneous remark: "I'm still here!" preserved her from further decompensation and we were able to work through her anxieties and aggressions. My exclamation had re-established a relationship that carried. Mr E experienced something similar when he caused a road accident and rode in the hearse. In the subsequent telephone interview it was important for me to feel what he had experienced so that I could look "in one direction" with him (p. 169 et seq.). Ms O had to interrupt analysis and walk out on myself and her daughter because she felt overpowered by me and was unable to clarify her hatred of me in the transference. Only later was she in a position to recognise her identifications with the aggressor.

One thing all these analyses have in common is that the acting out of destructive affect irruptions jeopardised the analytic relationship. The presence of the analyst ("I'm still here!"—"May I interrupt you?") prevented (further) derailments and helped integrate the hate. This procedure is indicative of my analytic stance and the implicit theory associated with it. The reactivation of a feeling of security in the relationship was able to bind the hatred so that we could work on it further at a later stage. This course of events corresponds to the development processes the patients had lived through in reverse order. Over-arousal and panic had *not* been taken up and bound by a protective other; *no* satisfactory equilibrium was established in early infancy between the development of healthy narcissism and trusting relatedness.

The analyses demonstrate the diversity of potential resistance phenomena (acting out, transference splitting, discontinuation of analysis, etc.). In every case, the point at issue is recognition of one's own hatred and the feelings of shame associated with it. The sheer force of destructiveness has the potential to destroy the relationship, which must of course be prevented at all costs. Both analysand and analyst aim at attaining a feeling of security that counteracts these tendencies, indeed they can tacitly agree to a joint level of resistance (Focke, 2010). If the feelings of hatred in the relationship can be identified and interpreted, then the integration of loving and hating affects in the transference object is conceivable (Henningsen, 2011c). There are many instances of this in the treatments we have been discussing, for example, Mr E discovering me as a "flesh and blood person" or referring to my "cuddly" pullover. The same is true of Ms O, who in the middle of a depressive crisis suffused with hatred suddenly said she would have killed herself if it hadn't been for me and her daughter. Invariably there is an—albeit reticent—degree of loving affection that prevents the worst. In this, the attachment to the transference object has an integrating and life-preserving function (Fonagy & Target, 2002). In my thoughts on compulsive repetition I have indicated that repetition and acting out are not only geared to pure destruction, they also contain the tacit hope of being understood (cf. Mentzos, 2009, p. 255 et seq.; p. 137 et seq. in this book).

There are however conditions under which it is impossible (or only partly possible) to activate these last vestiges of relatedness. In the case of severe personality disorders and extremely narcissistic and/or psychotic states, exclusive self-relatedness can thwart any kind of relationship. In her book *Escape from Selfhood* (2007), Ilany Kogan has impressively described the "breaking [of] analytic boundaries" (pp. 23–31) and "the craving for oneness" (pp. 63–65). She focuses on the mode of existence of severely traumatised individuals as one that cannot be coped with because they can neither live in a relationship nor stand to be alone. Borders are torn down, the analyst is swept into a maelstrom of affects and runs the risk of acting out countertransference feelings.

In her harrowing report, Kogan describes the depths plumbed by her patient David and her own fantasies and anxieties indicating how she (herself a survivor of the Holocaust) was in danger of succumbing to her patient's projective identifications, for example, when she almost cancelled a journey for fear of finding that her patient might be staying at the same hotel.

Neither his surviving parents nor David himself had been able to retain their extremely traumatic experiences, let alone mentalize and symbolise them. In the Nazi era, the patient's mother had been massively abused and threatened; after the birth of her son she became severely ill. Other menaces followed, including a cancer illness that was probably a further and crucial motive for her suicide at the age of fifty-four. David was also fifty-four when he came for analysis, himself entertaining thoughts of suicide. His desire was to be at one with his mother in the grave. The catastrophic development hit new heights when during the period of his analysis his son, Avi, killed himself. He too was obviously driven by menace and destruction, was unable to find support anywhere, and acted out what his father was feeling.

When in the further course of analysis the patient seeks out the place where his son took his own life and investigates the circumstances and the degree to which he may possibly be to blame for his son's act, he establishes something in the presence of his analyst: "Yes, that was the scene of the crime." This sentence can be directly related to the analysis and marks a turning point in treatment. The trauma is acknowledged, it becomes psychic reality (cf. p. 134 and Chapter Nine). The analysis becomes the scene of the crime or rather the many crimes compounded into each and every action handed down from one generation to the next and leaving their mark on the transference. As I see it, the patient now succeeds in changing his perspective, which makes him able to contemplate his own fate. The patient's manic defence changes to severe depression, opening up opportunities for the work of mourning. He can now recognise and work on his identifications as a potential murderer.

Again, this case gives us an opportunity to look at the fate of affect splitting (love and hate) in transgenerational terms. Under the conditions imposed by manic defence, the role of "oneness" was to save both parties (mother and son, in transference analyst and patient) from total collapse and intolerable affects. Presumably, the sick and severely traumatised mother had split off her untenable destructive experience and projected it on to the child; neither the mother nor the child could deal with the affects. Mother and child were doomed to fusion for life; it was a case of "self-object fusion as the core of the traumatic experience"

(Bohleber, 2007, p. 342). This fusion knows no transitional space (Winnicott, 1955), which is what makes the impulses appear so compelling in transference. The split-off affect cannot be mentalized and leads to enactment, symptoms, and unremitting defence strategies that bind the partners to one another all their lives. When David reaches the age at which his mother died, his defence collapses. He wants to unite with his mother via suicide and concretistically lie down with her in her grave. I have described this kind of oneness in the destructive affect as concretistic fusion and conceptualised it as a special form of projective identification (Henningsen, 2008; cf. thoughts on concretistic fusion in this book, Ms R, Ms S, Ms F, Ms O, and Mr V).

Emergence from this fusion is invariably bound up with special hazards because it is this that opens up "the journey to pain", as Ilany Kogan reminds us (Kogan, 2007, pp. 60–61). I can imagine that the concretistic fusion in which David lived with his mother was disrupted in his fifty-fourth year. The apparent inevitability of suicide made him seek analysis. It seems fair to assume that his son, Avi, was drawn into the apparently inexorable sequence of these fusions. In identification with his father he sought out highly perilous war scenes, seeking perhaps in this way (like his father) to externalise the inner part-objects so as to win control over them. This defence broke down. The psychoanalyst became the observer involved in the chain of disasters. She succeeded in resolving the destructive fusions with the patient, thus making the establishment of limits possible. But the father's progress came too late for his son.

Because the analytic relationship is invariably the medium in which analysis takes place, it is especially difficult to conceive of, and deal with, instances of extreme self-relatedness. In his model, Bion attempted to get a hold on these phenomena by conceptualising the split between the material and the immaterial world (Bion, 1962, p. 10; cf. Chapter Four). "Fear, hate and envy are so feared that steps are taken to destroy the awareness all feelings, although that is indistinguishable from taking life itself" (Bion, 1962, p. 10). Bion describes the materialisation of this splitting as a defence "enforced by starvation and fear of death through starvation on the one hand, and by love and the fear of associated murderous envy and hate on the other" (ibid., p. 11). He is patently describing the psychic conditions of infant traumatisation without actually using the word "trauma". These splitting processes culminate in structures in which the individual one-sidedly strives for material gratification and is driven by a desire to "to be rid of [...] a relationship with live objects" (ibid.). Severe addictions, suicidal states, anti-social tendencies, psychoses, and severe narcissistic personality disorders are syndromes in which these splitting structures play a role. Here the emphasis can differ, ranging from one-sided identification with the material side of things (as in addictions, adiposity, etc.) or a rejection of materiality manifesting itself in one-sided identification with the lifeless world of inanimate objects (anorexia nervosa, extreme narcissism, psychosis). In either case, the link between love and hate, self-love and object-love is disrupted.

Extreme forms of hatred—as exemplified today by rampage killers and terrorists running amok and seeing themselves as martyrs sacrificing their lives for some doctrine of redemption—are an example of the potential consequences of a state of total splitting between material and psychic reality (cf. Chapter Sixteen, "Trauma in society and politics"). In extreme narcissistic delusions of grandeur, existential tensions between psyche and soma, life and death are transformed into absolute certainties that dematerialise and dehumanise the world; hatred is lived out in an idea or a fantasy, and there is no *feeling* for what happens to the victims and the world.

In the patients discussed here, such extreme destructiveness only surfaces occasionally. In the case of Mr E (Chapter Ten), the abusive and perverted mother–child relationship triggered bodily dispossession that secured his survival. His narcissistic development and the not-feeling of his member as a part of his body can be construed as instances of splitting between material and immaterial reality. Studying theology and working out his own very personal version of Christian faith were certainly also helpful possibilities for sublimation creating links between love and hate.

With the help of the second dream she told me about, Ms A (Chapter Nine) took me into her split-off, narcissistically destructive world. The stone had become a symbol for inanimate material that had to be fluidised in analysis so that the traumatic experiences lodged in the patient's psychic space could be recognised, called by name, and retained.

In Ms O (Chapter Eleven) we find little of the splitting structure we have just described. This is only surprising at first glance because she largely bound her affects via fusion with persons close to her: as a child in the grave with dead mother (I have discussed this in terms of concretistic fusion), later via projective identification with her daughter, her animals, and other people. From this we can also draw conclusions about the severity of the disorder. In Ms O the object precursors were probably a little better internalised than, say, in the case of Mr E, whose mother, as he knew from reports by others, was prone to giving him a severe dressing-down while she was changing his nappies.

PART IV

EXPERIENCES OF VIOLENCE AND ABUSE
IN ADULTHOOD: TORTURE AND WAR

CHAPTER THIRTEEN

Post-traumatic stress disorder

Splitting processes in transference

The following sections examine the psychic consequences of severe traumas caused by war, torture, and involuntary exile (Henningsen, 2003, 2004a, 2004b). In my capacity as a psychological consultant for residential-permit issues (Haenel & Wenk-Ansohn, 2004), I have talked to and assessed many refugees applying for asylum in Germany. Assessors and their expert opinions are located in the institutional interzone between alien-registration offices, law courts, and the police. The analyst's job in such a context is the practice of "applied psychoanalysis", which is quite patently a task located in the socio-political sphere. It requires the analyst to modify her attitude and also, of course, to reflect very seriously on the role played by transference and countertransference. Difficulties encountered by other professionals involved in this process are frequently caused by unconscious transference and countertransference processes impacting on their perception of things and potentially influencing the accuracy of their assessments. It is frequently impossible for doctors, lawyers, psychologists, and psychotherapists inexperienced in dealing with severely traumatised individuals to recognise the severe disorders of the ego functions caused by trauma. Also, the expert opinion delivered by the analyst is an official document, and the non-private nature of the process leading to it contrasts with the intimacy of the analytic situation as it is normally understood. Probands interviewed to assess their entitlement to (continued) residence know that whatever they say can be made use of in court. Under certain circumstances, the opinion of the examining psychologist may be read by judges, lawyers, doctors, members of the foreign residents' authorities, and family members.

Although refugees are told that the institutions involved rely heavily on their statements, they may still—like any extremely traumatised individual—be unable to talk about their experiences. Typical of trauma is the severe nature of the dissociations involved, the inability to mentalize experiences, to give a logical account of temporal processes. This makes it near-imperative for trauma sufferers to be entrusted to the care of psychoanalysts, who after all are specifically schooled in the art of recognising traumatic processes, responding to unconscious communication and non-verbal enactments, gradually elevating them to the symbolic plane, and—where appropriate—helping their charges give a name to them. Psychoanalysts can help trauma sufferers decipher their traumas. During the assessment process they can help them bear witness to their own malady and thus acknowledge their traumas (Laub & Weine, 1994, p. 1118). In the diagnostic assessment of traumatised refugees applying for asylum, power and powerlessness are crucial modes of experience in transference and countertransference. The following influences need to be borne in mind:

- individually experienced intrusive traumas that cannot be mentalized and/or symbolised and thus have a direct impact on the assessor's subconscious;
- individually warded-off traumatisation and its latent effect on the interaction process;
- influences from collective memory and the individual's personal trauma history on present situations marked by persecution, torture, and war;
- influences from institutions and administrative courts, and difficulties in recognising the impossibility (for the victim) of putting the trauma into words.

This chapter is given over to systematic reflection on the specific transference processes characteristic of acutely traumatised individuals and a discussion of the intervention techniques that suggest themselves as a result. Chapter Fourteen illustrates appropriate procedures with reference to actual case histories.

Post-traumatic stress disorder (PTSD) was first described in the framework of the research and therapeutic attention dedicated to the veterans of the Vietnam War. In 1980 it found its way into the American diagnosis manual and ten years later into its international counterpart (ICD-10). All over the world, this process bestowed greater attention and recognition on psychic trauma as a cause of illness. The cases discussed in Parts I to III of this book would all qualify as cases of complex post-traumatic stress disorder, a concept introduced by Judith Herman (1992) to extend the range of symptomatologies covered by ICD-10. Psychoanalysts have trouble categorising their patients in terms of ICD-10 because the manual fails to take account of essential psychodynamic factors and ignores important dimensions of psychic disorder. Stavros Mentzos has pointed this out in no uncertain terms in his *Lehrbuch der Psychodynamik* ("Manual of Psychodynamics") (2009).

The distinction made by Mathias Hirsch between relational traumas and acute traumatisation is usually more meaningful (Hirsch, 2011, p. 41). But because the classifications in ICD-10 (or DSM-IV) are obviously necessary for political communication, and the clients I intend to discuss all suffered from PTSD in the narrower sense, let us first attempt to draw upon actual practice in this sector and reframe PTSD in a psychodynamic version that includes transference processes.

PTSD as set out in ICD-10 and DSM-IV is a descriptive diagnosis geared to the symptoms displayed. If the diagnostic findings are to be used for the indication guidelines and treatment planning of psychoanalytically oriented psychotherapy, it needs to be reframed in psychodynamic terms.

Table 1, an overview taken from Oliver Schubbe (2004, p. 15) and updated, sets out the most important features of PTSD. It lists specific features and makes reference to the time factor, that is, the beginning and end of the disorder. Accordingly, the emphasis is on objectifiability.

Reacting to a traumatic event (acute stress reaction, column 1) with a degree of decompensation is relatively normal and usually also appropriate. Some people manage to restore their psychic balance relatively quickly, some will react more extremely than others. But depending on the extent of the trauma, between ten and thirty per cent of the persons affected will suffer from lasting psychic damage. The likelihood of traumatisation in the form of PTSD is probably highest after aggression

Table 1. Psychic trauma sequels listed in ICD-10 and DSM-IV.

	1) Acute stress reaction	2) Post-traumatic stress disorder	3) Permanent personality change after extreme stress
	DSM-IV 309.8 ICD-10 F 43.0	DSM-IV 309.81 ICD-10 F 43.1	ICD-10 F 62.0
Symptoms	ICD-10: initial emotional numbing, then alternating depression, irritation, despair, hyperactivity, and withdrawal DSM-IV: dissociative reactions	Flashbacks, nightmares, avoidance behaviour, amnesia, emotional numbness, anhedonia, hopelessness, permanent over-arousal, heightened vigilance, disturbed sleep, poor concentration, memory lapses, increased apprehension, irritability	Suspicion, social withdrawal, feelings of emptiness and hopelessness, chronic nervousness plus constant feeling of threat, alienation
Time	ICD-10: some minutes to max. 3 days after the event DSM-IV: 2 days to max. 1 month	Longer than 1 month; may occur after latency periods of weeks, months or years	Symptoms lasting at least 2 years No previous personality disorder, no organic brain disorder

inflicted by humans on humans (abuse, torture, war). Severe illness and natural disasters figure somewhat less prominently. These patients are accounted for in the columns on PTSD and/or those on permanent changes to the personality. The distinction is important because it casts light on the question of when trauma therapists (in the narrower sense) are required and when they are not. In the first stage (column 1) I would consider it indicated to support the natural remedial forces of potential spontaneous remission. In the case of natural disasters, for example, the first things needed are warm blankets, food, finding relatives, etc. In other words, the prime requirement is to create conditions that restore security and trust in the workings of the world.

Collective trauma therapies as conducted, for example, after 9/11 appear to me highly dubious and indeed misguided. It transpires that many individuals only fell ill after "trauma exposure" or "debriefing" (cf. Ehlers, 1999; Fischer, 2000; Sachsse, 2004). When deciding on the indication issue, attention should be paid instead to the significance of resilience factors and the pre-traumatic personality for both diagnosis and therapy. In general, it is fair to say that people react highly individually to a traumatic event, essential factors being the severity of the trauma, the personality structure of the victim, the conditions prevailing in their lives, and the state of their development. The diversity of these dimensions manifests itself in the distortions and splitting processes of transference and countertransference. Here it is important to recognise and acknowledge two fundamental differences in the emotional situation of the assessor and the refugee that depend on the severity of the proband's disturbance and dictate the relation to the examiner: 1) the avoidant form of PTSD held in latency; 2) the intrusive, manifest form of PTSD.

These two "versions" of chronic PTSD should be envisioned as the endpoints of a continuum. The states may fluctuate in traumatised individuals, sometimes even within one and the same session. The kind of relationship conditioned by the respective manifestation form is also to be found outside the assessment situation, for example, with physicians, authorities, or the family. But therapists working with psychoanalysis and depth psychology are trained and conditioned to recognise these dynamics and to draw upon them for therapeutic purposes. Here it is essential to distinguish between feeling and reaction in the assessor. Tables 2 and 3 below indicate potential countertransference feelings and the countertransference reactions they engender.

PTSD: the avoidant variety

Processes keeping traumatic experiences and intrusions in latency or even encapsulating them have been frequently described in psychoanalytic literature (Bohleber, 2010, pp. 75–100; Henningsen, 1990, 2003; Chapter Seven). Holocaust research has also familiarised us with the

Table 2. PTSD with intrusions largely held in latency: potential transferences and countertransferences.

Symptoms	Countertransference feeling	Countertransference reaction
Somatisations	"(Pseudo-)normal feeling"	Disturbed empathy, distancing
High adaptation	Emptiness, admiration	Denial of illness
Partial thought disorders	Insecurity	Denial
Partial dissociations	Insecurity	Substitution or denial
Affective impoverishment	Depression, emptiness	Over-identification, distancing
Symbolisation disorders	Emptiness	Slight thought disorder, enactment
Avoidance behaviour	Anxiety (may recall own trauma)	Avoidance behaviour
General life restriction	Pressure, fatigue	"Bossing", neglect
Neurotic function level outside trauma sector	As with other patients	As with other patients

process of transgenerational identification: the warded-off trauma is transferred to the next generation and in the second or even third generation may lead to severe psychic disorders (Chapter Seven).

A patient suffering from acute trauma differs significantly from a traumatised patient whose traumatic experience lies in the past and who has succeeded in encapsulating the trauma or holding it in latency. Patients of the latter kind will come for frequent analysis; they suffer from a variety of symptoms, usually display a relatively restricted symbolisation disorder, and normally function at a neurotic level. In the course of analysis the trauma comes to the surface, and if patient and analyst succeed in mastering the extremely difficult transference relationship, the patient will be able to integrate and symbolise the trauma in a satisfactory manner. Confrontation with a traumatised patient suffering from a manifest, intrusive form of PTSD gives the therapist an opportunity to observe *in statu nascendi* what the avoidant patient is at such pains to ward off. As we have said, the two states—intrusive PTSD

Table 3. Intrusive PTSD: potential transferences and countertransferences.

Symptoms	Countertransference feeling	Countertransference reaction
Dissociations	Chaos	Thought disorders
Panic, intrusions	Overstimulation	Empathy disturbance
Stupor, rigidity	Rage, emotional restriction	Paralysis, over-reaction
Paranoid mistrust	Paranoid mistrust	Persecutory interview technique
Anxiety	Anxiety	Avoidance behaviour, flight
Motoric restlessness	Aggression, helplessness	Enactment, somatic reactions
Powerlessness, infantility	Shame, guilt, impatience, rage	Over-identification, bossing, helper syndrome
	Recalls own trauma?	Loss of distance, fending off depressive feelings
Borderline level/ psychosis	Lack of object-relation	Bossing the patient

as opposed to the avoidant form of chronic PTSD in which the trauma is held in latency or possibly even encapsulated—need to be regarded as two ends of a continuum. Reality for the individual patient is normally located between the two poles and may fluctuate. For example, a refugee may experience the assessment situation—the initial transference offer—as a repetition of an interrogation by the police or of actual persecution. The result is paranoid mistrust with intrusive symptoms. In others, the death of a family member at home may lead to renewed intrusions fully comparable to PTSD and hence to decompensation (reactualisation).

Refugee families frequently display the following structure: one family member (usually a parent) suffers from PTSD with all its manifestations, the others are occupied round the clock with looking after the trauma victim; by way of projective identification, these family members may project their own sufferings on to the seriously ill father or mother. They ward off their own anguish by caring for the patient. In such a case, the PTSD patient assumes the role of symptom-bearer for the whole family. Accordingly, it is important to include family-dynamic considerations in diagnosis and therapy for these patients.

Splitting-off or encapsulation can frequently be observed in refugee children. Normally they have experienced the same situations as their parents but feel the helplessness and panic bound up with them not only directly but also through the parents they identify with. Normally it is impossible to find words for the traumatic experiences they have been through together. In these children, attachment to the parents mobilises many successful efforts of a defensive and adaptive nature that help them to cope with life in their new environment. They frequently speak excellent German, their performance at school is unimpeachable, they function as auxiliary egos for the parents when they translate for them during appointments with the authorities or with doctors. The pressure on them is enormous, for example, when they have to describe their parents' illnesses to complete strangers or give an account of traumatic experiences in the war. What applies to interpreters (cf. p. 217 et seq.) applies equally to these children. They have to split off their affects in order to accomplish the task they have been set. As the children have an emotional attachment to their parents and have to provide them with protection and care, the long-term result of all this may be serious cases of parentification and attachments disfigured by guilt. Teachers frequently report that these children "function" extremely well, they never cause any trouble in class, they are over-adjusted and at the same time completely overtaxed because their own traumas are held in latency. Here we can observe development processes leading to results well-known from the accounts of the sufferings incurred by the second and third generations after extreme cases of traumatisation.

PTSD: the intrusive variety

Individuals suffering from the intrusive form of PTSD are mercilessly exposed to intrusions and have no adequate stimulus protection at their disposal. This exerts a very great strain on the people trying to help them. Trauma victims are completely unable to cope with their feelings, and those feelings become directly and intrusively manifest in their vis-à-vis without any protective membrane or cognitive processing. In the interview situation—sometimes only for brief moments—fusions occur that can trigger massive countertransference reactions. This is very probably the reason for the burnout syndromes affecting so many trauma therapists.

As we saw in Chapter Four, Splitting and fusion, these fusions are themselves defence mechanisms. The unbearable affect is split off and projected directly onto the therapist's unconscious. What this is designed to ward off is a state of total depletion tantamount to the experience of psychic non-existence. These are extreme existential experiences for which there are no words. Time stands still, there is no past, no future, no feeling. The only way of protecting the patient from such extreme states is to mobilise resilience. For this purpose, therapists must on the one hand empathise with the patient's psychic situation while at the same time maintaining their capacity for distance in order to be able to hold and understand the patient. This is most likely to succeed if the therapist draws upon her heightened sensitivity with regard to transference and countertransference.

Like quasi-psychotic micro-impulses, the split-off feelings of the trauma patient impinge directly on the feelings of the vis-à-vis and provoke rejective reactions. Also, the perception function in the interview situation is particularly susceptible to the effects of these splitting phenomena, and it is essential to be inwardly prepared to initially achieve no more than the recognition of individual parts of the person in question. To grasp the implications for countertransference, it is important to distinguish between the trauma patient's introjected or empathically perceived feeling and the analyst's subsequent reaction (emotional and mental processing). These crack points can often be identified and reconstructed in supervision. In the record of the session there is a sudden "blip" or *non sequitur* in the analyst's train of thought. Asked after her countertransference feelings, the supervisee remembers a whole range of overpowering feelings that she attempted to ward off in the real situation by means of avoidance.

In this context, the presence of interpreters is frequently helpful. The role they play merits closer scrutiny. As they act as a go-between, the analyst will not perceive the proband's facial reactions and the content of what he says at once but only after a delay. This can protect both of them from over-exposure to stimuli and the proband from renewed traumatisation. The fact that form and content are out of phase in this way is especially important as in connection with the description of a traumatic event it reflects a kind of splitting. The feelings of shock and/or expressive stasis are communicated directly, but analysts will be apprised of the appalling content a little later than it is uttered. In other words, they register the traumatic event in stages, which gives them time to "steel" themselves and thus protects them from sudden alarm and potential empathy inhibitions. Vice versa, probands can observe the analyst's out-of-phase perception. As they speak, they can observe the analyst's empathy, and later, when the interpreter speaks, the patient can recognise whether the analyst already has an inkling or premonition of the content enabling her to grasp the essential feeling and how much new, and perhaps dreadful, information the interpreter may later supply.

This latency period is marked by a special atmosphere engendered by processing at the preverbal level. In equal measure, but in opposite perceptual directions, both analyst and proband are concerned with piecing together content and emotion. This can initiate mentalization processes (Varvin, 2000). By contrast, the interpreter is permanently and unremittingly concerned with the communication of intrusive content and thus requires special supervision.

The seating arrangement for interpreter, proband, and therapist/ diagnostician should be a triangle with the chairs equidistant from one another. This needs to be "staged" beforehand, so that there is adequate space for the participants to look at or past each other, as they feel the need. One frequently observes that at the beginning of such sessions interpreter and proband automatically move closer together. This can lead to a fusion between the two native speakers. The therapist is left on the outside, while in the dual union essential affects are regulated, split off, or projected on to the therapist. Enactments of this kind can seriously interfere with the process of diagnosis and therapy.

At the beginning of the relationship, the trauma patient can hardly take advantage of the potential for successive perception. The analyst clearly senses the rupture of contact, the patient's withdrawal into hopelessness and inertia. But in time, when the hope of being understood has grown a little, the trauma patient can periodically take advantage of this space. By observing the analyst's face, the patient can see how a picture is forming in her mind, followed by a comment, a supportive intervention, another question, or an interpretation. Periodically, and then only temporarily, integrative processes may take place via identification. Accordingly, analysts can learn a great deal about dissociating processes and train themselves not to overlook, but to recognise and acknowledge, them (Gerzi, 2002). In so doing, they learn to restrict themselves to naming the split-off feelings only. They realise that they cannot obtain a unified picture of a refugee's personality in one sole session; they learn to work with fragments and to show the patients that they are fully aware of the fragmentary nature of the knowledge they can glean. They desist from forming things prematurely into wholes in order to reassure themselves, because if they did, they would certainly abandon these refugees to their anguish.

Therapists and diagnosticians working with traumatised individuals should always have worked through their own trauma histories before they start (Fischer & Riedesser, 1998). Only then will there be a chance for them to understand their countertransference and make constructive use of it (cf. Chapter Sixteen).

Structuring psychotherapy and probationary sessions

Therapists and diagnosticians need to listen to PTSD patients differently from the way they listen to psycho-neurotic patients. In each individual case, the degree of structuring required will make itself felt during the probationary sessions and subsequently (in the treatment phase) be a function of the modified psychoanalytic procedure. The technique appropriate for the verbal exchanges themselves will fluctuate between free-floating attention and exploration, as the case requires. The assessor plays things by ear; the patient is incapable of free association and, unlike the normal procedure with analysands, is not explicitly encouraged to attempt it. But assessors/therapists observe their transference and countertransference reactions, to which they then gear the exploratory questions and supportive interventions. Possible dissociations require special containment protecting the patient from further decompensation while preserving at all costs the security of the setting.

Much as in initial psychoanalytic interviews, the investigator's job is to find out what level the patient is functioning at—regression or defence. Assessor analysts need to keep a close eye on their own activities if they are to correctly establish diagnosis and indication. Crucial is the assessment of dissociative disorders. The severity of the disorder and the nature of the task in hand (assessment or therapy) calls for a structuring of the interview along the following lines:

- introductory stage: symptomatology, present life situation (recognition of dissociations)
- biographic details: pre-traumatic development

- specific trauma anamnesis
- closing stage: explanation of the diagnosis plus counselling.

In the interests of a good relationship, it is advisable, once the patient's present life situation has been mapped out, to talk to the patient about his life history *prior to* traumatisation. If patients can indicate that the life they led before trauma was different from what it is now, this is tantamount to informing the therapist that what has happened to them is an irruption, it has nothing to do with the way they had originally planned their lives. They may even be able to recognise how their development has been stunted, how and to what degree they have lost their identity. Here resilience factors identifiable in anamnesis play a major role. In certain situations, they may help patients to mobilise their own resources and regain dignity. Also, the analyst will obtain some idea of the patient's pre-traumatic personality structure. This is of course essential for differential diagnosis, but if the therapist knows how patients coped with earlier crises and what their life situation was before the trauma struck, then it will also be easier, when working on the trauma at a later stage, to match the therapeutic approach to the individual client. In this way, patients will be less suspicious of the situation and sense that the analyst is interested in their entire personalities. It establishes a kind of working alliance that will make it easier to weather the stormier passages in later therapy. The recourse to affectionate experiences, good inner objects, and successful instances of self-assertion in the analytic procedure is quite definitely comparable to the establishment of the "secure inner place" propagated by Luise Reddemann (2011).

Both in the diagnostic phase and later during psychotherapy proper it may be necessary to employ trauma-specific interventions such as directly addressing patients to jolt them out of a dissociative state. It may be both appropriate and necessary to apply a variety of stabilisation techniques described in detail in the literature (Plassmann, 2007; Reddemann & Wöller, 2011; Rosenberg, 2010; Sachsse, 2004). Where depth-psychological psychotherapy is indicated, I would suggest proceeding in line with the motto "as little as possible, as much as necessary". This will help ensure that the integration process proper is not disturbed and can proceed at a speed appropriate for individual patients so that they have time to grow and to grieve over their fate. Where modified psychoanalytic psychotherapy is indicated, active used of relaxation technique is not normally required because the transference processes provide support and orientation and can be interpreted accordingly. When the therapeutic relationship has been placed on a solid footing and the patient experiences the analyst as reliable, supportive, and fully involved, the time has come to start addressing the trauma. In this process, "trauma exposure" enacted or planned by the therapist is detrimental rather than beneficial (cf. p. 213). This exposure takes place more or less automatically as a function of the analytic or depth-psychology-oriented procedure, which I believe to be more organic and more conducive to the patient's recovery. "Trauma exposure" along more or less well-defined lines invariably establishes the therapist as an omnipotent object. The patient is relegated to inferiority and powerlessness, which in its turn is harmful to the necessary development of autonomy and ego-strength.

CHAPTER FOURTEEN

Negative countertransference: depletion and resilience

The resolution passed by the Conference of German Ministers of the Interior (23–24 November 2000) has created a new basis for deciding on applications by refugees from former Yugoslavia for the right of residence in Germany. It states that refugees from Bosnia-Herzegovina, Sandžak, and Kosovo are entitled to such a permit if they have been traumatised by the events of the civil war. The investigations discussed in this chapter took place in my practice in the framework of my activity as an assessor for refugees applying for asylum in Berlin. I had been asked to act in this capacity by the administrative court.

Common to all these cases is that they initially triggered in me a negative countertransference that I had to reflect on if I intended to acquit myself responsibly of the task in hand. It was also particularly necessary to recognise resilience factors so that they could be referred to at an appropriate point in the patient-therapist exchange. To encourage a feeling of security and a good working alliance during the sessions, it is necessary to explain the setting and clarify the parameters.

At the start of the first session, I would say something like this:

> You know that the administrative court has asked me to act as an assessor in connection with the traumas you have suffered. I know from the files that

you have been through some very difficult experiences in the past few years and I also know how hard it is for you to talk about them. But if you want to obtain recognition as a refugee traumatised by the war, I need to learn as much as I can about your experiences and your present condition. I should like to talk to you about all this in as relaxed a manner as possible. We have plenty of time. One session always lasts fifty minutes, we'll be meeting a number of times, the interpreter will always be on hand. That means that you can speak your native language. This is very important, so that you can express yourself precisely as you feel.

I then inform the patient that as an agent of the court I am not sworn to silence.

Normally the trauma patients respond to this offer with extreme suspicion, or they say things like "I have lost all faith in the future" or "I don't believe you can help me."

Mr D: suspicion and splitting-off of violence

First session: recognition of dissociations

Mr D (Henningsen, 2003, p. 113 et seq.) came to me for an assessment commissioned by the administrative court pertaining to his right of residence. I had been asked to determine whether he was suffering from PTSD.

In his home country he had been a crane-driver. He arrived at the first session making a contemptuous gesture in my direction. Like a pubescent teenager he wore a baseball cap with the peak turned backwards. He was in his early thirties, very thick-set; my countertransference was marked by antagonism and suspicion. With his wrong-way-round baseball cap, he came across as cynical and scornful, an adolescent attitude that did not fit in at all with his overall appearance. He weighed 115 kilos, his massive physique gave him an air of brutality, as if he might be a dangerous criminal. For one brief moment I asked myself whether this might not be someone fully prepared to pull the wool over my eyes in order to obtain a residence permit. But my suspicions quickly evaporated. I soon realised that I was in the presence of a fragmented self that came at me in ways that were both disparate and contradictory. He was in such a state of tension that he could not sit still, he trembled violently from time to time, wept, clenched his fists to work off his arousal. His diction was terse, his delivery staccato, his gaze dismissive.

He was unable to give a temporally cogent account of his experiences, only incoherent bits and pieces.

I attempted to obtain an overview of his present situation, his life in Berlin, his symptoms, his experiences with the authorities. He was one of those refugees who had initially been allowed to work for a few months, but now that the administrative regulations had tightened, he had been out of a job for quite a while. This had made him contemplate emigrating to America. He displayed the classical symptoms of severe PTSD: anxieties, sleep disorders, flashbacks, depressive episodes. Since his arrival in Germany (1993) his original weight (68 kilos) had doubled. He had tried in vain to assuage the constant tension that tormented him day and night with guzzling bouts.

Brutality, fear, adolescent scorn, criminal leanings, temporal chaos, and helplessness were the main fragments I sensed within myself. The manner of speaking was jerky and incoherent. I tried to give a name to the self-parts that I registered. Sometimes I succeeded in connecting them with the feelings I perceived. I offered myself as a mirror and tried to piece together a picture of his present situation, the facts of which were (partly) recorded in his file.

I feel it to be essential that at the initial contact one should not expect too much of oneself or the situation. Verbal exchange is repeatedly interrupted by hiatuses in which dissociations are at work. Glib "understanding" will encourage an inappropriate, omnipotent countertransference situation and harry the refugee further still into a position of hopelessness and powerlessness.

I concluded the first session with Mr D like this: "You have experienced terrible things, things that are beyond words. You would like to forget everything, but you cannot, again and again the tension mounts within you and you try to calm yourself down by eating. I want us to try to understand what you have experienced. That will take time, and if I am to see what significance the war events have for you, I also need to know something about your life before the war. I think the first thing we should talk about next time is your earlier development."

Second session: pre-traumatic biography—pre-traumatic personality

Mr D came to the next session without his baseball cap, thus indicating his willingness to co-operate. My suggestion that we might talk first about his early childhood obviously came as a relief. He may also have sensed that I was interested in him as a whole person, although he could not have put this into words.

Mr D comes from a very ordinary family. Even before the war he had not been accustomed to talking about feelings, but emotional actions were quite common with him. In this session his narrative style was more coherent than in the first, though here again he was not able to give an ordered, sequential account of his life: accordingly, many supportive interventions were necessary on my part.

Mr D was born in 1969 as the first of two same-sex, non-identical twins. His father worked in a factory, his mother in a textile mill. The parents were very proud of their two boys, they were often spoiled and given preferential treatment over and against their older sisters (two years and four years older). They wore the same clothing, were in the same class at school, and played with each other a great deal. Mr D's brother resembled his father, Mr D was more like his mother. He was always the livelier of the two, his brother was quieter and frequently ill. As the parents both went out to work, the brothers were looked after by their grandmother, who lived close by. The whole set-up was very similar to an extended family. Mr D spoke of his parents in an idealising manner, describing them as kind, helpful, and much respected in the village community. After attending school for twelve years, Mr D embarked on his training as a building machine operator.

Two traumatic events left a serious mark on his development. Playing cowboys and Indians at the age of six, he shot a stone at a glass plate and the shards injured one of his eyes. Despite a remedial operation he lost the sight of his damaged eye. Throughout his three-month stay in hospital his mother was with him at all times. At the age of sixteen, his brother was killed in a road accident. The family were on the way home from a wedding celebration in two different cars. His brother and a cousin died in the accident. I was able to show Mr D how much he had been suffering from unconscious guilt feelings, as it was a complete coincidence that his weaker brother had been in the doomed car. He wept and insisted that while he could live with the partial loss of his sight, his brother's death was much harder to take. My interpretation visibly took much of the strain off Mr D and he began to talk about his brother. It had never occurred to him that his wildness in comparison with his brother might cause feelings of guilt or that he might feel to blame for being in the other car. It now became possible for him to speak critically about the way his mother had narcissistically idolised him as the first-born son. The further course of the session proved how helpful it had been to address this part of his biography before coming round to the wartime events.

Third session: traumatic development during the war

Mr D arrived at the third session with an air of grim determination. During his description of the traumatic wartime events his verbal delivery was frequently accompanied by trembling and tension. He clenched his fists, periodically jerked a leg forward or moved his knee back and forth. These physical impulses were motoric reactions stemming from his introjected experiences of violence, the emotional force of which was beyond his powers of verbal communication. They ran parallel and were split off, he spoke monotonously, his voice displaying no emotional modulations, his delivery was staccato, the sentences often incomplete, and he avoided eye contact. Details from his file enabled me to put things in the proper chronological order and to frame my questions accordingly. Mr D attempted to give an account of himself without any emotional involvement. I responded supportively to what he said, thus enabling him to continue. With my help I wanted him to give an eye-witness report, a documentary account of what had happened. The reconstruction of past reality is an important precondition for the success of integration processes (cf. Laub & Weine, 1994).

In 1987 Mr D did his national service, taking part in 1990 in an exercise for reservists that put him in touch with Albanians fighting for independence. He wanted to help these people and became politically active. In 1990 (at the time of the establishment of the political parties prior to the war), Mr D was arrested for the first time. He joined the Democratic Action Party (SDA), pasted up their posters, and was sent further afield to recruit new members. His father had forbidden him to engage in these activities because they were too dangerous, but his mother and one of his sisters relented and secretly gave him the fare money he needed.

As he spoke, I suddenly realised why Mr D had come to the first session wearing his baseball cap. At an unconscious level he was harking back to his earlier life. Life had come to a standstill for him when he was still a boy rebelling oedipally against his father. Mother and sister had surreptitiously financed his exploits to support him in his boyishness. He belonged to a clique and felt strong as a result. He had failed to recognise the extent of the danger he was in. He obviously wanted to show me something of this oedipal side of his character. In the present, by contrast, Mr D was completely devastated and disempowered, the baseball cap was merely a quote from the distant past. When Mr D could no longer go on, I said: "I believe that as a boy you were a livewire and as a young man also very hard-hitting. As a child you miscalculated the dangers of playing cowboys and Indians and you paid for it by losing the sight of your eye. That was dreadful, of course, but it was nothing compared to what you are going through now." Mr D resumed his account without looking at me. The essential facts were as follows:

On 30 December 1990 Mr D was arrested for the first time. He was interrogated and beaten for fifteen days then sentenced to six months' hard labour, in which time he and his fellow inmates were frequently lined up against the wall, cuffed, and kicked in the ribs.

After discharge he went on working for the SDA. The police had a list of all the members and conducted surprise raids to see if they had weapons. But Mr D never owned a weapon. In 1992 Mr D resisted his conscription to the Serbian military reserve because as a Moslem he did not want to be sent to Bosnia to shoot at other Moslems. Shortly after that he was arrested a second time.

One evening a Serbian neighbour visited the family. Mr D had gone into hiding, his father stood in the doorway, there were plans to kill him. The son was found, both men were marched off and interrogated and beaten by the police for two days. Mr D suffered a head injury from an iron rod. His father had shouted: "Leave him, take me!" Then they were taken to a big room in a barracks and tortured further. After seven days, Mr D was taken to a "House of Health" so that his head injury could be stitched. He never saw his father again. The general assumption is that he was killed.

Mr D was singled out for special attention every day. His tormentors wanted him to give them the names of SDA members who owned firearms and held leading positions in the party: "I didn't know who they were and I never made any lists." He was beaten every day. At the end, only twenty-three of the other fifty prisoners were left. The prisoners were given one meal a day and one litre of water for five persons. One day, he was taken to Priboj in a lorry and managed to escape from there to Berlin via Macedonia.

Fourth session: final counselling

At the fourth session, Mr D was appreciably more relaxed. He was relieved that he had told the whole story. He had resolved to apply for emigration to America, relatives of his life partner lived in the States, he intended to look them up and then start a new life. Ideally, he wanted to forget everything and leave it all behind, but he knew that he could not.

I told him that psychotherapy was a possibility he might envisage and explained my diagnosis in simple terms. He had experienced things that no ordinary person had ever been through, but he had probably been goaded to extreme anger by his treatment at the hands of the Serbian militiamen. But because one cannot truly perceive such feelings, they make themselves felt in the form of tension, sleep disorders, general nervousness. His guzzling had been an attempt to calm himself down. I told him that as a young man he had committed himself to the cause of democracy and justice but now felt that he had done a great wrong. In my view, he required psychotherapeutic help in getting over the loss of his father and his home country. He then told me that to that very day neither his mother nor his sister had been able to talk to him about his decision to become politically active. The consequences had made not only him speechless but the whole family.

Mr D was obviously able to develop some kind of notion of his psychic situation and to some small extent see it separately from the massive violence he had been subjected to. At the time, he had been involved in an oedipal entanglement with his father, and had incurred guilt by rebelling against his father's instructions. But this had nothing to do with the murder of his father, his own imprisonments and torture experiences. The father himself had indicated as much by offering to sacrifice himself. It was necessary to distinguish between internal and external reality.

Mr D thanked me for all the trouble I had taken and said: "I have to get rid of those nightmares somehow. But I don't know how. When I talk about them, I am dead and cold. But if I were really so dead, I'd have a stone inside me, not a heart." This poetic turn of phrase suggested to me that he had achieved at least some awareness of his dissociations.

Ms W: overleaping the trauma

Dissociations often manifest themselves as a loss of the feeling for time. Trauma sufferers can no longer describe the relevant events in the correct order and veer back and forth in their account of them. This evasive strategy frequently means that no reference is made to what it is precisely that determines the severity of the trauma. Inexperienced assessors run the risk of conniving in this defence strategy. Doubt may then be cast on the traumatisation itself, as happened in the case of Ms W (Henningsen, 2004a, 2004b).

Ms W displayed all the symptoms of PTSD, her file referred to various traumatic experiences, and she had lost many relatives. Despite all this, the assessment process was instituted. I had been told quite casually (and orally): "She wasn't raped." During the interviews Ms W was frank and co-operative. When in the third session I asked her to talk about the war period, her response was terse: "Yes, war broke out and I went to Berlin." Her facial expression told me she had finished her account before it had started. For a brief moment I felt relieved and hesitated. But then I took a deep breath and encouraged her to tell me about her experiences. I had felt internal resistance, a feeling frequently encountered in investigative situations involving refugees with traumas.

What had happened? In countertransference I had been tempted not to probe any further. After all, she had made it to Berlin, we could leave it at that. What unconscious factors were operative in this situation?

Alongside the bouts of depression caused by the loss of her relatives and her home country, Ms W also suffered from massive feelings of shame and guilt. In her native village all the Bosnian houses had been destroyed, the women retreated to the cellars that were still accessible, living there with the elderly and the children. At regular intervals, the Serbs came down into the cellars and raped the women—"all except me."—"Do you know why you were spared?"—"The troop leader went to the same school as I did. We were in the same class for ten years."

In my unconscious, I was exposed to a complex transference relationship that I initially refused to acknowledge. The association between the patient, the interpreter, and myself was characterised by solidarity and the desire to help; it was as if we were down in the cellar of the ruined house, determined to stand by one another. Unconsciously, Ms W had felt like a traitor for benefiting from the preferential treatment given to her by her former schoolmate. This betrayal was split off and projected on to me. The initially positive attachment to her classmate had turned into a perverted relationship that protected her from rape, as if she had entered into a pact with the devil. These destructive introjections were split off and manifested themselves in psychosomatic symptoms and bouts of depression.

At the point when Ms W had to defend her life and speak up for herself to obtain a residence permit for Berlin, this aspect of the situation repeated itself. I had been on the point of sparing her questions that might have led to retraumatisation, but that would have meant that her sufferings would not have been recognised for what they were: she would have been sent back. The danger, in transference, was that I might fail to perceive the projected destruction, identify unconsciously with the dual betrayal, and act in accordance with a projective countertransference response (Grinberg, 1991). It is entirely conceivable that their doubts about her traumatisation and the casual remark—"She wasn't raped"—indicated that the authorities had fallen for this projective identification.

Ms B: depletion and absence of defence

Before Ms B (Henningsen, 2004a, 2004b) came to me for the first time, I had received an unrequested report from the (woman) therapist treating her. The therapist had been seeing the patient once a week for several months. She was obviously greatly concerned for her patient's welfare and at this early stage already I felt that pressure was being put on me.

Ms B is a carefully groomed, well-proportioned woman. She arrived for the first interview with an interpreter she had obviously been paired off with by her personal supervisor outside my front door. During our exchanges Ms B was repeatedly overcome by tears and trembled all over. She was completely unable to give a chronological account of the relevant events. She complained about having to come to me and told me that her therapist knew everything there was to know and I should get my information from her. She was angered by the fact that five appointments were necessary in all and wanted the whole process to be over as quickly as possible. When I asked her about her daughter, she merely repeated the account of her sufferings and showed me the rings of sweat under her armpits.

Ms B quickly aroused a negative countertransference in me; I experienced her as demanding and infantile. She was unable to distinguish between herself and her daughter, and in much the same way I was in danger of feeling exposed to her destructive intrusions. I felt an urge to put her in her place and show her that the interpreter and I were both doing our best to help her. I became aware of shame and guilt feelings of my own. In the interventions required to enable Ms B to speak at all, I attempted to put a name to her sufferings and with her assistance to put her experiences in the correct chronological order. I did my best to acknowledge the dissociative states and her avoidance behaviour. References to reality were acquitted by Ms B with criticisms of me or renewed lamentations about her physical complaints and anxieties.

> I said to her: "I know you can hardly speak about your sufferings and that this situation in which you need to speak up for yourself is difficult for you. I want to help you overcome those difficulties."
> Ms B told me that she suffered from severe anxieties, nightmares, and flashbacks and often screamed at night: "I close my eyes and all the pictures of the war come back."

She was constantly assailed by bouts of depression, cold sweat, pains in her head, back, and stomach. Her blood pressure fluctuated so severely that she was sometimes unable to mount the stairs. Gastroscopic examinations had revealed ten stomach ulcers. In addition, Ms B complained of respiratory and cardiac irregularities. Her memory was seriously affected: "I have a barrier in my head." She was unable to concentrate and suffered from explosive emotional outbursts: "My brain just goes inert. Recently, on the street, I asked my daughter something and she didn't reply immediately. I blew my top. I just can't control myself." She showed me a large plastic bag full of medicines, including psychoactive drugs.

Ms B lived in a two-room flat with her daughter, who was in the last year of primary school. Ms B could not tell me the name of the school. In the afternoons, her daughter attended a daycare centre after school. Ms B was able to cook for the child and eat with her but she could not prepare meals for herself alone. She was looked after eight hours a week by a personal assistance provider (PAP), who accompanied her to doctors, the social welfare department, and other institutions because Ms B was afraid of travelling on the underground.

Ms B had been living in Berlin for ten years. From the outset she had only been given temporary residence permits of six months' duration, and the uncertainty of the situation was a major source of stress for her.

Some biographical details are significant. She was born in Croatia in 1958 as the youngest of three children (brother born in 1949, sister in 1954). Her father died of a brain tumour when she was five months old. She reported that she had not suffered from her father's early death because her childhood had been so idyllic (this may be the encapsulation of an early trauma). She "inherited" her father's cheerful character and was a great consolation to her mother. She worked as an administrative clerk and married a Serb at the age of twenty. She is Catholic but not religious, so the mixed marriage had little significance for her. The marriage remained childless for ten years; at first she and her husband had not wanted a baby, later there were problems. When war broke out, Ms B became pregnant "although at a time like that, we definitely didn't want a baby."

Trauma anamnesis

Ms B reports that when the war broke out, she noticed the first signs of an anxiety syndrome. All around her people were losing their jobs, she and her husband had been in constant jeopardy. They were forced to go into hiding and felt threatened by both ethnic groups (her husband was Serbian, she was Croatian). When her husband was recruited to dig trenches, she was in constant fear for his safety because the hatred of people living in mixed marriages could flare up at any time.

But the worst shock she experienced was when one evening ten men forced their way into their house, where she was alone. She was forced at gunpoint to go and make her female neighbours come to the house. The men were not clearly identifiable as soldiers, nor could Ms B tell what ethnic group they belonged to. They sang bawdy songs, drank alcohol, and forced the women first to strip and then to dance naked in front of them. Ms B repeatedly pleaded for mercy because she was quite obviously six months pregnant. This made no impression on the men whatsoever, she had to obey their commands like the other women (four Croatians, one Serbian woman). It went on like this all night. Ms B heard the other women screaming. In flashbacks she is still haunted by the screams and her own memories of what the men looked like. After more thoroughgoing exploration I gained the impression that during these events Ms B was in a state of shock and was thus unable to give a precise account of what had gone on. It is however probably safe to assume that the other women were raped. On various occasions the men made slighting references to her mixed marriage: "You've got a chetnik in the oven." The next morning, "real soldiers" came to the women's rescue: "I don't know who was who, Sarajevo was one big mix-up."

Later Ms B told her husband about this traumatic experience, although she was afraid how he might react. But her husband was unable to appreciate the enormity of what she had been through; he was himself completely intimidated and "just stared at one point all the time."

She gave birth to her daughter under dramatic circumstances and without medical assistance. Her legs trembled all the time, she was unable to frame one single coherent thought, everything was unhygienic. She developed no feelings for her little daughter, she could neither caress her nor breast-feed her. Panic and fear were dominant.

After the birth of her child she escaped to Germany. On the way grenades were fired at them, they found refuge with friends, continued their trek through forests, and were finally taken up by a lorry-driver. For money, he was prepared to take them to Austria via devious routes: "I don't know where we ended up, my daughter was crying, I had no milk to give her." "At the beginning I was strong, I wanted to get everything organised. But in the end it was just too much for me." Later the family travelled by bus from Austria to Berlin because they had friends living there.

Once in Berlin, she and her family were given a room in a flat they shared with another family. After things had relaxed a little, Mr B and their daughter fell seriously ill. Mr B had had severe pains in the legs for some time, the assumption being that they were the after-effects of the hard labour involved in digging the trenches. But the symptoms worsened dramatically and Mr B was diagnosed with bone cancer.

Shortly after that, their little daughter's eating disorders (she was eighteen months old) became so extreme (including vomiting) that both the mother and the underweight child had to be taken to hospital. Ms B was completely unable to cope: "I had ceased caring." "I just wanted to die, I couldn't carry on any longer." After discharge, Ms B spent the next eighteen months in the room they lived in looking after her husband until he died. Their little daughter slept in the same room. Ms B shut herself away, took tablets, and mechanically acquitted all the tasks required of her. At one point the electricity was turned off and the doctor had to examine her husband by the light of an electric torch: "I couldn't think about it." "Since then I have a tremor in my hands, I only weighed ninety pounds." In that period she lost her respect for physicians, was frequently at the end of her tether, and sometimes just shoved her daughter into bed. In accordance with his parents' wishes, her husband was buried in home soil. The social services centre organised the transport. Ms B was not present at the burial; she would like to visit the cemetery with her daughter and put roses on her husband's grave.

Her daughter, Vanessa, was put in nursery school very early (before she was two years old). Ms B believes that this is what saved her, because at least during the daytime she was spared the atmosphere of death pervading the flat. A social worker said: "We've got to get this child out of here." At nursery school she was the smallest child and hardly ever ate. Ms B says she was unable to give her child any love and never hugged or cuddled her. Today Vanessa is in the last year of primary school, she is conspicuously neat and tidy, her grades are excellent. She more or less taught herself to speak and write Serbo-Croatian after her mother had given her an initial grounding. No one noticed that she was not German.

Whenever Ms B lapsed into a dissociative trance (probably caused by flashbacks) and "simply stared at one point", Vanessa would jolt her out of her lethargy by saying "Hallo, Mama, we're going to the doctor's." In the doctor's surgery she would perform the requisite interpreting tasks if the PAP was not there. Ms B shared with her daughter a five-foot-wide bed supplied by social services. The daughter was regularly woken by her mother's nocturnal screams and then did her best to calm her down. "She knows when I can't take any more [...] Today she told me not to get all worked up because of the appointment with you and then caressed me."

As stated earlier, I very quickly developed a negative countertransference vis-à-vis Ms B which I had to keep under control. Her therapist's letters announcing her arrival, the interpreter who led her by the hand at our first interview, and her repeated injunctions to leave her in peace and ask her therapist if there was anything I wanted to know all conspired to arouse in me feelings of impatience, shame, and guilt. I started querying the point of my work. What are you doing here? I asked myself. I found it entirely understandable that she had lost her respect for doctors and the authorities, but at the same time I had to concede that as an assessor I was in a position of power and the patient was bound to feel that she was at my mercy. I had the impression that her therapist, who was employed by a public institution and was only able to see the patient once a fortnight, was completely unable to cope with the situation. Over-identification with the appalling sufferings of her patient and guilt feelings caused by the restricted scope she was forced to operate in presumably made her fear confronting the patient in a more sequestered setting. The personal assistance provider was there to help the patient deal with everyday matters. In the initial scene, the interpreter had unconsciously assumed the daughter's role and led the patient by the hand, just as the daughter did when she took her mother to the doctor's.

At the end of the first session I resolved to stick to the roles as they had been distributed so as to maintain a modicum of order. After the session, I asked the patient to go downstairs on her own, I shook her firmly by the hand, and said: "You can do it, your PAP is waiting for you outside." She had no trouble complying. I had the impression that I needed to defend the setting for the assessment. If the interpreter continued to be involved in the patient's unconscious transferences and actively accepted her involvement, her impartiality as a translator might be at risk.

When I realised how badly Ms B needed her daughter as a protective parent object and how impossible it was for her to give her child warmth, I felt an upsurge of serious anger. I was in danger of identifying with the parentified daughter and losing sight of the mother's anguish. I had to make it clear to myself that Ms B had no alternatives for her behaviour.

In the concluding counselling session, Ms B asked me whether she would ever regain the cheerful attitude to life she had once had. I told her that her life could never be the same as it had been because the things that had happened would not simply go away. What was necessary was that she should recognise and acknowledge her sufferings for what they were. For this she required therapeutic aid and in addition much time and patience. I suggested that she undertake the attempt in small stages.

We returned to the subject of her sleeping arrangements. Ms B defended the present arrangement with the words: "I don't want to be a nuisance to the social services people." I answered: "I'm not sure that's the real reason. Your daughter is a great help to you, she calms you down in the night. It's as if you were the child and your daughter the mother. I think you have to learn to be a good mother yourself." Ms B resolved to go to the social services department with her PAP immediately after the session and ask them to give her two smaller beds in exchange for the one she had so that she and her daughter could sleep in separate rooms. Then she expressed her profound gratitude for the interviews with me, which greatly surprised me because she had always regarded the assessment process as a constant torment. Obviously it had done her good to withstand her regressive tendencies. This gave her an opportunity to acknowledge her traumas and the dissociations bound up with them and to see herself more clearly as separate from her daughter.

In Ms B's case, depth-psychological or modified psychoanalytic psychotherapy was indicated; the interventions on my part were understandable as trial interpretations promising some success. I discussed this assessment with the therapist treating Ms B and in the case of analytic treatment recommended a setting with one to two sessions a week in a sedentary position.

Ms C: cultural containment

One crucial effect that therapy can have is a product of the attitude assumed during the documentation process. Refugees experience how the assessor empathises with them in order to write an account of the things they have been through. The assessor is a witness of the devastated inner world of the patient. Containment is necessary and can indeed be helpful, as the case of Ms C demonstrates (Henningsen, 2004a, 2004b).

Ms C, an overweight woman with very little education, displayed all the symptoms of PTSD. She responded to my greeting on the occasion of our first meeting with barely pent-up anger and an aggressively defensive attitude: "Nobody can help me. There's no point in trying." The strong smell of nicotine that she emanated indicated that smoking was the resource she fell back on in her attempts to reduce her enormous tensions. She was not allowed to smoke in my office, so instead she tore up several paper handkerchiefs into very small pieces during the first session. In the following sessions she had a linen bag with her that she kneaded throughout the meeting. She had become psychotic during the escape with her children. She had endangered both her own life and the lives of her children, had immigrated and then emigrated again, destroyed documents, and made any number of contradictory statements that made her suspicious in the eyes of the registration office. It took nine sessions to clear up the various stages of her escape route and understand her pre-traumatic personality development.

At the seventh session she said to me: "I know all the stages of hell." After a pause, she added: "At school we read a book where a person goes through all the stages of hell. I know them all." In my mind's eye I immediately saw Botticelli's illustrations (2000) for Dante's *Divine Comedy*. At the same time, I thought of Primo Levi (1959) and his description of the way learning the verses of Dante's "Inferno" by heart had kept him alive. I asked Ms C: "Are you referring to Dante's 'Inferno'?" "I can't remember what it was called. But I can remember the words." The interpreter (a native speaker) confirmed that Dante's "Inferno" was one of the titles on the list of set books for school usage. I was greatly moved and said to Ms C: "It's true. You've been through all those stages of hell, but now you're here with me and we're trying to remember everything you've been through, and it's very tormenting for you. But Dante didn't go through all those stages alone, he was accompanied by Vergil, and I'm here with you. I believe that with this memory you have created an image that can help you. If you have someone with you, it's easier to look hell in the face. With Dante there's redemption at the end. It may not be your redemption but it can be a relief, for example, if you should decide in favour of psychotherapy." After this session, Ms C inquired into the possibilities of finding a course of therapy for herself.

PART V

CONCLUSION

CHAPTER FIFTEEN

Consequences for psychoanalytic technique

This chapter summarises and discusses the essential conclusions that can be drawn from what we have said about dealing therapeutically with traumatised patients.

First of all, it is necessary to adhere to the distinction between patients who have been through psychic trauma(s) in childhood and PTSD sufferers traumatised in adulthood by experience(s) of violence and/or abuse. This distinction is meaningful and necessary for the indication issue. The first of these groups (dealt with in Parts I to III) display a variety of relational traumas, a transgenerational legacy of un-coped-with affects, severe illnesses, and/or other disasters that have etched themselves into their minds in the course of their development. Their personality structure is marked by an abundance of trauma-motivated defence strategies and adjustments. These internalisations lead to severe symptoms and massive restrictions to the patients' lives and have to be worked on in long-term therapy. The patients may develop a plethora of personality disorders as well as neurotic and psychotic conditions. According to ICD-10, they would need to be categorised under the heading "complex post-traumatic stress disorder (PTSD)".

The variety of pathologies and the very different courses taken by therapy show how rough-hewn the "complex PTSD" diagnosis is and prompt us to ask ourselves what we need it for. An indication for psychoanalytic therapy can only derive from a system of diagnosis geared to psychodynamic insights. It will always be essential to regard the individual case on its own merits. Many of the patients discussed in these chapters had already been through a course of therapy based on depth psychology; in other cases we had to go through an initial low-frequency phase before I could confidently say that analytic treatment was called for. In retrospect, however, it is fair to say that high-frequency analytic psychotherapy clearly benefited these patients.

On the question of indication, I feel it is important to inquire to what degree the development of object- and self-relatedness has been impaired by traumatisation in early childhood. If the sequels are minor or hard to discern, it may well be sufficient to work with the patient largely on the present conflict situation. A procedure based on depth psychology or modified, low-frequency analytic therapy in the sedentary position may then lead to lasting success. But there are cases (like the ones described in the early chapters of this book) where the experience of trauma pervades the patient's entire life, as we can see from diverse repetitions, somatisations, or patent personality disorders. Then it is essential to offer the patient a course of treatment in which regression and integration processes are possible so that in the transference relationship these patients can better understand themselves and their lives and work out new ways of coping with their conflicts. This is where high-frequency analysis comes into its own. In such cases, the relevant experiences are usually nonverbal and the patients require secure containment if they are to square up to the traumatic relational constellations. This being the case, four one-hour sessions a week make better sense than three. In my experience, the four-hour format is both faster and more reliable, an assessment confirmed by my long years of supervision experience and my activities as an assessor for psychotherapy in the German health insurance system. Of course, there are analysts who dislike high-frequency therapy and patients who are not suited to it. Dyad formation between patient and therapist is a highly sensitive matter and should therefore be treated with the necessary respect and circumspection and not regimented in any way.

The diagnosis of a so-called "complex" post-traumatic stress disorder requires a thorough prior examination, which may then (depending on the individual case) lead to various indications. Not all patients are suited to the psychoanalytic process. However, my own therapeutic efforts centre on analytic psychotherapy, the classical psychoanalytic method, and (where necessary) modified analytic techniques geared to transference processes. From this perspective I now intend to discuss a number of fundamental issues and to indicate how the approaches I have just listed differ from other methods.

In Part IV I have discussed cases of acute or chronic PTSD with the typical symptoms this involves: intrusions, avoidance behaviour, hyperarousal. These cases are not suitable for high-frequency analysis on the couch. Modified analytic and depth-psychology-based procedures are more likely to help these patients because they strengthen cognitive processes and reality control. The states of severe dissociation and emotional depletion that these patients suffer from have to be mitigated before a therapeutic relationship of any resilience can come about. The essential precondition is to establish an adequate feeling of security for the patient.

If the control functions of the ego and affect regulation are seriously impaired, I normally offer the patient modified analytic psychotherapy taking place once a week in a sedentary position. Within the limits that the health insurance schemes are prepared to extend to (normally 160 sessions, at most 240–300), these patients then have a chance to profit from the protective nature of a therapeutic relationship to develop new adjustment strategies and work on their traumatic experiences in the space of the four to seven years available to them. This approach takes full account of transference processes and, above all, projected, split-off affects and acting out. Frequently it is best to make use of a trial course of therapy (twenty-five sessions, short-term therapy, once a week, sedentary) to arrive jointly at the correct indication in conjunction with the patient. In my experience, differentiating between the indication for psychoanalysis proper and for depth-psychology-based psychotherapy should take place at the discretion of the therapist and be based on due concern for a variety of factors. Largely speaking, modified analytic treatment tends to be indicated when the following features are especially prominent: complexity of the disorder; compulsive repetition of internalised traumatic relations; childhood traumas with repercussions on the present.

These syndromes normally require intensive work on transference processes and should largely be entrusted to trained psychoanalysts. Another factor is the "match" between patient and therapist. Usually, trial therapy gives sufficient opportunity to decide whether one can build up a helpful relationship with a particular patient. Sometimes, however, both parties require more time to decide on this. In such cases it is probably best to agree on an initial course of short-term therapy. This is also true for psychotherapists operating on the basis of depth psychology but not pursuing an approach closely geared to transference.

With these patients, psychoactive drugs may also be helpful. Of course, this should always be supervised by a psychiatric colleague so that the transference relationship does not suffer as a result. Most patients desist from taking the medication once a secure transference relationship has been established. In these cases, identification with a reassuring object enhances their capacity for stabilisation. Other patients may not be so fortunate.

Adherence to the setting

For both groups of patients, adherence to the setting is of the utmost importance (cf. Hirsch, 2004, p. 177 et seq., 216 et seq.). Traumatised individuals entrusting themselves to a therapist are venturing out of their inner withdrawal. This step involves very considerable risks for them, risks that they intuit without being able to verbalise them. Accordingly, the parameters of treatment must be especially transparent: clearly defined agreements on the nature of the working alliance; respectful engagement with feelings of shame; acknowledgement of suffering from a position of non-neutral abstinence (Fischer & Riedesser, 1998; Henningsen, 2003); respect for human dignity; readiness to go in search of truth; no abuse of professional skill in the form of manipulation or superiority. All this is necessary to gain the patient's trust.

The setting is the consistent framework in which analyst and patient operate. For example, the therapist displays reliability by adhering to the time-scheme involved. With a view to getting closer to his anxieties and conflicts, the patient has agreed to treatment and all that it implies for a session period of fifty minutes. Realising that the therapist will invariably ensure that this period is not exceeded makes it easier for the patient to relinquish control and defence strategies and engage with his traumatic experiences. Adhering to time limits helps the patient achieve the indispensable feeling of security. Many trauma therapists dealing with PTSD patients favour flexible session durations, talking to their patients for between one and two hours, depending on how things are going, and then saying things like: "We really got to grips with the trauma." These therapists are so impressed by the suffering and high affectivity reflected in what their patients have to say to them that they are apprehensive about interrupting them. I call this misguided empathy. With this approach there is a danger of the patients feeling re-exposed to their intrusions. The therapist is perceived as the person in charge, steering the process by means of time management. The patient is at the mercy of this procedure, and aspects of his role as a victim of traumatic experiences may be reactivated. In the long term, patients encountering this in therapy will return to the next sessions with increasing apprehension. They may believe that this is all a part of their traumatisation and a necessary part of the treatment, unable to recognise that patient and therapist are falling victim to a species of enactment in which the triangulating function of the setting gradually gets lost.

Instead, trauma therapists should keep a close eye on the limited stretch of time available. As the end of the session approaches, they should help the patient "arrive back" in the present by saying something like: "Yes, you went through some terrible things in …, but now we're in Berlin and the end of the session is approaching." It also helps to activate experiences in which the patient was able to assert his autonomy, for example: "That is very different from …, when you were able to assert yourself so successfully. Unfortunately, the session is drawing to a close so we'll have to stop there this time …"

Of course, transference can never be the centre of attention in low-frequency, depth-psychology-based therapy. Dealing with frightening situations and the links between such situations and unprocessed internal conflicts and anxieties will rather tend to be examined from the perspective of adjustment and autonomy, an approach that helps many patients and does not require profounder engagement. But here too transferences take place. The danger is that the revival of the trauma may find its way unnoticed into the relationship with the therapist, who may then seek to defuse the unpleasant situation by changing the setting. Here is an example from a supervision group.

> A female patient traumatised by incest suffered from severe work disruptions, a plethora of psychosomatic complaints, sleep disorders, and massive anxiety. After a few weeks of one-session therapy the patient appeared to have become calmer and the therapist (also female) interpreted this as a sign that her work was beginning to bear fruit. Despite the severity of the disorders she felt quite sanguine about the direction the therapy was taking.

But then things started grinding to a halt; the patient no longer spoke, some impediment was operative. To "loosen the patient up", the therapist suggested a few sessions devoted to catathymic image perception. The patient consented willingly but the symptoms got progressively worse and the patient no longer attended the sessions regularly. The relationship with the therapist and the stabilisation already achieved began to crumble.

What had happened? When the transference line was reconstructed in the supervision group, the question was answered relatively quickly. After the patient had gained trust, she unconsciously brought her traumatisation and all the speechlessness it involved into the relationship. The therapist had not grasped and interpreted this "blockade". Instead, she had acted out her countertransference. She changed the setting and abandoned her role, which in the patient's unconscious was equivalent to a re-enactment of the earlier traumatic situation. The patient was told to lie down (as her father had done?) and with her instructions on catathymic image perception (associations of compulsive repetition and transference) the therapist had assumed the role of the rapist.

As an assessor for the Association of Statutory Health Physicians I am frequently confronted with applications from therapists to have female patients who have suffered sexual abuse transferred to a psychosomatic hospital at a decisive stage in their treatment, that is, when they are beginning to find access to their trauma. Frequently (but not invariably), reports on their progress indicate that they did not have much benefit from inpatient care. In retrospect, and with due concern for the transference processes involved, one can see that hospitalisation was a repetition of an essential part of the trauma. At the very point when they have started to talk about and engage with the trauma, these patients are "sent away" by their (female) therapists in the same way as the mother did by closing her eyes and ears and leaving her daughter to her fate at the hands of some perverted father, grandfather, neighbour, or uncle. The feelings of shame that assail a child when she turns to a trusted person or even her own mother for help and is uncomprehendingly turned away are unbearable and reinforce the trauma. In certain cases, this rejection can effect renewed traumatisation or may even be the actual subject of the trauma. If a patient is unthinkingly "sent away" after having established sufficient attachment to the therapist, this part of the trauma is repeated and the original trauma topic reinforced. Once again, patients experience the fact that they have no one understanding and supportive to turn to, that they and/or their experiences are so menacing that they cannot be dealt with in a therapeutic relationship outside hospital.

In analytic therapy proper, these critical stages can also be denied by means of acting out or enactment. Patients with severe traumas in early childhood who decide to undergo analysis also need time to build up a trustful therapeutic relationship. As we have seen, at the beginning of therapy they have no words for the loss of the object. The weekend or the end of the session may trigger memories of the trauma. But frequently the brute force of the destruction they have experienced only comes to full fruition when the relationship as such appears to be at stake, for example, when a new application has to be submitted to the insurance scheme after the eightieth or 160th session, that is, at a stage when the transference neurosis has normally established itself.

The following supervision example shows how the end of the number of sessions sanctioned by the insurance scheme activated a patient's early separation trauma. While he knew that his mother had killed herself, her suicide with all its threatening affective implications had not been worked through. Neither the analyst nor the patient were able to recognise the unconscious destructiveness revealing itself in the patient's anxieties, in a dream, and in his sleep disorder, and relate it to his insecure prospects for the future. The feelings and fantasies were jointly warded off and repressed. The patient began criticising the analyst (without any apparent warning) and contemplated breaking off therapy. After heated controversy, the two parties finally agreed on the continuation of therapy with fewer sessions. This was also advocated by the external assessor as a way of ensuring that the course of therapy be brought to a useful and meaningful conclusion after 240 or (at the most) 300 sessions.

We can interpret this course of events as a large-scale enactment. In his awareness, the patient draws closer to the fact of having lost his mother in early childhood. There were no words to express this at the time, and this has not changed now. The patient senses that he might lose the therapist and in anticipation of this terminates the relationship himself. At the same time he entertains gargantuan feelings of rage at the object for abandoning him; the affects thronging in on him are irreconcilable and are projected directly into the analyst's unconscious. If the analyst grasps the situation in his countertransference he will interpret it (i.e., see the connection between the present situation and the infant trauma). Then the likelihood is greater that the scenario will calm down, transference will cut deeper, and the analysis can be continued in the accustomed setting and without any further upsets. Ideally, analyst and patient will have shared the experience of bearing up to not-knowing and acknowledging helplessness in the face of loss, an experience that may help the patient to institute maturation processes.

But if the analyst lets herself be affected by the threat, she will also advocate a reduction in the number of sessions and have all kinds of serious, realistic arguments in favour of that step. The analysis will be impoverished in terms of its potential depth. The patient's suffering has not been fully fathomed. What remains is a diffuse feeling of not being properly understood. Via projective identification and counter-identification (Grinberg, 1990) the split-off affect will be handed on unprocessed, possibly even to the assessor acting for the insurance scheme, and ultimately returned to the patient unprocessed (or at best slightly mitigated). Then, if therapy is discontinued, the patient is abandoned all over again, and even if he is only partly abandoned, the relationship will be watered down. At all events, the patient will see his unconscious, guilt-ridden conviction confirmed that he was to blame for the loss of his mother and will now have to take the consequences. This attitude should not be confused with doubt about whether, after working through the trauma, the patient will be capable of looking after himself and facing up to his fate. If he is able to look after himself, he will be capable of thinking about terminating therapy and also reducing the number of sessions.

When the trauma impinges on transference, a frequent reaction on the parts both of analyst and patient is to start querying or modifying the setting. In the case of patients with traumas one should think very carefully before putting a change of setting into practice. It is absolutely crucial in these critical phases of treatment to keep a close eye on the transference situation, weigh up the pros and cons, and not make any rash decisions. Often it makes good sense to suggest to the patient a stretch of time in which one could think about a change of setting so that one can fully grasp what it would mean for the treatment process before putting it into practice. In other cases it might be best to suggest spending two or three months with fewer sessions per week so as to sound out the conceivable repercussions and then come to a final decision.

If changes do have to be made to the setting, the immense fear of defenceless exposure that traumatised patients will have makes particular clarity and transparency imperative. These changes should be clearly announced and discussion of them should ideally take place at the beginning of a session so there is time to think about the significance of the change. If the patient in question is undergoing therapy on the couch, these exchanges should take place in a sedentary or standing position before the patient resumes the reclining posture. Owing to their traumatic experiences, these patients are at constant risk of the boundaries between inner and outer reality losing definition or fading altogether. A change of setting is part of the working alliance, it belongs to the relationship between analyst and patient and is rooted in reality. To assess the significance of the new arrangement, it will be necessary to see what influence it exerts on internal reality, something that can be explored with the patient on the couch subsequent to discussion of the changes envisaged.

Another frequently practised change of setting consists in the combination of various procedures. The implication of such a change of setting is that the psychoanalyst does not consider it possible to work through the trauma in transference (cf. Eckert, 2011; Ehlert-Balzer, 1996; Reddemann & Sachsse, 1998).

When trauma-therapeutic techniques (in the extended sense of the term) are incorporated into the analytic process, the essential thing is for patient and therapist to engage with the trauma in a planned and pre-structured way, either via EMDR,[1] screen technique,[2] or some other form of trauma exposure. In the last analysis it is the therapist who takes charge of the proceedings, not least by discussing his proposals with the patient, ensuring a feeling of security, etc. Frank Rosenberg describes such a procedure (albeit without EMDR) in his treatment of an adolescent (2010). Andrea Eckert takes her bearings from Oliner and advocates the use of EMDR and trauma exposure, conceding, however, that "many questions still remain unanswered […] in connection with the integration of this approach into ongoing outpatient therapy" (Eckert, 2011, p. 261). For Eckert, the use of EMDR is also indicated in cases of complex PTSD, whereas Klaus M. Wackernagel has misgivings:

> The present author no longer uses EMDR with these patients because it necessarily places the therapist in a dominant position that makes the patients feel dependent and subjected. In the face of reactivated traumatic feelings and memories, it triggers destructive transferences and countertransferences and confronts these patients too quickly, too uncontrollably and too unpredictably with intensive traumatic affects. (Wackernagel, 2011, p. 228)

In my view, the integration of trauma therapy (in the extended sense of the term) into long-term analytic therapy often irresponsibly jeopardises the therapeutic relationship because such a change of setting massively interferes with the transference relationship. In outpatient settings, such changes should accordingly be given very careful consideration. It may help the patient to acquire relaxation techniques such as autogenic training, yoga, certain breathing exercises, motion therapy, and artistic activity. This will strengthen the patient's body-self and support the integration of psychic and physical processes. These techniques should however be conducted under the supervision of a different therapist, not by the analyst or psychotherapist in charge of long-term therapy, because then the patient can talk to the analyst about his experiences with the body psychotherapies. The big advantage of inpatient settings is that they normally facilitate a division of tasks between a number of different reference persons.

Transference and countertransference

As I have already emphasised, the recognition and acknowledgement of trauma is a sine qua non for patients with traumas. Frequently the extent and the nature of the traumatisation only become fully apparent in the course of long-term therapy. In comparison with "classical" transference neuroses, therapists treating patients with traumas as the decisive cause of illness will need to pay special attention to the preservation or reinforcement of their autonomy. This will protect the patients from excessive dependency and the feeling of being entirely at the mercy of the circumstances they find themselves in, a feeling that may well trigger malign regressions transforming the therapeutic alliance into a traumatising relationship. Nonetheless, in a course of therapy geared to psychoanalysis, engagement with transference processes will remain a core concern, even though modification will be necessary.

This feature of the psychoanalytic approach contrasts starkly with the so-called "dynamic procedures", which, though based on psychoanalytic insights, are explicitly concerned to prevent the resuscitation of traumatic constellations in transference. Reddemann and Wöller (2011) are very clear on this point:

> Traditional psychoanalytic approaches encourage regressions and as such are not suitable for the treatment of traumatised patients.

> Instead of integrating pathological elements into the therapeutic relationship, care should be taken *not* to let traumatic experiences find their way into the relationship because this may lead to transference-conditioned distortions in the therapist's perception. Instead of bringing infantile patterns of subjective experience back to life, patients should be encouraged to take their lives in their own hands and to be successful in doing so. In psychodynamic therapy worthy of the name, this would be the justification for psycho-education and explanatory methods. (Ibid., p. 582)

The cases discussed in this book and in many other psychoanalytic publications demonstrate the utility of including transference processes in therapeutic work. It is however also true to say that analytic work with traumatised patients occasionally requires a shift of emphasis in the therapeutic attitude that derives from the permanent necessity to ensure that patients feel secure enough to build up an active engagement with traumatic experiences and their sequels. There are phases in these analyses where the therapist will tend to interpret more actively than in other cases.

In Chapter Eight, Acting out and compulsive repetition, I have indicated the creative potential inherent in the scenic representation of traumatic experiences. Today, knowledge of the mechanisms of projective identification, of action dialogue (Klüwer, 1983, 1995) and the complications invariably occurring between analyst and patient enable us to draw upon these processes in our attempts to dispel symbolisation disorders. When "traumatising transference" (Holderegger, 1998) ensues via enactment, it may be necessary for the therapist to undertake quite concrete translation steps by recognising present aspects of the original traumatic situation as repetition and calling them by name. In this way, patients can learn to get an idea of their own histories, gain a concrete notion of what has really happened, and integrate it more effectively.

Another central issue is how to deal with split-off affects. In real traumatic situations, the splitting-off of affects is a strategy for survival. In the case of a relational trauma in early childhood, it serves the preservation of the object, indeed usually the preservation of the object's love. This is why in analytic therapy we frequently have phases of (necessary) idealising transference that need to be perceived as such and dissipated carefully in stages that the patient can relate to.

Trauma in early childhood can also lead to a permanent fusion of affects in a concretistic form (Chapter Four). This happens when the child is either not sufficiently separated from the mother, has not developed adequate symbolisations, or these symbolisations have been destroyed in the traumatic situation. This defence structure is preserved along with its bodily memory traces (embodiment) and protects the child from the experience of potential annihilation, should the province of traumatic memories be activated. To some extent, this will hinder further emotional growth. When this fusionary defence cracks open in analysis and the patient's self emerges from the fusion, it is imperative to be aware of the danger the patient is in and to strengthen his vital, self-protective forces.

Another important requisite to be borne in mind with traumatised patients is the higher dosage of genetic (i.e., biography-related) interpretations. Given that such patients are very often highly intelligent, this aspect tends to be neglected. Even though they gain cognisance of the essential traumas in their life histories, they do not have a memory of them at their disposal in the same way as non-traumatised individuals when the traumatising aspects manifest themselves in transference.

Marion Oliner (2010) and others have pointed out that many psychoanalysts tend to accord acknowledgement of the historical reality of the trauma too little space, a point that I have discussed in the Introduction. Interventions dedicated to the clarification of historical reality and biography should be given just as much attention as interpretations geared to the here-and-now. Of course, too much in the way of genetic interpretation can be detrimental for the curative process (as in any analysis) because the past is then pressed into service as a defence resource. But when squaring up to their central conflicts, traumatised patients are quicker to dissociate or to be overwhelmed by their affects. This means that they need more guidance than others and also more time to find their way around in their own past and achieve greater continuity. Time and again, they also need to assure themselves of their autonomy vis-à-vis the transference object. Accordingly, more genetic interpretations tend to be required than with other patients, and maintenance of the setting is especially important.

Preliminary therapy in a one-hour setting is often very helpful because in this way patients can acquire a cognitive idea of their histories and experience and internalise the analyst as a real object. Probationary sessions should also be used for this purpose if the indications favour analysis. A trial, surface-level interpretation of the trauma and its links with the patient's symptoms and the present assures the patient that the therapist has a notion of what he has been through. As such, it encourages trust. At the same time, therapists can recognise how the patient responds to interpretation and fine-hone their diagnostic approach accordingly.

Flashbacks and dissociations

Patients suffering from intrusions and flashbacks are not suited for analysis in a classical setting but require a modified form of psychoanalysis. As we have seen, they normally need special assistance to achieve the requisite distance from their traumatic experiences. For patients suffering from PTSD, I suggest a modified, low-frequency analytic or depth-psychology-based setting in a sedentary posture. Relaxation techniques and other trauma-therapeutic techniques should be used as little as possible and as extensively as necessary.

In all the cases we have discussed, however, there were situations during analysis when the patients were overwhelmed by their traumatic experiences and lost their capacity for contemplation. They began to act out massively, developed thoughts of suicide, contemplated terminating treatment, or dissociated. Wherever possible, their acting out was interpreted. In connection with the severe decompensations in which reality bore in on them in all its bitterness, transference in its more genetic form receded (Bohleber, 1997; Grubrich-Simitis, 1984, 2008). The points at issue were acknowledgement, calling by name, providing support, joint silence. Injunctions (systematically addressing the patient directly) were sometimes necessary. In each and every case the main thing was to acknowledge the frequently unspeakable external reality. Here the analyst must take the lead. If she can find words for what the patient has been through, the patient can regain security and embark on a corrective experience. In technically difficult situations, the preservation of the analytic relationship is the curative element that must be assured at all costs.

These repercussions may be less violent. In such cases they can be observed proceeding in small stages from session to session as the patient gradually gets closer to the traumatic experiences. Here the analyst becomes a present object providing support. The patient sees that he is not abandoned. This is analytic work *in* transference. When greater distance has been established, work continues *on* transference, quickly reverting to the other mode. Every patient and every analyst-patient relationship have a rhythm of their own which must be respected. Peter Fonagy (1991) distinguishes between two mutually complementary approaches, the representation model (restructuring internal representation via interpretation) and the process model (reintegrating excluded or inhibited psychic processes). The research team headed by Fonagy were inspired by the work of Wilfred Bion and Hanna Segal to look more closely at thought disorders and the pathological processing of affects in transference processes. Fonagy demonstrates that if a restructuring of representations is to be a feasible proposition, work on psychic processes is indispensable for borderline patients and patients with severe personality disorders. In my view, the same is true of the work on psychic traumas.

Traumas that are warded off or, worse still, encapsulated, are life-restricting and lead to "psychic retreat" (Steiner, 1993). In all the cases we have looked at, split-off elements of a traumatic relational constellation manifested themselves in actions and/or bodily symptoms and hardly, if at all, at the level of psychic reality (Cournut, 1988; Henningsen, 1990). A "theory of the psychic" (Fonagy, 1991) has yet to materialise. In analysis, the stepwise reintegration of traumatic modes of experience invariably culminates in the question: When does the trauma turn into conflict and the conflict into trauma? In every course of therapy, this interim zone implies both opportunities (for integration) and dangers (of termination). When the trauma is revived in transference, the analyst can turn into a (potentially) traumatising object. Incomprehensible aggression and the feelings of guilt attendant upon it are communicated via acting-out and may be misinterpreted as a result of counter-acting-out by the therapist.

But in analytic therapy the very point is to identify these enactments and use them productively for the interpretation process. They are unconscious enactments of the trauma triggered by compulsive repetition, and as such they deserve special attention. If the therapist succeeds in recognising the creative potential and the hope for a better solution contained in the enactment, then she can formulate an interpretation (Chapter Eight).

Symbolisation deficits on the part of traumatised patients are frequently restricted to topics and areas of experience that have some kind of connection with the trauma. Despite the life-restrictions they suffer from, many such patients hold down highly qualified jobs and are creative and imaginative in their dealings with the world, as long as those dealings have nothing to do with their trauma. But despite their remarkable intelligence there is one part of their psyche (the part associated with the trauma) where they have no words, no chance of affect regulation, and are forced to enact their experiences. The need to control their objects when traumatic memories are activated may exacerbate the situation. If the analyst fails to recognise in time that the patient is enacting what needs to be understood, she runs the risk of an over-involvement with the patient that can culminate in an enactment on the part of the therapist.

Notes

1. EMDR (eye movement desensitization and reprocessing) is a method of "bilateral stimulation" introduced by Francine Shapiro. By moving a finger back and forth before the patient's eyes, the therapist stimulates the connections between the two hemispheres of the brain. As the patient engages with his traumatic experiences, the method is designed to reinstate adaptation processes and introduce the processing of the trauma (Shapiro, 2001).
2. The screen method is an imaginative method in which the patient is asked to look at a blank surface and, as in a film, imagine and recount experiences from the past (Reddemann, 2011; Sachsse, 2004).

CHAPTER SIXTEEN

Trauma in society and politics: an outlook

Even if they know which external event is to blame for their condition, individuals with traumas are all but incapable of talking about their traumatic experiences. Patients suffering from transgenerational identifications are equally unable to gauge and understand the extent of the harm involved. Accordingly, these people need special protection and specific networks providing them with support and assistance. In short, there must be sectors in society where traumas are acknowledged for what they are. The parameters required for the purpose (legislation, social security, sickness benefits, networks, institutions, etc.) are policy-dependent. Here psychoanalysts can play a special part as counsellors, supervisors, or assessors because they are trained to recognise the unconscious processes operative in relationships and in institutions that distort the perception of traumatic circumstances or lead to their being denied altogether.

Franziska Lamott and Günter Lempa (2011) have demonstrated that both in the last century and in the present, the nosology and diagnosis of war-induced traumas have been influenced for politically motivated reasons in a way that militates against the acknowledgement of trauma.

In such cases, the victim is left alone with his trauma—a situation that leads to renewed traumatisation—while society divests itself of its responsibility.

In the following I want to indicate a number of instances where traumatic processes make themselves felt in society and also point to subject areas where politicians and society must face up to their responsibility. Psychoanalytic knowledge about the significance of extreme traumatisation for individuals, groups, and societies has achieved a degree of indisputable clarity that makes it essential to discuss this knowledge with representatives of other psychotherapeutic/medical approaches and with help groups and also to seek a dialogue with politicians.

Collective memory and collective resistance

In Germany, the consequences of Nazi dictatorship are still vividly present in our collective memory and have a great deal of impact on political action. The truth of this assertion is borne out by the way in which refugees from former Yugoslavia have been welcomed and looked after.

Fifty years after the end of the Second World War, a state in southeastern Europe collapsed as a result of nationalist and ethnic conflicts. Ethnic purges, concentration camps, labour camps, war, rape, and displacement were the order of the day. Many refugees came to Germany. The city of Berlin,[1] still marked by the sequels of National Socialism, Holocaust, and war, and extended to its limits by the integration of East and West, appeared unable to handle the never-ending influx of refugees. The medical services under the aegis of the police authorities resorted to an investigation strategy that rode roughshod over anything resembling human dignity. The refugees were subjected to expulsion practices that made retraumatisation more or less inevitable.

Depending on the generation we belong to, accounts from individuals traumatised by wartime occurrences evoke images and memories that we have either experienced ourselves or that we can more or less immediately relate to because they are reminiscent of what we have heard from our parents (transgenerational identification, Gampel, 1994; Kogan, 1990, 1995). These images and memories may never have been explicitly referred to, but whether they were mentioned or not, engagement with them is bedevilled by very formidable verbalisation and symbolisation barriers. Bosnian men describing the horrors of war remind us of our fathers and grandfathers. The images on show at the

Wehrmacht exhibition come flooding back. Displaced persons, prisoners, and victims of ethnic purges remind us (specifically in Germany) of the Nazis' treatment of Jewish citizens. Feelings of shame ensue. In our collective preconscious or unconscious, other accounts recall escape or expulsion from the former German areas in Eastern Europe. Manifest violence triggers psychotic states both in the victims and (differently) in the perpetrators. The question arises here whether at a societal level there is a split-off, unprocessed trauma or an encapsulated psychotic introject involved that must never reach the conscious level (although this would in fact initiate societal discourse on the subject) but has to be ejected. In other words, is this kind of defence partly a product of the way the legal fraternity and the police go about things (Henningsen, 1990; Laub & Weine, 1994)?

In this connection, one particularly tragic incident is worthy of mention. One police psychologist greatly feared by asylum applicants and their helpers refused point-blank to acknowledge the significance of post-traumatic stress disorder (PTSD). Assessments by physicians and psychotherapists referring to this disorder by name were rejected by her outright. She told the refugees that she herself had been severely traumatised in her youth by being confined to a concentration camp and that they should take an example from her. Protests from doctors, psychotherapists, and the press proved powerless to convince the authorities or the Senate that this woman's actions were dictated by her own severe disorder and that she could not possibly be equal to the responsibilities of her position. Only when she developed decompensated psychotic delusions and had to be put in psychiatric care was she suspended from office. But by then, many applicants (probably about 400) had been wrongfully denied temporary one-year residence as a result of their traumatisation. This is certainly not the place to speculate on the nature and severity of the traumas haunting this desperately sick psychologist. But the event proves once again very poignantly and graphically how absolutely essential it is for trauma researchers and trauma therapists to be fully aware of their own trauma history and to engage with any such condition that may exist in a way that ensures that their view of their patients is neither one-sided nor distorted (Fischer & Riedesser, 1998, p. 180 et seq.). Doctors, psychologists, and psychotherapists acting for the medical services provided by the police must be placed by law under the aegis of the Medical Association. No administrative official or politician can accurately assess the competence of a physician or psychologist working in this field.

This incident is also indicative of persistent collective trauma defence. Despite all the highly qualified protests they were faced with, the politicians and administration officials were unable to see how irresponsibly they were behaving vis-à-vis the refugees, the psychologist herself, and the Holocaust victims. In a manner reminiscent of the atrocities of the last century, destructive and psychotic features were split off and ejected in favour of the desire for smoothly operating bureaucracy.

In connection with the assessment of traumatised refugees from former Yugoslavia, I have indicated elsewhere the profession-specific transferences that occur and shown how lawyers, administrative officials, and authorities tend to make unconscious use of bureaucratic regulations to protect themselves from potentially overpowering feelings. This is in no way commensurate with the needs of trauma sufferers and undermines the intentions of the legislation promulgated by the ministers of the interior. Trauma therapists dealing with political refugees will come into contact with un-coped-with traumas stored in the collective memory of our society and thus perhaps have a chance to do something for integration. This would not only be relevant for all of us, it would also cast light on the societal defence constellations and compulsive repetitions that we encounter so frequently (Henningsen, 2003).

The return of a further collective-resistance phenomenon becomes apparent when we look at the petty officialdom that ran rife in post-war Germany in connection with the implementation of the Federal Compensation Law. It led to the denial of firmly established facts and thus prevented swift and humane treatment for the victims (Klein, 1984; Krystal, 1968; Niederland, 1981; Pross, 2001; Wangh, 1965). Only in 1965, for example, was the Federal Republic prepared to recognise the severe distress of people with traumas patently deriving from their confinement in concentration camps although they were not able to provide "watertight" evidence of the fact. This was how long it took to desist from a hair-splitting and extremely dubious assessment procedure. The new criterion was that the victim in question had been imprisoned for at least one year in a concentration camp (Pross, 2001, p. 143 et seq.). The important thing here is that (although it happened too late and not extensively enough) the mere fact of having been in a concentration camp was finally accepted as the clinching factor. But even today it is still not enough for Bosnian refugees to prove where they come from, whether they were incarcerated in a camp, etc. If these simple facts were acknowledged as being traumatic by their very nature, most applicants could be spared the time-consuming and tormenting assessment procedure that invariably involves the risk of retraumatisation. The refugees could be given quicker assistance, the taxpayer could save a lot of money. In other European countries such as Sweden, Bosnian refugees were able to acquire the respective nationality as early as the mid-90s. In Germany, mass traumatisation appears to be something that hardly anyone can imagine, perhaps because it is too painfully reminiscent of Germany's own history, perhaps because we cannot really believe that genocide can take place outside Germany and after 1945. Officials and the legislator appear to have succumbed to compulsive repetition, as if they were waiting for another twenty years to elapse before the traumas these people are suffering from can be acknowledged as such.

At present we are finding it particularly hard to recognise that we too are a nation that due to its western alliances is involved in wars. It took some fifteen years before these things could be called by name. Since the 1990s, soldiers of the Federal Armed Forces have been sent to scenes of hostilities and increasingly often exposed to extremely traumatic situations. The army hospitals are full of soldiers requiring psychotherapeutic treatment (Zimmermann, Ströhle, & Hahne, 2009). "According to the official records, 2,200 soldiers have been treated for PTSD since 1996. A study by the Technical University of Dresden suggests that the real figure is twice as high" (Seliger, 2011, p. 8). The PTSD figures in the armed forces are constantly on the rise. The medical corps (www.sanitaetsdienstbundeswehr.de: PTBS) officially reports that in 2010, 729 soldiers were suffering from PTSD and 368 others from a psychic disorder caused by foreign deployment experiences. A soldier returning home from a war venue is a revenant from another world, a world that people living in security and the lap of affluence would prefer to know nothing about. In Germany, this aversion to acknowledging that we are a nation involved in hostilities may be subject to special defence mechanisms deriving from the atrocities of the Nazi period. The last surviving veterans of the Second World War are eking out their final years in old people's homes, tormented by the paranoid fears caused by the delayed consequences of PTSD. We would obviously prefer not to be confronted with these pathological cases all over again (cf. Böwing & Schröder, 2009).

The interest in the stories soldiers, war reporters, and auxiliaries have to tell is correspondingly meagre. Frequently, the social isolation of these trauma sufferers is heightened by their feelings of shame. Individual soldiers with PTSD also have to anticipate substantial financial and professional disadvantages if they admit to their condition. Attempts to obtain compensation by way of expert assessment are frequently fraught with unforeseeable bureaucratic obstacles and a refusal to acknowledge the suffering these soldiers have been through. Applications take between twelve and eighteen months to deal with. Only in 2011 did the Federal Parliament pass a law to the effect that soldiers with a thirty-per cent reduction of their ability to earn a living are entitled to further employ with the armed forces.

In Germany the word "veteran" is indissolubly linked with the Second World War, one essential reason why it has taken twenty years of foreign deployment for them to organise themselves in two associations both established in 2010 (the Association of German Veterans in Berlin and the German Veteran Association in Saarbrücken). These organisations emphasise that they have nothing to do with the associations formed by Second World War veterans. One of the goals they have set themselves is to support traumatised soldiers in their quest for medical support, assessors, and lawyers (Friederichs, 2010).

In all the cases presented in this book—and this is something that all therapists agree on, regardless of the kind of therapy they espouse—the first thing to be done was to establish a feeling of security firmly anchored in external reality before psychotherapy could make any leeway at all. In the treatment of traumatised refugees, one is frequently confronted by the following paradox: asylum seekers are "tolerated" (i.e., given temporary right of residence) so that they can undergo therapy in Germany, albeit with the explicit proviso that after successful treatment they must return to their home countries. Under these parameters, successful therapy is inconceivable. Patients from elsewhere embarking on psychotherapy in Germany under the impact of their traumatic experiences will never be able to build up a relationship of trust with the therapist if the latter's job is to get them back on their feet double-quick so that they can be sent back to the very environment that is indissolubly bound up with the traumas assailing them.

Accordingly, asylum is the conditio sine qua non for successful therapy. Patients who can mourn for the relatives they have lost may sometimes express the wish to pay a visit to their home country under the protection of the transference. And there are people who find it so difficult to reconcile themselves to a different system of values that they give up the effort and return home at a later date. But this is not something that can be enforced or categorically declared to be the ultimate goal of therapy before it has even begun.

A similar problem poses itself in connection with traumatised soldiers. Traumatised soldiers of the Federal Armed Forces and their families are looked after by the *Familienbetreuungsstelle* (Family Assistance Office), a clearly salutary institution established in connection with the increase in the incidence of foreign deployment missions (Hägler, 2011). With regard to assessment processes (pension claims, employability) and psychotherapy in the narrower sense of the term, I believe it necessary to undertake a critical review of the parameters conditioning the way these decisions are taken. I contend that assessment and therapy should not be conducted by representatives of the Federal Armed Forces. The employer under whose aegis traumatisation has occurred will always—even if "only" covertly—have an interest in ensuring that soldiers can be declared fit to return to their duties at the front as quickly as possible. He will also have an interest in seeing to it that the working conditions under which his soldiers operate are declared humane and above board in terms of the provisions laid down by employment legislation. This tendency can seriously impair transference processes both in connection with diagnostics and with therapy itself. It may easily militate against an unswerving concern for the truth and also vitiate the chances of lasting recovery. The patient cannot "open up" and will hardly be able to establish a trusting relationship with the person examining his case if that person is himself a member of the armed forces. The therapist is also likely to be subject to the same pressures. These unfortunate circumstances have recently been impressively described by Timmermann-Levanas and Richter (2010) and Lamott and Lempa (2011).

Spurred on by the flaws bedevilling the assessment of refugees with war traumas from former Yugoslavia, a group dedicated to the establishment of standards for the assessment of individuals with psychotraumas (SPBM) consisting of Hans Wolfang Gierlichs, Ferdinand Haenel, Franziska Henningsen, Helga Spranger, Eva van Keuk, Mechthild Wenk-Ansohn, and Waltraud Wirtgen elaborated a system of relevant standards that in the meantime has been recognised by the Federal Medical Association and the Federal Psychotherapy Association and put into practice in the form of certification and continuing education classes. In 2012 they were updated with the assistance of Gisela Scheef-Maier and adjusted to conform with the official UN document known as the Istanbul Protocol (United Nations High Commissioner for Refugees, 2001) (Gierlichs et al., 2012). In my view, the resultant network of certified assessors with special extra training could be emulated in other fields as well. It would be possible to create corresponding curricula and certification for other groups of traumatised individuals, for example, soldiers suffering from PTSD. The extra training necessary should not focus solely on trauma-specific content but should extend to the soldiers' cultural, psychosocial, and contractual circumstances and backgrounds, all of which are pertinent to the assessment process. Accordingly, such a curriculum for dealing with soldiers with traumas could only be elaborated in conjunction with the Federal Armed Forces. Appropriate assessment of traumatised individuals calls for clinical and psychotherapeutic experience. Training in forensic psychology and/or psychiatric diagnostics is not enough. It would make very good sense to place these assessments under the aegis and supervision of medical and psychotherapeutic associations.

Childhood traumas and child welfare

Harald Schickedanz and Reinhard Plassmann have evaluated a large-scale American study on morbidity based on information from 55,000 members of American health insurance schemes. Their results can be found in the *Handbuch der Psychotraumatologie* ("Manual of Psychotraumatology") (Schickedanz & Plassmann, 2011). They demonstrate that traumatic stress in childhood is a central cause of later physical ailments. "If left untreated, the consequences of traumatic experiences in childhood and adolescence will live on (traumatic schema), generate further physical, mental and social disorders, and in the worst case be passed on to later generations (psychosocially and epigenetically)" (ibid., p. 448 et seq.). The authors emphasise: "Illness prevention and health support start at the beginning of life and should be societally promoted and politically assured by attachment security and the absence of violence and abuse" (ibid., p. 448). Here we have a further indication of the necessity at the political level of implementing scientifically sound findings for the welfare of children.

Another fact that needs to be acknowledged is that in all societies there will be instances of abuse and violence in families, schools, churches, and associations. Experts surmise that the number of undisclosed cases is particularly high in the case of domestic violence. Uncontrollable hatred, affective irruptions, destructiveness, and perverted actions are part of human nature; curbing the crimes deriving from these unfortunate characteristics calls for a political system specifically geared to the purpose. The horror and indignation aroused by abuse scandals in Germany have led to a statutory initiative: "Children are entitled to non-violent upbringing" (cf. §1631 Para. 2 German Civil Code, in force since December 2000). Social, health, and educational policies on the one hand and the press and the public on the other are especially called upon to make this statement reality. We are justified in hoping that the newly created networks and counselling centres will help lift the taboo on investigating offences leading to traumatisation and assist victims in finding help for themselves.

During the 1960s and 1970s, the publication of studies by Anna Freud and Dorothy Burlingham (1942, 1943), René Spitz (1965), John Bowlby (1973), and others triggered greater public awareness of the way in which the separation of mother and child in infancy can qualify as a potentially traumatic event. Concrete measures for the improvement of mother–child relations were implemented on the political plane. In the German Democratic Republic (GDR), the *Wochenkrippe*, a crèche where children were deposited on Monday morning and only collected on the following Friday or Saturday, was then abolished (cf. p. 83 et seq.) on account of the realisation that many children reacted negatively to day-long or week-long separation from their mothers. They frequently reported sick and/or developed severe psychic disorders. A new diagnostic category was created for these cases: crèche compatibility. If a child was not "crèche-compatible", the mother was not expected to go out to work.

In the Federal Republic of Germany (BRD), the hitherto restrictive visiting hours in children's hospitals were loosened and opportunities created for rooming-in. Mothers with new babies now spend much less time in the maternity ward than was previously the case. In some of today's hospitals, the parents and the newborn baby are given a room to themselves (unless they elect to leave the hospital more or less immediately after the birth).

In the light of these gratifying developments it would make very good sense to systematically draw upon the insights produced by modern attachment theory to enhance child welfare and the feeling of security within families (Fonagy, Gergely, Jurist, & Target, 2002; Grossmann & Grossmann, 2004; Leuzinger-Bohleber et al., 2011). Midwives, infant pedagogues, paediatric physicians, and teachers should be trained and encouraged to look out for signs of inadequate attachment patterns. Notably in social flashpoint areas, preventive projects should be initiated and promoted. The new (German) child protection laws make it easier than before for doctors, teachers, and social workers to inform the youth welfare office of circumstances endangering child welfare that they have observed.

In this connection, care also needs to be taken in increasing the number of crèches in Germany (cf. memorandum of the German Psychoanalytic Association, DPV, 2008). Nursery-school educators should be given thorough schooling (not mere "crash courses") in the special requirements of infants and very small children. Conditions need to be created that strengthen children's attachment capacities. For most small children, spending more than half the day in a crèche, kindergarten, nursery school, etc., involves considerable stress. Physiological stress indicators can be detected in children up to the age of fifteen (Roisman et al., 2009). Children from unstable families, on the other hand, tend to profit in their development from whole-day attendance of such institutions. Accordingly, it is essential to proceed discriminatingly and create more opportunities for part-time jobs and flexible working hours for fathers and mothers. In the long term, it will almost definitely be necessary to include issues involved with crèche-compatibility in the routine examinations of young children, probably ending up with a testing and seal-of-approval system for nursery schools similar to the one already in place for old people's homes.

There is frequent debate about the necessity of providing children with as ideal an education as possible in view of the fact that they will be the mainstays of tomorrow's society, not least in terms of pension security. But this discussion tends to lose sight of one thing: the importance of *emotional* and *social* growth for a balanced development of the intelligence. Nor is there adequate appreciation of the joys that children can vouchsafe to their parents and other adults. Public spaces where children are welcome and where parents and children have time for one another plus family-friendly working conditions can contribute to a "climate change" of the positive variety, and support the development of sound attachment patterns.

Note

1. In December 2001, there were 5,327 Bosnian refugees still living in Berlin. The highest number was in December 1996 (28,719). In December 2001, there were 2,747 applications for residence on grounds of traumatisation, of which 743 had been decided on (Berlin Senate: Commissioner for Foreign Nationals).

REFERENCES

Abraham, K. (1924). A short study of the development of the libido, viewed in the light of mental disorders. In: *Selected Papers* (pp. 418–501). London: Hogarth, 1927.

Abraham, N., & Torok, M. (1986). *The Wolf Man's Magic Word: A Cryptonymy*. Minneapolis: University of Minnesota Press.

Alexander, F. (1950). *Psychosomatic Medicine: Its Principles and Applications*. New York: Norton.

Amati, S. (1987). Some thoughts on torture. *Free Associations*, 1: 94–114.

Amati, S. (1990). Die Rückgewinnung des Schamgefühls. *Psyche: Zeitschrift für Psychoanalyse und ihre Anwendungen*, 44: 724–740.

Bergmann, M. V. (1982). Thoughts on superego pathology of survivors and their children. In: M. S. Bergmann & M. E. Jucovy (Eds.), *Generations of the Holocaust* (pp. 287–309). New York: Basic Books.

Bick, E. (1968). The experience of the skin in early object-relations. *International Journal of Psychoanalysis*, 49: 484–486.

Bion, W. R. (1962). *Learning from Experience*. London: Heinemann.

Bion, W. R. (1970). Lies and the thinker. In: *Attention and Interpretation* (pp. 97–105). London: Tavistock.

Bohleber, W. (1997). Trauma, Identifizierung und historischer Kontext. Über die Notwendigkeit, die NS-Vergangenheit in den psychoanalytischen

Prozeß einzubeziehen. *Psyche: Zeitschrift für Psychoanalyse und ihre Anwendungen, 51*: 958–995.

Bohleber, W. (2007). Remembrance, trauma and collective memory: The battle for memory in psychoanalysis. *International Journal of Psychoanalysis, 88*: 329–352.

Bohleber, W. (2010). *Destructiveness, Intersubjectivity and Trauma: The Identity Crisis of Modern Psychoanalysis*. London: Karnac.

Bollas, C. (1987). *The Shadow of the Object: Psychoanalysis of the Unthought Known*. London: Free Association.

Boris, H. N. (1984). On the treatment of anorexia nervosa. *International Journal of Psychoanalysis, 65*: 435–442.

Botticelli, S. (2000). *Sandro Botticelli: Der Bilderzyklus zu Dantes Göttlicher Komödie* (exhibition catalogue). Berlin: Staatliche Museen zu Berlin, Preußischer Kulturbesitz.

Böwing, G., & Schröder, S. G. (2009). Spätfolgen von Kriegserlebnissen. Brückensymptome, Trauma-Reaktivierung und Retraumatisierung. *Trauma & Gewalt, 3*: 294–203.

Bowlby, J. (1973). *Attachment and Loss, Vol. 2: Separation: Anxiety and Anger*. London: Hogarth.

Britton, R. (1995). Psychic reality and unconscious belief. *International Journal of Psychoanalysis, 76*: 19–23.

Bruch, H. (1978). *The Golden Cage: The Enigma of Anorexia Nervosa*. Cambridge, MA: Harvard University Press.

Carhat-Harris, R. L., & Friston, K. J. (2010). The default-mode, ego functions and free-energy: A neurobiological account to Freud ideas. *Brain, 133*: 1265–1283.

Chasseguet-Smirgel, J. (1988). Vorwort. In: P. Zagermann, *Eros und Thanatos. Psychoanalytische Untersuchungen zu einer Objektbeziehungstheorie der Triebe* (pp. ix–xix). Darmstadt: Wissenschaftliche Buchgesellschaft.

Cohen, J. (1980). Structural consequences of psychic trauma: A new look at *Beyond the Pleasure Principle*. *International Journal of Psychoanalysis, 61*: 421–432.

Cohen, J. (1989). The two classes of psychoanalytic reconstruction: Why analysis requires both. (Unpubl. paper. German publication: Die zwei Arten der psychoanalytischen Rekonstruktion: warum Analysen beide benötigen. *Jahrbuch der Psychoanalyse, 30, 1993*: 65–100).

Cournut, J. (1988). Ein Rest, der verbindet. Das unbewußte Schuldgefühl, das entlehnte betreffend. *Jahrbuch der Psychoanalyse, 22*: 67–98.

DPV (2008). Memorandum der Deutschen Psychoanalytischen Vereinigung (DPV). Krippenausbau in Deutschland—Psychoanalytiker nehmen Stellung. *Psyche: Zeitschrift für Psychoanalyse und ihre Anwendungen, 62*: 202–205.

Dreher, A. U. (2000). *Foundations for Conceptual Research in Psychoanalysis*. London: Karnac.
Drewermann, E. (1990). *Kleriker. Psychogramm eines Ideals*. Freiburg: Walter.
Ebrecht-Laermann, A. (2009). Symbolverwendung und Symbolzerstörung. Was es bedeutet, zwischen Realität und Fiktion zu unterscheiden. *Semester-Journal des Karl-Abraham-Instituts, 17*: 9–26.
Eckert, A. (2011). "Zimmer mit Aussicht". Erinnern als unverzichtbares therapeutisches Element. *Forum der Psychoanalyse, 27*: 239–262.
Ehlers, A. (1999). *Posttraumatische Belastungsstörung*. Göttingen: Hogrefe.
Ehlert, M., & Lorke, B. (1988). Zur Psychodynamik der traumatischen Reaktion. *Psyche: Zeitschrift für Psychoanalyse und ihre Anwendungen, 42*: 502–532.
Ehlert-Balzer, M. (1996). Das Trauma als Objektbeziehung. Veränderung der inneren Objektwelt durch schwere Traumatisierung im Erwachsenenalter. *Forum der Psychoanalyse, 12*: 291–314.
Fenichel, O. (1932). Outline of clinical psychoanalysis (iii–iv). *Psychoanalytic Quarterly, 1*: 545–652.
Ferenczi, S. (1909). Introjection and transference. In: *First Contributions to Psycho-Analysis* (pp. 35–93). London: Maresfield, 1980.
Ferenczi, S. (1949). Confusion of tongues between adults and the child (1933). *International Journal of Psychoanalysis, 30*: 225–230.
Ferenczi, S., Abraham, K., Simmel, E., & Jones, E. (1921). *Psycho-Analysis and the War Neuroses* (Introduction by Sigmund Freud). London: The International Psycho-Analytic Press.
Fischer, G. (2000). *KÖDOPS. Kölner Dokumentations-und Planungssystem für dialektische Psychotherapie, Psychoanalyse und Traumabehandlung*. Köln/Much: Deutsches Institut für Psychotraumatologie (DIPT).
Fischer, G., & Riedesser, P. (1998). *Lehrbuch der Psychotraumatologie*. München: Reinhardt.
Focke, I. (2010). Widerstand, Übertragung und die Gefährdung des psychischen Gleichgewichts. *Psyche: Zeitschrift für Psychoanalyse und ihre Anwendungen, 64*: 34–58.
Fonagy, P. (1991). Der Prozess der Veränderung und die Veränderung psychischer Prozesse. In: H. Luft & G. Maas (Eds.), *Kurative Faktoren in der Psychoanalyse* (pp. 127–148). Proceedings of the DPV Meeting, Wiesbaden, 1991.
Fonagy, P., & Target, M. (2002). Neubewertung der Entwicklung der Affektregulation vor dem Hintergrund von Winnicotts Konzept des "falschen Selbst". *Psyche: Zeitschrift für Psychoanalyse und ihre Anwendungen, 56*: 839–862.
Fonagy, P., Gergely, G., Jurist, E. L., & Target, M. (2002). *Affect Regulation, Mentalization and the Development of the Self*. New York: Other Press.

Freud, A. (1937). *The Ego and the Mechanisms of Defense* (rev edn). New York: International Universities Press, 1966.

Freud, A., & Burlingham, D. (1942). *Young Children in War-Time*. London: Allen & Unwin.

Freud, A., & Burlingham, D. (1943). *Infants without Families*. London: Allen & Unwin.

Freud, S. (1890a). Psychical (or mental) treatment. *S. E.*, *7*: 281–302. London: Hogarth.

Freud, S. (1900a). *The Interpretation of Dreams*. *S. E.*, *4/5*. London: Hogarth.

Freud, S. (1901b). *The Psychopathology of Everyday Life*. *S. E.*, *6*. London: Hogarth.

Freud, S. (1916/17). *Introductory Lectures on Psycho-Analysis*. Lecture XVIII: Fixation to traumas—the unconscious. *S. E.*, *16*: 273–285. London: Hogarth.

Freud, S. (1918b). From the history of an infantile neurosis. *S. E.*, *17*: 7–122. London: Hogarth.

Freud, S. (1919d). Introduction to *Psycho-Analysis and the War Neuroses*. *S. E.*, *17*: 207–210.

Freud, S. (1920g). *Beyond the Pleasure Principle*. *S. E.*, *18*: 7–64. London: Hogarth.

Freud, S. (1923b). *The Ego and the Id*. *S. E.*, *19*: 12–59. London: Hogarth.

Freud, S. (1927e). Fetishism. *S. E.*, *21*: 152–157. London: Hogarth.

Freud, S. (1939a). *Moses and Monotheism: Three Essays*. *S. E.*, *23*: 1–138. London: Hogarth.

Freud, S. (1940e). Splitting of the ego in the process of defence. *S. E.*, *23*: 271–278. London: Hogarth.

Friederichs, H. (2010). Die Bundeswehr-Veteranen organisieren sich. *Zeit online*, www.zeit.de, 25/08/2010.

Gaddini, E. (1998). *"Das Ich ist vor allem ein Körperliches." Beiträge zur Psychoanalyse der ersten Strukturen* (Ed. by G. Jappe, & B. Strehlow). Tübingen: Edition diskord.

Gampel, Y. (1994). Identifizierung, Identität und generationsübergreifende Transmission. *Zeitschrift für psychoanalytische Theorie und Praxis*, *9*: 301–319.

Gergely, G. (2000). Reapproaching Mahler: New perspectives on normal autism, symbiosis, splitting and libidinal object constancy from cognitive developmental theory. *Journal of the American Psychoanalytic Association*, *48*: 1197–1228.

Gerzi, S. (2002). Integration holes into the whole: To live the absence in the memories of patients who were children during the Holocaust. In: S. Varvin & T. Stajner Popovic (Eds.), *Upheaval: Psychoanalytical Perspectives on Trauma* (pp. 101–132). Belgrade: International Aid Network.

Gierlichs, H. W., Haenel, F., Henningsen, F., Van Keuk, E., Scheef-Maier, G., Schaeffer, E., Spranger, H., Wenk-Ansohn, M., & Wirtgen, W. (2012). *Standards zur Begutachtung psychisch reaktiver Traumafolgen (in aufenthaltsrechtlichen Fragen)*. http://sbpm.web-com-service.de/downloads/SBPM_Standards_und_Curriculum_2012.pdf.

Green, A. (1975). The analyst, symbolization and absence in the analytic setting (on changes in analytic practice and analytic experience). *International Journal of Psychoanalysis, 56*: 1–22.

Green, A. (2001). The dead mother. In: *Life Narcissism, Death Narcissism* (pp. 170–200). London: Free Association.

Greenacre, P. (1967). The influence of infantile trauma on genetic patterns. In: *Emotional Growth (Vol. I)* (pp. 260–299). New York: International Universities Press, 1971.

Greenacre, P. (1971). *Emotional Growth*. New York: International Universities Press.

Grinberg, L. (1990). Projective counteridentification. In: *The Goals of Psychoanalysis: Identification, Identity and Supervision* (pp. 83–97). London: Karnac.

Grinberg, L. (1991). Countertransference and counter-identification in non-verbal communication. *Bulletin of the European Psychoanalytic Federation, 36*: 11–23.

Grossmann, K., & Grossmann, K. E. (2004). *Bindungen—das Gefüge psychischer Sicherheit*. Stuttgart: Klett-Cotta.

Grubrich-Simitis, I. (1981). Extreme traumatization as cumulative trauma—Psychoanalytic investigations of the effects of concentration camp experiences on survivors and their children. *Psychoanalytic Study of the Child, 36*: 415–450.

Grubrich-Simitis, I. (1984). From concretism to metaphor: Thoughts on some theoretical und technical aspects of the psychoanalytic work with children of Holocaust survivors. *Psychoanalytic Study of the Child, 39*: 301–319.

Grubrich-Simitis, I. (1988). Trauma or drive—drive and trauma: A reading of Sigmund Freud's phylogenetic fantasy of 1915. *Psychoanalytic Study of the Child, 43*: 3–32.

Grubrich-Simitis, I. (2007). Trauma oder Trieb—Trieb und Trauma. Wieder betrachtet. *Psyche: Zeitschrift für Psychoanalyse und ihre Anwendungen, 61*: 637–656.

Grubrich-Simitis, I. (2008). Realitätsprüfung an Stelle von Deutung. Eine Phase in der psychoanalytischen Arbeit mit Nachkommen von Holocaust-Überlebenden. *Psyche: Zeitschrift für Psychoanalyse und ihre Anwendungen, 62*: 1091–1121.

Grunberger, B. (1979). *Narcissism: Psychoanalytic Essays*. New York: International Universities Press.

Haenel, F., & Wenk-Ansohn, M. (Eds.) (2004). *Begutachtung psychisch reaktiver Traumafolgen in aufenthaltsrechtlichen Verfahren.* Weinheim: Beltz.

Hägler, M. (2011). Wenn der Krieg nach Regen kommt. *Süddeutsche Zeitung*, 05/03/2011, p. R17.

Henningsen, F. (1976). *Ulcus pepticum. Psychosomatische Aspekte.* Freiburg i.Br.: Alber.

Henningsen, F. (1980). Die psychische Belastung des Knochenmarkspenders und die Bedeutung begleitender Psychotherapie. *Praxis der Kinderpsychologie und Kinderpsychiatrie, 29*: 37–42.

Henningsen, F. (1988). "... aber die Gespräche mit Ihnen waren so interessant." Eine Behandlung über Bilder. *Zeitschrift für Theorie und Praxis der Psychoanalyse, 3*: 23–47.

Henningsen, F. (1990). Psychisches Trauma—Psychische Realität. *Zeitschrift für psychoanalytische Theorie und Praxis, 5*: 204–227.

Henningsen, F. (1993). "In diese Hölle will ich nicht." Zur Psychoanalyse eines Homosexuellen mit latenter Perversion. *Zeitschrift für psychoanalytische Theorie und Praxis, 8*: 374–388.

Henningsen, F. (2002). Inszenierung von Todesängsten in der Kindertherapie. Aspekte der Symbolbildung bei psychischem Trauma. *Semester-Journal des Karl-Abraham-Instituts*, Wintersemester 2002/03: 33–49.

Henningsen, F. (2003). Traumatisierte Flüchtlinge und der Prozess der Begutachtung. Psychoanalytische Perspektiven. *Psyche: Zeitschrift für Psychoanalyse und ihre Anwendungen, 57*: 97–120.

Henningsen, F. (2004a). Übertragung und Gegenübertragung bei der Begutachtung traumatisierter Flüchtlinge. In: F. Haenel & M. Wenk-Ansohn (Eds.), *Begutachtung psychisch reaktiver Traumafolgen in aufenthaltsrechtlichen Verfahren* (pp. 184–207). Weinheim: Beltz.

Henningsen, F. (2004b). Macht und Ohnmacht in Übertragung und Gegenübertragung bei der Begutachtung traumatisierter Flüchtlinge. In: A. Springer, A. Gerlach & A.-M. Schlösser (Eds.), *Macht und Ohnmacht* (pp. 321–340). Gießen: Psychosozial-Verlag.

Henningsen, F. (2004c). Angst und konkretistische Fusion bei frühem Trennungstrauma. In: A.U. Dreher, M. Juszczak & M. Schmidt (Eds.), *Theorie und Klinik der Angst* (pp. 55–61). Proceedings of the DPV Meeting, Bad Homburg, 2004.

Henningsen, F. (2005). Early infantile trauma and concretistic fusion: On transforming objectless anxiety into separation anxiety. IPA 44th Congress, Rio de Janeiro.

Henningsen, F. (2008). Konkretistische Fusion, Agieren und Symbolisieren. Zum psychoanalytischen Prozeß bei schwerem frühkindlichem Trauma. *Psyche: Zeitschrift für Psychoanalyse und ihre Anwendungen, 62*: 1148–1169.

Henningsen, F. (2011a). Zur Transformation objektloser Angst in Trennungsangst—Frühkindliches Trauma und konkretistische Fusion. In: A. Ludwig & U. Bahner (Eds.), *Festband zum Symposium zum 20jährigen Bestehen des Sächsischen Institutes für Psychoanalyse und Psychotherapie* (pp. 33–41). Leipzig: Web Pro Medico.

Henningsen, F. (2011b). Eine Antwort auf Helmut Thomäs Gedanken zu meinem Vortrag: "Zur Transformation objektloser Angst in Trennungsangst—Frühkindliches Trauma und konkretistische Fusion." In: A. Ludwig, & U. Bahner (Eds.), *Festband zum Symposium zum 20jährigen Bestehen des Sächsischen Institutes für Psychoanalyse und Psychotherapie* (pp. 80–84). Leipzig: Web Pro Medico.

Henningsen, F. (2011c). Widerstand. Eine Frage der analytischen Haltung? *Psychotherapeut*, 56: 118–127.

Henningsen, F., & Ullner, R. (1981). Die psychotherapeutische Betreuung sterbender und lebensbedrohlich erkrankter Kinder und ihrer Familien. In: G. Biermann (Ed.), *Handbuch der Kinderpsychotherapie (Vol. IV)* (pp. 610–623). München: Reinhardt.

Herman, J. (1992). *Trauma and Recovery*. New York: Basic Books.

Hirsch, M. (2004). *Psychoanalytische Traumatologie—das Trauma in der Familie. Psychoanalytische Theorie und Therapie schwerer Persönlichkeitsstörungen*. Stuttgart: Schattauer.

Hirsch, M. (2011). *Trauma*. Gießen: Psychosozial-Verlag.

Holderegger, H. (1998). *Der Umgang mit dem Trauma* (2nd edn). Stuttgart: Klett-Cotta.

Kardiner, A. (1941). *The Traumatic Neuroses of War*. New York: Hoeber.

Keilson, H. (2011). *Da steht mein Haus. Erinnerungen*. Frankfurt/Main: Fischer (English edition: *There Stands My House: A Memoir*. Melbourne: Scribe, 2012).

Kernberg, O. F. (1975). *Borderline Conditions and Pathological Narcissism*. New York: Aronson.

Kernberg, O. F. (1976). *Object Relations Theory and Clinical Psychoanalysis*. New York: Aronson.

Kernberg, O. F. (1991). Sadomasochism, sexual excitement, and perversion. *Journal of the American Psychoanalytic Association*, 39: 333–362.

Kernberg, O. F. (1992). *Aggression in Personality Disorders and Perversions*. New Haven: Yale University Press.

Kestenberg, J. S. (1989). Transposition revisited: clinical, therapeutic, and developmental considerations. In: P. Marcus & A. Rosenberg (Eds.), *Healing Their Wounds: Psychotherapy with Holocaust Survivors and their Families* (pp. 67–82). New York: Praeger.

Khan, M. M. R. (1974). *Privacy of the Self: Papers on Psychoanalytic Theory and Technique*. New York: International Universities Press.

Khan, M. M. R. (1979). Fetish as negation of the self: Clinical notes on foreskin fetishism in a male homosexual. In: *Alienation in Perversion* (pp. 139–176). London: Hogarth.

Kinston, W., & Cohen, J. (1986). Primal repression: Clinical and theoretical aspects. *International Journal of Psychoanalysis, 67*: 337–355.

Klein, H. (1984). Wiedergutmachung—Ein Akt der Retraumatisierung. In: Evangelische Akademie Bad Boll (Ed.), *Die Bundesrepublik Deutschland und die Opfer des Nationalsozialismus* (pp. 51–52). (Protokolldienst, 14). Bad Boll: Evangelische Akademie.

Klein, M. (1946). Notes on some schizoid mechanisms. *International Journal of Psychoanalysis, 27*: 99–110.

Klein, M. (1952). Some theoretical conclusions regarding the emotional life of the infant. In: *Envy and Gratitude and Other Works 1946–1963* (pp. 61–93). London: Hogarth.

Klüwer, R. (1983). Agieren und Mitagieren. In: S. O. Hoffmann (Ed.), *Deutung und Beziehung. Kritische Beiträge zur Behandlungskonzeption und Technik in der Psychoanalyse* (pp. 132–145). Frankfurt/Main: Fischer.

Klüwer, R. (1995). Agieren und Mitagieren—zehn Jahre später. *Zeitschrift für psychoanalytische Theorie und Praxis, 10*: 45–70.

Klüwer, R. (2005). M.C. Escher—Spielen mit Bildern und Gedanken. Psychoanalytische Assoziationen zu einem dimensionalen Modell der inneren Realität. *Jahrbuch der Psychoanalyse, 50*: 191–224.

Kogan, I. (1990). Vermitteltes und reales Trauma in der Psychoanalyse von Kindern von Holocaust-Überlebenden. *Psyche: Zeitschrift für Psychoanalyse und ihre Anwendungen, 44*: 533–544.

Kogan, I. (1995). *The Cry of Mute Children: A Psychoanalytic Perspective of the Second Generation of the Holocaust*. London: Free Association.

Kogan, I. (2007). *Escape from Selfhood: Breaking Boundaries and Craving for Oneness*. London: International Psychoanalytic Association.

Köhle, K., & Simons, C. (1982). Anorexia nervosa. In: Th. v. Uexküll (Ed.), *Einführung in die Psychosomatische Medizin* (pp. 529–556). München: Urban & Schwarzenberg.

Krejci, E. (2011). Zur Relevanz von Freuds "Ichspaltung im Abwehrvorgang" als Brückenkonzept für die Erweiterung des Neurosenmodells der Psychoanalyse. *Psyche: Zeitschrift für Psychoanalyse und ihre Anwendungen, 65*: 1–29.

Krystal, H. (Ed.) (1968). *Massive Psychic Trauma*. New York: International Universities Press.

Künzler, E. (1992). Der homosexuelle Mann in der Psychoanalyse. Theorie und Praxis im Wandel. *Forum der Psychoanalyse, 8*: 202–216.

Lamott, F., & Lempa, G. (2011). Zwischen Anerkennung und Zurückweisung. Das Kriegstrauma im politischen Kontext. *Forum der Psychoanalyse, 27*: 263–277.

Laub, D., & Weine, S. M. (1994). Die Suche nach der historischen Wahrheit: Psychotherapeutische Arbeit mit bosnischen Flüchtlingen. *Psyche: Zeitschrift für Psychoanalyse und ihre Anwendungen, 48*: 1101–1122.

Leuzinger-Bohleber, M., Fischmann, T., Läzer, K. L., Pfenning-Meerkötter, N., Wolff, A., & Green, J. (2011). Frühprävention psychosozialer Störungen bei Kindern mit belasteten Kindheiten. *Psyche: Zeitschrift für Psychoanalyse und ihre Anwendungen, 65*: 989–1022.

Levi, P. (1959). *If this is a Man*. New York: Orion.

Lipin, T. (1955). Psychic functioning in patients with undiagnosed somatic symptoms. *AMA Archives of Neurology & Psychiatry, 73*: 329–337.

Loch, W. (1985). Anmerkungen zur Pathogenese und Psychodynamik der Hysterie. *Jahrbuch der Psychoanalyse, 17*: 135–174.

Lorenzer, A. (1965). Ein Abwehrsyndrom bei traumatischen Verläufen. *Psyche: Zeitschrift für Psychoanalyse und ihre Anwendungen, 18*: 685–700.

Lorenzer, A., & Thomä, H. (1965). Über die zweiphasige Symptomentwicklung bei traumatischen Neurosen. *Psyche: Zeitschrift für Psychoanalyse und ihre Anwendungen, 18*: 674–684.

Mahler, E., & Thomä, H. (1964). Über die simultane Psychotherapie einer Anorexia-nervosa-Kranken und ihrer Mutter. *Jahrbuch der Psychoanalyse, 3*: 174–211.

Mahler, M. (1968). *On Human Symbiosis and the Vicissitudes of Individuation*. New York: International Universities Press.

Mahler, M., Pine, F., & Bergman, A. (1975). *The Psychological Birth of the Human Infant*. London: Hutchinson.

Marty, P. (1958). Die allergische Objektbeziehung. In: K. Brede (Ed.), *Einführung in die psychosomatische Medizin* (pp. 420–445). Frankfurt/Main: Fischer, 1974.

McDougall, J. (1982). *Plea for a Measure of Abnormality*. New York: International Universities Press.

McDougall, J. (1989). One body for two. In: *Theaters of the Body: A Psychoanalytic Approach to Psychosomatic Illness* (pp. 140–161). New York: Norton.

Meltzer, D. (1966). The relation of anal masturbation to projective identification. *International Journal of Psychoanalysis, 47*: 335–342.

Meltzer, D. (1975). Adhesive identification. *Contemporary Psychoanalysis, 11*: 289–310.

Meltzer, D. (1984). *Dream-Life: A Re-Examination of the Psycho-Analytical Theory and Technique*. Perthshire: Clunie.

Meltzer, D. (1990). *The Claustrum: An Investigation of Claustrophobic Phenomena*. London: Karnac.

Mentzos, S. (2009). *Lehrbuch der Psychodynamik. Die Funktion der Dysfunktionalität psychischer Störungen*. Göttingen: Vandenhoeck & Ruprecht.

Milner, M. (1952). Aspects of symbolism in comprehension of the not-self. *International Journal of Psychoanalysis, 33*: 181–195.

Milner, M. (1969). *The Hands of the Living God*. London: Hogarth.
Mitscherlich, A. (1966/67). *Krankheit als Konflikt. Studien zur psychosomatischen Medizin*. Frankfurt/Main: Suhrkamp.
Money-Kyrle, R. (1971). The aim of psychoanalysis. *International Journal of Psychoanalysis*, 52: 103–106.
Morgenthaler, F. (1974). Die Stellung der Perversionen in Metapsychologie und Technik. *Psyche: Zeitschrift für Psychoanalyse und ihre Anwendungen*, 28: 1077–1098.
Müller-Pozzi, H. (1982). Trauma und Neurose. In: R. Berna-Glantz & P. Dreyfus (Eds.), *Trauma, Konflikt, Deckerinnerung* (pp. 102–120). Stuttgart: Frommann-Holzboog.
M'Uzan, M. de (1977). Zur Psychologie der psychosomatisch Kranken. *Psyche: Zeitschrift für Psychoanalyse und ihre Anwendungen*, 31: 318–332.
Niederland, W. G. (1981). The survivor syndrome: Further observations and dimensions. *Journal of the American Psychoanalytic Association*, 29: 413–425.
Nissen, B. (2008). On the determination of autistoid organizations in non-autistic adults. *International Journal of Psychoanalysis*, 89: 261–277.
Ogden, T. H. (1989). On the concept of an autistic-contiguous position. *International Journal of Psychoanalysis*, 70: 127–140.
Oliner, M. M. (1996). External reality: The elusive dimension of psychoanalysis. *Psychoanalytic Quarterly*, 65: 267–300.
Oliner, M. M. (2010). Life is not a dream: The importance of being real. *Journal of the American Psychoanalytic Association*, 58: 1139–1157.
O'Shaughnessy, E. (2003). Eine invasive projektive Identifizierung. Wie Patienten in Denken und Fühlen des Analytikers eindringen. *Jahrbuch der Psychoanalyse*, 46: 9–28.
Parsons, M. (2011). Discussion of Franziska Henningsen's paper: Destruction and consolation in one Person. 4th British German Colloquium, Hamburg. (Unpubl. paper).
Plänkers, T. (2008). Die Verbindung von Trauma und Konflikt: das Konzept der intrusiven Identifizierung. *Semester-Journal des Karl-Abraham-Instituts*, 17: 29–44.
Plassmann, R. (2007). *Die Kunst des Lassens. Psychotherapie mit EMDR für Erwachsene und Kinder*. Gießen (Psychosozial-Verlag).
Pross, C. (2001). *Wiedergutmachung. Der Kleinkrieg gegen die Opfer*. Berlin: Philo.
Quinodoz, J.-M. (1999). Dreams that turn over a page. Integration dreams with paradoxical regressive content. *International Journal of Psychoanalysis*, 80: 225–238.
Reddemann, L. (2011). *Psychodynamisch Imaginative Traumatherapie PITT. Das Manual: Ein resilienzorientierter Ansatz in der Psychotraumatologie* (6th edn). Stuttgart: Klett-Cotta.

Reddemann, L., & Sachsse, U. (1998). Welche Psychoanalyse ist für Opfer geeignet? *Forum der Psychoanalyse, 14*: 289–294.

Reddemann, L., & Wöller, W. (2011). Psychodynamische Verfahren. In: G. H. Seidler, H. J. Freyberger, & A. Maercker (Eds.), *Handbuch der Psychotraumatologie* (pp. 580–589). Stuttgart: Klett-Cotta.

Reiche, R. (1990). *Geschlechterspannung. Eine psychoanalytische Untersuchung.* Frankfurt/Main: Fischer.

Rhode, M. (2005). Mirroring, imitation, identification: The sense of self in relation to the mother's internal world. *Journal of Child Psychotherapy, 31*: 52–71.

Roisman, G. I., Susman, E., Barnett-Walker, K., Booth-LaForce, C., Owen, M. T., Belsky, J., Bradley, R. H., Houts, R., & Steinberg, L. (NICHD Early Child Care Research Network) (2009). Early family and child-care antecedents of awakening cortisol levels in adolescence. *Child Development, 80*: 907–920.

Rosenberg, F. (2010). *Introjekt und Trauma. Einführung in eine integrative psychoanalytische Traumabehandlung.* Frankfurt/Main: Brandes & Apsel.

Rosenfeld, H. (1987). *Impasse and Interpretation: Therapeutic and Anti-Therapeutic Factors in the Psychoanalytic Treatment of Psychotic, Borderline and Neurotic Patients.* London: Tavistock.

Sachsse, U. (2004). *Traumazentrierte Psychotherapie. Theorie, Klinik und Praxis.* Stuttgart: Schattauer.

Sandler, J., Dreher, A. U., & Drews, S. (1991). An approach to conceptual research in psychoanalysis illustrated by a consideration of psychic trauma. *International Review of Psycho-Analysis, 18*: 133–141.

Schacht, L. (1987). Der imaginäre Planet. Zur Nutzung des intermediären Raumes in der Initialphase einer Kinderpsychotherapie. *Zeitschrift für psychoanalytische Theorie und Praxis, 2*: 88–107.

Scharff, J. M. (2002). Zur Zentrierung auf innere und äußere Faktoren als zwei Perspektiven des klinischen Verstehens. *Psyche: Zeitschrift für Psychoanalyse und ihre Anwendungen, 56*: 601–629.

Schickedanz, H., & Plassmann, R. (2011). Belastende Kindheitserfahrungen und körperliche Erkrankungen. In: G. H. Seidler, H. J. Freyberger & A. Maercker (Eds.), *Handbuch der Psychotraumatologie* (pp. 435–449). Stuttgart: Klett-Cotta.

Schore, A. N. (2003). *Affect Regulation & the Repair of the Self.* New York: Norton.

Schöttler, C. (1981). Zur Behandlungstechnik bei psychosomatisch schwer gestörten Patienten. *Psyche: Zeitschrift für Psychoanalyse und ihre Anwendungen, 35*: 111–141.

Schubbe, O. (2004). Störungskonzepte und Neurobiologie. In: F. M. Haenel & M. Wenk-Ansohn (Eds.), *Begutachtung reaktiver Traumafolgen in aufenthaltsrechtlichen Verfahren* (pp. 11–36). Weinheim, Basel: Beltz.

Segal, H. (1957). Notes on symbol formation. *International Journal of Psychoanalysis, 38*: 391–397.
Seliger, M. (2011). Im Frühling kam der Tod. Traumatisiert in Afghanistan. *FAZ.Net*, www.faz.net, 07/04/2011.
Shapiro, F. (2001). *Eye Movement Desensitization and Reprocessing: Basic Principles, Protocols, and Procedures* (2nd edn). New York: Guilford.
Sharpe, E. F. (1937). *Dream Analysis: A Practical Handbook for Psychoanalysts*. London: Hogarth.
Sperling, E., & Massing, A. (1970). Der familiäre Hintergrund der Anorexia nervosa. *Zeitschrift für psychosomatische Medizin, 16*: 130–141.
Spitz, R. (1965). *The First Year of Life: A Psychoanalytic Study of Normal and Deviant Development of Object Relations*. New York: International Universities Press.
Steiner, J. (1993). *Psychic Retreats: Pathological Organisations in Psychotic, Neurotic, and Borderline Patients*. London: Routledge.
Stephanos, S. (1981). Das Konzept der "pensée operatoire" und das "psychosomatische Phänomen". In: Th. v. Uexküll (Ed.), *Lehrbuch der psychosomatischen Medizin* (2nd edn) (pp. 217–241). München: Urban & Schwarzenberg.
Stern, D. N. (1995). *The Motherhood Constellation: A Unified View of Parent-Infant Psychotherapy*. New York: Basic Books.
Stoller, R. J. (1985). Research on homosexuality: The rules of the game. In: *Observing the Erotic Imagination* (pp. 167–183). New Haven, CT: Yale University Press.
Thomä, H. (1961). *Anorexia nervosa. Geschichte, Klinik und Theorien der Pubertätsmagersucht*. Bern: Huber; Stuttgart: Klett.
Thomä, H. (1981). Über die psychoanalytische Behandlung eines magersüchtigen Mädchens. In: *Schriften zur Praxis der Psychoanalyse: Vom spiegelnden zum aktiven Psychoanalytiker* (pp. 267–316). Frankfurt/Main: Suhrkamp.
Thomä, H. (2011). Einige Gedanken zum Vortrag von Franziska Henningsen "Zur Transformation objektloser Angst in Trennungsangst— Frühkindliches Trauma und konkretistische Fusion." In: A. Ludwig & U. Bahner (Eds.), *Festband zum Symposium zum 20jährigen Bestehen des Sächsischen Institutes für Psychoanalyse und Psychotherapie* (pp. 76–79). Leipzig: Web Pro Medico.
Timmermann-Levanas, A., & Richter, A. (2010). *Die reden—wir sterben. Wie unsere Soldaten zu Opfern der deutschen Politik werden*. Frankfurt/Main: Campus.
Trimborn, W. (1999). Der analytische Prozeß und die Fähigkeit zur Destruktion. *Zeitschrift für psychoanalytische Theorie und Praxis, 14*: 17–30.
Tustin, F. (1986). *Autistic Barriers in Neurotic Patients*. London: Karnac.

United Nations High Commissioner for Refugees (2001). *Istanbul Protocol. Manual on the effective investigation and documentation of torture and other cruel, inhuman or degrading treatment or punishment.* New York, Geneva: United Nations.

Van der Kolk, B. (1996). Trauma and memory. In: B. van der Kolk, A. McFarlane & L. Weisaeth (Eds.), *Traumatic Stress: The Effects of Overwhelming Experience in Mind, Body and Society.* New York: Guilford.

Varvin, S. (2000). Die gegenwärtige Vergangenheit. Extreme Traumatisierung und Psychotherapie. *Psyche: Zeitschrift für Psychoanalyse und ihre Anwendungen, 54*: 895–930.

Wackernagel, K. M. (2011). Psychoanalyse und Traumatherapie. Das Gewalttrauma als Einbruch in die innere Realität. *Forum der Psychoanalyse, 27*: 223–237.

Wangh, M. (1965). Verfolgungsgeschädigte vor deutschen Gutachtern. *Psyche: Zeitschrift für Psychoanalyse und ihre Anwendungen, 25*: 716–719.

Winnicott, D. W. (1953). Transitional objects and transitional phenomena. *International Journal of Psychoanalysis, 34*: 89–97.

Winnicott, D. W. (1955). Metapsychological and clinical aspects of regression within the psycho-analytical set-up. *International Journal of Psychoanalysis, 36*: 16–36.

Winnicott, D. W. (1958). The capacity to be alone. In: *The Maturational Processes and the Facilitating Environment: Studies in the Theory of Emotional Development* (pp. 29–36). London: Karnac, 2007.

Winnicott, D. W. (1971). *Playing and Reality.* London: Tavistock.

Zimmermann, P. L., Ströhle, A., & Hahne, H. H. (2009). Psychiatrische Erkrankungen bei Bundeswehrsoldaten. Veränderungen in der Inanspruchnahme medizinischer Versorgungssysteme im Vergleich der Jahre 2000 und 2006. *Trauma & Gewalt, 3*: 316–327.

Zwiebel, R. (2010). *Der Schlaf des Analytikers. Die Müdigkeitsreaktion in der Gegenübertragung* (3rd edn). Stuttgart: Klett-Cotta.

INDEX

abandoned child, 185
abnormal child, 86
abortion, 99, 156, 163, 198
abortive separation, 38
Abraham, K., xxii, 73
Abraham, N., 73
abusive, 205
acting-out, 21, 23, 38, 83, 132, 184–185, 254
action symptoms, 110, 114
acute stress, 211–212
acute traumatisation, 211
addiction disorders, 68
adolescence, 24, 40, 84, 135, 264
adult analysis, 4
adulthood, xvii, 26, 35, 38, 40, 74, 165, 209, 241
affect-splitting, 65, 69, 74
aggression, 46, 50, 58, 90, 92, 102, 109, 111, 122, 131, 166, 209, 211
  see also: anxiety
alacritous cooperation, 69
Alexander, F., 105

altruistic life, 106
Amati, S., 23, 76
amenorrhoea, 44
analytic theory and practice, xv, xxiii
anamnesis, 11, 44, 61, 220, 233
anxiety, 22, 27–28, 33, 38, 41, 65, 76, 81, 95, 110, 157, 181, 183, 214–215, 233
  annihilation, 72, 83
  massive, 172, 245
  objectless, 38, 40–41, 73, 81, 83, 95
  separation, 81, 84, 92, 199
asceticism at puberty, 62
Association of Statutory Health Physicians, 246
autism, reactive, 44
autistic-contiguous position, 76
autistic features, 82, 198
autistic objects, hard, 72, 73
autistic phenomena, 61, 62, 72, 74, 76
avoidance behaviour, 212, 214–215, 232, 243 *see also*: anxiety

281

behaviour(al), 28, 31, 45–46, 51, 86, 147, 162, 212, 214–215, 232, 236, 243
  avoidance, 212, 214–215, 232, 243
  controlling, 185
  emphatic, 86
  perverted, 198
  play, 18
  promiscuous, 103
  refined, 165
  transvestite, 125
behavioural therapists, xxiv *see also*: psychoanalysis
behaviour patterns, 198
Bergmann, M. V., xxiv
Bick, E., 76
Bion, W. R., 22, 67–68, 82, 131, 168, 254
Bohleber, W., xii, xxv, 22, 76, 109, 204, 213, 253
Bollas, C., xxiv
Boris, H. N., 52, 62
Botticelli, S., 238
Böwing, G., 261
Bowlby, J., xxiii, 265
breastfeeding, 94, 128
Britton, R., 63
Bruch, H., 61
bulimia, 83–84, 87, 93, 116
Burlingham, D., xxiii, 265
burnout syndrome, 71, 217

Carhat-Harris, R. L., 134
case studies
  childhood traumas, 143–159
  children with traumas, 4–18
  concretistic fusion, 23–41
  destruction and consolation, 179–196
  destruction and guilt, 115–132
  perversion structures, 161–178
  separation traumas, 83–96
  concretistic fusion and denial of object loss, 97–108
  suspicion and splitting-off of violence, 224–229
  withdrawal and communicating in images, 43–64

Caucasian Chalk Circle, 175
central traumatic affliction, 137
Chasseguet-Smirgel, J., 131
chemotherapy, 34–35, 37
child
  analysis, xxiii, 148
  therapy, 40
childhood traumas, 25, 38, 143, 243, 264
children's feelings, 113
child's anxieties, 22, 81
chronic diarrhoea, 110, 130
chronic nervousness, 212
claustrum theory, 74
Cleric: A Psychoanalytic Study of Clergymen and Religious Orders, The, 174
clinical experience, xxv, 73
cognitive awareness, 70
Cohen, J., 113, 137, 139–140, 155, 167, 169–170
compulsive-neurotic defence syndrome, 65
compulsive repetition, xxvi, 132–133, 137–139, 149, 171, 202, 243, 246, 251, 254, 260–261
concretistic fusion, xviii, xxvi, 17, 21, 26, 28, 66, 70, 83–84, 86, 108, 110, 134, 183, 199, 206
conjunctivitis, 33, 36
conscious *see also*: unconscious
  analyst's, 21, 24, 72, 74–75, 83, 104, 135–136, 209, 217–218, 247
  child's, 135
  patient's, 74, 83, 136, 153, 167, 200, 236, 246
  pre-, 3, 259
consoling objects, 107
coprophagic children, 86
countertransference, xvii, xxvii, 4, 16–17, 21–23, 26–28, 31–32, 70, 85, 110, 143, 213–215, 217 *see also*: transference
  emotional, xviii
  identifications, 21
Cournut, J., 113, 117, 130, 254

crippling fatigue, 87
cumulative trauma, 23, 130, 135, 164, 177

debriefing, 213
defence mechanism, xviii, xxiii, 21,
    65–66, 145, 147, 217, 261
degree of dissociation, 4
Democratic Action Party (SDA), 227
dental disorders, 155
depression, xxvi, 30, 46, 50, 75, 82, 98
development(al) *see also*: conscious
    balanced, 266
    infant, xxiii, 63, 139
    mental, 68, 134
    narcissistic, 205
    personality, xviii, xxv, 237
    pre-traumatic, 70, 219, 227
    psychology, xxiii, 95, 129, 139
    psychoneurotic, 25, 38
    psychotic, 47
    relationship, 135
    theories, 69
diabolical creatures, 182
diagnosis and indication, 138, 219
diagnostic assessment, 210
dissociative reactions, 212
Dreher, A. U., xxiii
Drewermann, E., 174
Drews, S., xxiii

early-childhood trauma, 61
Ebrecht-Laermann, A., 74
Eckert, A., 249
ego, xxi–xxiii, xxvii, 22, 26, 35,
    39, 65–67, 69, 71, 82, 100,
    108, 153
  -centric, 46
  conflict, xxii
  -development, 7, 164
  -distortions, 135
  function(s), 82, 155, 176, 209
  peace-, xxii
  -regression, 61
  restriction, 69, 134, 198
  -splitting, 65–66, 69, 100
  -strength, 221

Ehlers, A., 213
Ehlert, M., 171
Ehlert-Balzer, M., 249
EMDR *see* eye movement
    desensitization and
    reprocessing (EMDR)
emotional
    care, 131
    hyperarousal, 70
    modulations, 227
    numbness, 212
    physical impulses, 227
    significance, 143, 158
    tensions, 170
enuresis, 164
ergotherapists, xxiv
*Escape from Selfhood: Breaking Boundaries
    and Craving for Oneness*, 74
extricating, 41, 89
eye movement desensitization and
    reprocessing (EMDR), 249, 255

fatigue, 50, 87, 214
fear of death, 204
Federal Armed Forces, 261, 263–264
Federal Medical Association, 263
Federal Psychotherapy Association,
    263
Federal Republic of Germany (BRD),
    265
feeling of pressure, 119
feelings of guilt, 28, 109–111, 130–131,
    156, 187, 226, 254 *see also*:
    unconscious
    aggression, 131, 254
    parental, 130
    unconscious, 109, 111
Fenichel, O., 62
Ferenczi, S., xxi, xxii, 73
Fifth International Psychoanalytic
    Conference, xxi
Fischer, G., 213, 219, 244, 259
Fixation to traumas—the unconscious
    (Freud), xxi
Focke, I., 202
Fonagy, P., 22, 39, 82, 135, 202, 254, 265

free association, 69, 117, 219
Freud, A., 62, 82
Freud, S., 105, 130, 133–134, 154, 167, 265
Freudian Marxism, xxiv
Friederichs, H., 262
Friston, K. J., 134

Gaddini, E., 60, 73, 82–83, 94
Gampel, Y., xxiv, 130, 258
Gergely, G., 22–23, 39, 82, 135, 265
German Democratic Republic (GDR), 265
Gerzi, S., 217
Gierlichs, H. W., 263
Green, A., 75, 82, 147, 164, 199
Greenacre, P., 83, 129, 134
Grinberg, L., 21, 231, 248
Grossmann, K., 265
Grossmann, K. E., 265
Grubrich-Simitis, I., xxv, 21, 110, 130, 150, 252
Grunberger, B., 164
guilt, xxii, 27–28, 87, 102, 109, 120–123, 156, 215–216, 229–230, 234–235, 254 *see also*: unconscious

Haenel, F., xii, 209, 263
Hägler, M., 263
Hahne, H. H., 261
hallucination, 35, 82
healing, xxi, 37, 41
Henningsen, F., 3, 17, 21, 23, 28, 32–33, 40, 43
Herman, J., 211
Hirsch, M., 68, 211
Holderegger, H., 251
Holocaust victims, xxiv, 260
homoeroticism, 31, 40, 94, 157, 169, 171, 177
hormone treatment, 98
hyperactivity, 212
hyperarousal, 70, 134, 243 *see also*: emotional: hyperarousal

ICD-10, xxii, 211–212, 241
idealisation phase, 194

implicit-procedural memory, 139
impulsive action, 122
incestuous component, 36
incipient symbolisation, 89, 95
infancy, xxiii, xxvi, 21, 28, 39, 69, 73, 81, 134–136, 139, 161, 163, 197, 199–200, 202
infant trauma, xxiii, 70, 77, 90, 135, 138, 201
infant traumatisation, 69, 204
intensive care, 26
interactional concatenation, 81
International Journal of Psychoanalysis, 109
interpretive technique, 4, 39
intrusive traumas, 210
investigation of narcissism, xxiv
Istanbul Protocol, 263

Jacobson, E., 66
Jones, E., xxi–xxii
Jurist, E. L., 39, 135, 265

Kardiner, A., 66
Keilson, H., xiii
Kernberg, O. F., xxiii, xxiv, 6, 22, 66–67, 82, 164
Kestenberg, J. S., xxiv
Khan, M. M. R., 23, 126, 131, 135, 161, 164, 166, 172, 176
Kinston, W., 137, 155, 167
Klein, H., xxiii, 66–67, 154, 260
Klüwer, R., 76, 83, 114, 251
Kogan, I., xxiv, 74–75, 202, 204
Köhle, K., 44, 61
Krejci, E., 65, 69
Krystal, H., 260
Künzler, E., 177

Lamott, F., 257, 263
Laub, D., 210, 227, 259
Leuzinger-Bohleber, M., 265
Levi, P., 238
Lempa, G., 257, 263
leukaemia, xxvi, 4, 6, 33–34, 37, 71, 124
Lipin, T., 28, 109, 139

Loch, W., 57–58, 153
Lorenzer, A., 65–66, 69, 132, 158
Lorke, B., 171

Mahler, E., 106, 148
Mahler, M., 44, 63, 66
manic defence, 25, 94, 183, 203
Manual of Psychodynamics, 211
Manual of Psychotraumatology, 264
marital disputes, 184
Marty, P., 61
Massing, A., 44, 61
masochistic sexual fantasies, 125
masochistic ties, 117
masturbation, 132, 175
McDougall, J., 39, 110
Meltzer, D., 74, 76, 130, 155, 167–168
memory lapses, 212
memory traces, 252
mentalization, 21, 23, 73, 76, 77, 82, 107, 132, 134–135, 137, 158, 203, 204, 210, 218
Mentzos, S., xxv, 65–67, 70, 198, 202, 211
Milner, M., 57–58, 153
Mitscherlich, A., 154
modulation, 81, 135
Money-Kyrle, R., 129–130
Morgenthaler, F., 161
mother–child relationship, xxvi, 59, 66, 128, 131, 135–136, 138, 176–177, 198, 205, 265
M'Uzan, M. de, 61
Müller-Pozzi, H., 136
mute phase, 158

narcissism, xxiv, 117, 202, 205
narcissistic cathexis, 35
narcissistic equilibrium, 198
narcissistic object, 86, 177, 198
neonates, 22
neurobiological foundations, 70
neuropsychological insights, 70
neuropsychology, xxiii
neuroscientific research, 134, 139
neurotic disorders, 65

newborn baby, 170, 265
Niederland, W. G., 260
nightmares, 34, 180, 184, 212, 229, 232
Nissen, B., 76
non-neutral abstinence, 244
non-verbal affects, 70

object, xviii
    autistic, 72–73
    inanimate, 155, 205
    legitimate, xxiv
    narcissistic, 86, 177, 198
    paranoid, 199
    -self, 22–23, 35, 73, 76, 82, 131, 195, 203
    -splitting, 81, 148, 154–155
    transference, 135, 140, 182, 185, 202, 252
    traumatising, 22, 124, 195, 254
objectal anxiety, 95
object-splitting, 81, 147, 154–155
oedipal level, 65
oedipal phase, 23, 26
Oedipus complex, 153, 176
Ogden, T. H., 76–77
old age, 26, 106
Oliner, M. M., xxv, 22, 117, 120, 249, 252
omnipotence, 124, 126, 131, 146, 154–155, 158, 163, 201
ontogenetic level, xxv
O'Shaughnessy, E., 74
outpatient clinic, 4, 19
over-identification, 214–215, 235

paedophilia, 161, 177
panic attacks, 33, 35, 116
paranoid mistrust, 48, 215
Parsons, M., 195
partial dissociations, 214
paternal protection, 129
pathogenesis, xxv, 100
pathological
    cases, 22, 81, 261
    fusions, 81
    integrating, 251
    maturity, 67

mourning, 105–106
  precocity, xxii
  problematic, 66
  separation, 40
peace-ego, xxii
permanent personality change, 212
perpetrators, 120–121, 259
personal assistance provider (PAP), 232
personality development, xviii, xxv, 237
personality disorder, 68, 202, 205, 212, 241–242, 254
perversion, 124–125, 161, 164, 176–177
phantasy, 64 see also: unconscious
phobia, 110, 132
phylogenetic dimension, xxv
physical, xxvi, 24–25, 29, 39, 61, 89, 95, 134, 137, 139, 152, 164, 180, 198, 264
  abuse, 198
  ailments, 264
  deficits, 24–25, 29
  disability, xxvi
  impotence, 39
  pain, xxiii, 89, 95, 137, 152, 164
  reactions, 95
  symptoms, 134, 139
  traumatic, 61
  violence, 180
physiological stress indicators, 265
Plänkers, T., xii, 74
Plassmann, R., 220, 264
play-therapy session, 7
post-traumatic stress disorder (PTSD), xii, xxii, xxvii, 209, 211–212, 241–242, 259
premature birth, xxvi, 24
pre-traumatic, xxvi, 4, 22–23, 39, 70, 213, 219–220, 225–226, 236
  biography, 225–226
  development, 70, 219
  infancy, 39
  personality, 4, 213
  personality structure, 220
  stage, 236
primal repression, 169–170

primitive fusions, 22
profound loneliness, 24, 26
Pross, C., 259–260
pseudo-adjustment, 65, 69, 76
pseudo-normality, 66, 158
psychic development, 117
psychic trauma(s), xv, xxiv–xxv, 152, 192, 211–212, 241, 254
psychoactive drugs, 29, 180, 232, 244
psychoanalysis, xiii, xv, xviii, xxi–xxii, xxiv, 65, 88, 101, 109, 113, 134, 209, 213, 243, 250, 253, 269, 272
  applied, 209
  clinical, 269, 272
psychoanalytic, xii–xiii, xvi–xix, xxi, xxv–xxvi, 33, 64, 70, 97, 99, 133–134, 177
  conflict model, xxv
  development theory, 70
  journals, xii
  knowledge, xiii, 258
  literature, xix, 213
  process, 242
  psychotherapy, 220, 237
  technique, xvi, xxvii, 241
  theory, xiii, xv, 133
  trauma research, xxii–xxiii
  treatment, xviii, xxvii, 33, 97
psychological processes, 166
psycho-neurotic patients, 219
psychosomatic counselling, 13, 44
psychosomatosis, 61
psychotic development, 47
pylorospasms, 170, 173–174

Quinodoz, J.-M., 114
quotations of trauma, 28

radiation therapy, 6–7, 34
Reddemann, L., 220, 249–250, 255
Reiche, R., 161, 164
relational trauma, 133, 135–137, 161, 168, 211, 241, 251
relationship triggers, 134
relaxation techniques, 250, 253

repression, 62, 66, 169–170 *see also*: unconscious
   primal, 169–170
resilience factors, 138, 213, 220, 223
respiratory and cardiac irregularities, 232
rheumatism, 144, 146, 155, 159
Rhode, M., 74
Richter, A., 263
Riedesser, P., 219, 244, 259
Roisman, G. I., 266
role play, 6, 93, 209
Rosenberg, F., 220, 249
Rosenfeld, H., 163

Sachsse, U., 70, 213, 220, 249, 255
Sandler, J., xxiii
Schacht, L., 56
Scharff, J. M., 22, 35
Scheef-Maier, G., xii, 263
Schickedanz, H., 264
Schore, A. N., xxiii, xxiv, 70, 73, 134, 139
Schöttler, C., 61
Schröder, S. G., 261
Schubbe, O., 211
Segal, H., 36, 254
self, xviii, 21–26, 35, 39, 46, 60, 67, 73, 76, 81–82, 184, 194–198, 203, 220, 225, 242, 252
   -analysis, 194
   -assertive admonitions, 196
   -delimitation, 26
   -demarcation, 60
   -destruction, 150
   -image, 198
   -object, 22–23, 35, 73, 76, 82, 131, 195, 203
   -object fusion, 23, 35, 76, 82, 203
   -preservation, 73, 183
   -relation, 67
   -representations, 22, 39, 81
Seliger, M., 261
separation anxiety, 81, 84, 92, 199
separation trauma, xviii, xxvi, 45, 92–93, 106, 148, 183, 200, 247

sexual, xxii, 25, 35–36, 46, 99, 113, 167, 184, 198–199, 246
   abuse, xxii, 198–199, 246
   excitement, 126
   gratification, 167
   identity, 36, 198
   maturity, 46
   problems, 35
   relationship, 25, 99, 113, 184
   sense, 175
sexualisation, 40, 101, 103
sexually transmitted diseases, 103
Shapiro, F., 255
Sharpe, E. F., 153
short-term therapy, 243–244
Simmel, E., xxi–xxii
sleeping disorders, 110–111, 131
Socialist Unity Party, 84
somatisation, 38, 73, 92–93, 95, 214, 242
speechlessness, 63, 71, 89, 246
Sperling, E., 44, 61
Spitz, R., xxiii, 86, 117, 199, 265
split-off, 17, 26, 38, 57, 82, 102, 118, 131, 140, 158, 176, 185, 190, 243, 248, 251–252, 254, 259
   affects, 69–70, 72, 74–76, 140, 158, 185, 204, 243, 248, 251
   aggression, 109, 180
   destructiveness, 114
   elements, 71, 254
   feelings, 217, 219
   fusional cores, 134
   paranoid, 102, 155
   trauma, 93, 112, 146, 168
splitting, xxvi, 22, 25, 70–71, 75, 91, 130–131, 144, 149, 158, 176, 183–184, 197–201, 204, 209, 213
   and fusion, xxvi, 65, 217
spontaneous healing, xxi
Spranger, H., 263
starvation, 68, 204
Steiner, J., 254
Stephanos, S., 61
Stern, D. N., xxiii, 32
Stoller, R. J., 177

Ströhle, A., 261
structural theory, 65
symbolic language, 3–4, 32, 63, 72, 109, 140, 153
symbolisation disorder, 22, 39, 70, 81, 214, 251
symptomatology, xxi, 61, 200, 211, 220

Target, M., 22, 39, 82, 135, 202, 265
therapeutic interventions, 71
therapeutic rider, 168, 200
Thomä, H., 44, 61, 65, 83, 158
Timmermann-Levanas, A., 263
Torok, M., 73
transference, xvii, xxvii, 4, 16, 26, 37, 46, 62, 70, 143, 211, 217
   see also: countertransference; unconscious
   ancillary, 109, 122
   relationship, xvii, 23, 31, 59, 69, 90, 107, 114, 135, 151, 157, 167, 181, 192, 230, 242, 250
   splitting, 27, 165, 168, 190, 202
   traumatising, 251
transgenerational identifications, xxiv, 76, 200–201, 257
transplant operation, 14, 19
trauma-conditioned, xviii, 23
trauma exposure, 213, 221, 249
trauma history, 21–26, 33, 35, 98, 134, 158, 180, 210, 259
trauma-specific content, 264
trauma-therapeutic techniques, 249, 253
traumatic childhood, 4
traumatic constellations, 4, 130, 250
traumatic processes, xvii, 17, 21, 65, 77, 93, 129, 158, 210, 258
traumatic relationship, 101, 134
traumatic separation, xxiii, xxvii

trauma victims, 215, 216
Trimborn, W., 119
Tustin, F., 61, 72, 74

Ullner, R., 4, 33
unconscious *see also*: anxiety, behaviour, conscious
   analyst's, 21, 24, 72, 74–75, 83, 104, 135–136, 209, 217–218, 247
   child's, 135
   patient's, 74, 83, 136, 153, 167, 200, 236, 246
   pre-, 3, 259
unconscious guilt feelings, 106, 226
unconscious processes, 70, 201, 257
United Nations High Commissioner for Refugees, 263
unresolved conflicts, 26

Van der Kolk, B., 69
Van Keuk, E., 263
Varvin, S., xii, 218
victims, trauma, 216
Vietnam War, xxiv, 211

Wackernagel, K. M., 249
Wangh, M., 260
war, xxi–xxii, xxvii, 84
   neuroses, xxi–xxii
weaning, 130
Weine, S. M., 210, 227, 259
Wenk-Ansohn, M., 209, 263
Winnicott, D. W., 26, 56, 58, 62–63, 76, 137–138, 147, 168, 204
Wirtgen, W., 263
Wöller, W., 220, 250

Zimmermann, P. L., 261
Zwiebel, R., 27